HERESY IN THE HEARTLAND

MARY JUDE BROWN

HERESY IN THE
HEARTLAND

THE CONTROVERSY AT THE

UNIVERSITY OF DAYTON,

1960–1967

THE CATHOLIC UNIVERSITY
OF AMERICA PRESS
WASHINGTON, D.C.

Cataloging-in-Publication Data available from

the Library of Congress

ISBN 978-0-8132-3502-8

CONTENTS

IMAGES

ACKNOWLEDGMENTS

Work on this book began over twenty years ago when I encountered a lengthy footnote in Philip Gleason's *Keeping the Faith: American Catholicism Past and Present* that referred to a University of Dayton faculty committee calling for the secularization of the institution. The footnote piqued my curiosity. I wanted to know what had happened to trigger such a response. My research led me to the "Heresy" Affair.

This book would not have been possible without the assistance of those directly involved in the "Heresy" Affair who shared their materials and memories: in particular, Eulalio Baltazar, Stephen Bickham, Dennis Bonnette, Thomas Casaletto, John Chrisman, Edward Harkenrider, William Doane Kelly, Theodore Kisiel, Father Matthew Kohmescher, Randolph Lumpp, Neil McCluskey, Father Thomas Stanley, and Lawrence Ulrich.

Members of the Society of Mary (the Marianists) at the University of Dayton also assisted me in numerous ways: in particular, Brother Raymond L. Fitz, Father James Fitz, Brother Don Hebeler, Father James L. Heft, Father François E. Rossier, and Father Paul Vieson.

Current and former members of the University of Dayton administration who provided support and encouragement include Paul H. Benson, Daniel J. Curran, F. Thomas Eggemeier, Paul J. Morman, Fred P. Pestello, Eric F. Spina, and Mary Morton Strey. Other current and former members of the University of Dayton community who were invaluable to the writing process include Jennifer Brancato, Ryan O'Grady, Kristina Schulz, Amy Rohmiller, Julie Weinel, and Thomas Westendorf. A special thank you is due to archivist Kerrie Cross, who early in the process helped me locate many sources within the University of Dayton archives.

Scholars who assisted me along the way include Michael Barnes, Erving Beauregard, Una Cadegan, Michael Cuneo, James Davidson, Timothy Dillon, Dennis Doyle, Robert Fastiggi, Isabel Fernandez, Father Robert Hater, Joseph Jacobs, Joseph Kunkel, M. Therese Lysaught, Judith G. Martin, SSJ, Father Jack McGrath, Vernon Meyer, Cecilia Moore, David O'Brien, Raymund O'Herron, Phyllis Scholp, Anthony B. Smith, Maureen Tilley, Terrence W. Tilley, William V. Trollinger, Norbert Wethington, and Sandra Yocum. A special thank you goes to Father James L. Heft and William L. Portier, who have encouraged and mentored me for many years.

It would have been impossible to write this book without the assistance of archivists who helped me locate materials: Andrew Armstrong (Christendom College), Shelley Barber (Boston College), Elise D. Bochinski (Fairfield University), Lynn Conway (Georgetown University), Sheila Conway (Santa Clara University), David E. Crawford (Creighton University), Deborah E. Cribbs (St. Louis University), Alan Delozier (St. Peter's College / Seton Hall University), Antonio Gascón (Archivi Generali Marianisti), Patricia Higo (University of Detroit Mercy), Ann M. Kenne (University of St. Thomas), Mary E. Kenney (National Archives Marianist Province of the United States), Anne Knafl (University of Chicago), Michael Knies (University of Scranton), Elizabeth T. Knuth (College of St. Benedict / St. John's University), Anne LeVeque (Catholic News Service), Lauren Zuchowski Longwell (Loyola Marymount University), Peter Lysy (University of Notre Dame), Shane T. MacDonald (the Catholic University of America), Kyle McMorrow (Santa Clara University), Deborah A. Malone (University of San Francisco), Carlo Alberto di Muro (Archivi Generali Marianisti), Sarah L. Patterson (Archdiocese of Cincinnati), Blythe E. Roveland-Brenton (St. John's University), Anne Ryckbost (Xavier University), David Schoen (Niagara University), Elizabeth B. Scott (Saint Michael's College), William John Shepherd (the Catholic University of America), and Massimiliano Vidili (Archivi Generali Marianisti).

Throughout the years, special friends have encouraged and supported me: Gina de Groote, Cathy Emley, Brother Joseph J. Fisher, Lindsey

Green, Judith Hecht, Dee Irwin, Jane Krites, Bambi Markham, Mark Masthay, Jean Masthay, Judy Owen, Don Pair, Karen Pettus, Don Polzella, and Urška Vintar. I am grateful to all of them for their friendship and support. In particular, I thank Niki Johnson for her friendship and her editing and proofreading skills, which improved this manuscript immensely.

Finally, this book would not have been possible without the love and support of my family: my parents (Bob and Vivian Wahrer), seven siblings (Kath, Tom, Joe, Dan, Pat, Fran, and Paul) and their spouses, my son Jason Brown, daughter Heidi Brown, grandchildren Kameron Brown, Destiny Brown, and Ben Brown, and especially my husband, Gary Brown, who has always provided me with love and support. Without him, this book would not have happened.

It goes without saying that any errors in the manuscript are my own.

ABBREVIATIONS

AAC   Archives of the Chancery. Archdiocese of Cincinnati, Cincinnati, Ohio.

ACUA   American Catholic History Research Center and University Archives. Catholic University of America, Washington, D.C.

AGMAR   Archivi Generali Marianisti. Rome, Italy.

ASM(CIN)   Archives of the Society of Mary, Cincinnati Province, Dayton, Ohio. The collection has been moved to San Antonio, Texas, and is known as the National Archives of the Marianist Province of the United States.

ASM(E)   Archives of the Society of Mary, Eastern Region, Dayton, Ohio. The collection has been moved to San Antonio, Texas, and is known as the National Archives of the Marianist Province of the United States.

AUD   University Archives and Special Collections, University of Dayton, Dayton, Ohio.

INTRODUCTION

On a fair, chilly March afternoon in 1967, Marianist Father Raymond
A. Roesch, president of the University of Dayton, waited nervously in the
wings of Boll Theatre in the recently completed John F. Kennedy Memorial Union located in the center of the campus. He had been president of
this major Catholic university since 1959, but had never faced any crisis
quite like what now preoccupied him. The address he was about to give
to the University of Dayton faculty was arguably the most important of
his then nine-year presidency. His faculty, both Marianist and lay, insisted
on meeting to find out more about a controversy involving philosophy
and theology lay faculty members that has since become known as the
"Heresy" Affair. The faculty's written request came in the form of a letter from Dr. Ellis A. Joseph, chairman of the Ad Hoc Committee for the
Study of Academic Freedom at the University of Dayton, and was "strongly endorsed" by the presidents of the university's American Association of
University Professors (AAUP) chapter, the student council, and the chairman of the university's faculty forum. In the letter, the faculty asked Father
Roesch to address ten items. Some were specific questions about the faculty controversy. Others were general questions dealing with secularization,
academic freedom, and Catholic identity. These latter issues were relevant
not only to the University of Dayton in the late 1960s, but to all institutions of Catholic higher education in the United States then and now.

How Father Roesch and the University of Dayton weathered this particular storm was important for a number of reasons. Prior to the contro-

versy, the administration of the university was entirely Marianist, and the faculty forum was an advisory body that included Marianist administrators appointed by the president. The lay faculty wanted UD to be a "real" university. This meant responding to the issues and challenges faced by most Catholic colleges and universities at the time—in particular, faculty governance, academic freedom, tenure, due process, and academic quality.

As such, the history of the "Heresy" Affair is an interesting case study of Catholic higher education in the United States during the turbulent sixties. Notre Dame historian John T. McGreevy has called for such case studies in order to animate the abstractions of the "Catholic 1960s."[1] What follows in this book is anything but an abstraction, especially to the people who were involved in it, suffered because of it, and have never forgotten it.

The events known as the "Heresy" Affair are also important because they are part of the then ongoing intense conversation swirling within the Roman Catholic Church about how to deal with modernity. In four sessions from 1962 through 1965, the world's bishops met in Rome for the Second Vatican Council, surely the most significant event of the Catholic Church in the twentieth century. The Council fueled change within the church and within Catholic intellectual thought. The controversy stems in part from the energy that was "in the air" prior to and during the Council.

Finally, the history of the "Heresy" Affair helps us to understand today's context of American Catholic higher education. In the sixties, American Catholic universities wanted more than ever to be respected by the secular academy. The Dayton controversy was the second of three academic controversies to erupt in the mid-sixties; those of St. John's University and the Curran affair at the Catholic University of America were the others. The three conflicts were very public, which embarrassed the universities involved and most of American Catholic higher education.

The desire to be respected by the secular academy led to actions that turned Catholic institutions toward the secular academy and away from their religious mission and identity. It should be asked whether at this critical point in history some Catholic universities gave up more than

1. John T. McGreevy, "Productivity and Promise: American Catholic History Since 1993," *U. S. Catholic Historian* 21 (Spring 2003): 125.

they had to give to gain respectability within the larger academy. By the 1980s, the Vatican began to examine closely the question of the mission and identity of Catholic higher education. *Ex Corde Ecclesiae*, Pope John Paul II's 1990 apostolic exhortation on Catholic higher education, offered corrective measures to clarify what it means to be a Catholic university.

Catholic higher education continues to discuss and surely will continue to discuss what it means to be a Catholic university when most of these universities now do not look anything like the Catholic universities of the sixties. We still struggle with our identity, with our relationship to the church, and with church teachings that conflict with the culture we live in, such as immigration, the environment, and sexual ethics. Furthermore, the divide between traditionalists and progressives in the church, as evidenced in the Dayton controversy, continues to this day, now fueled by social media and websites. The conflict at Dayton reminds us to take each other seriously, avoid exaggerations, and tone down the rhetoric.

Chapter 1 sets the stage and describes the context and origins of the affair in the early 1960s. Lay faculty were hired, sometimes over the phone, with backgrounds in newer philosophies leading to conflicts with the Thomists in the Philosophy Department. Chapter 2 explores the escalation of the controversy from 1964 to 1966, leading to the actual crisis in the fall of 1966 as described in chapter 3. Chapters 4 through 7 follow the outline of Father Roesch's address to the faculty. Chapter 8 looks at Roesch's resolution of the controversy, the Ad Hoc Committee for the Study of Academic Freedom at the University of Dayton, while chapter 9 covers the actions of the church behind the scenes. Media coverage is explored in chapter 10. The book concludes with a synopsis of what happened at the University of Dayton and draws some lessons for the future of Catholic higher education.

The story is told in chronological order by the participants in the controversy—faculty, administrators, students, and clergy—using the words of those involved. In particular, it is important that the students of that era be heard. As the controversy unfolds, the Thomists/traditionalists are motivated to oppose the progressives primarily because the students are being affected.

HERESY IN THE
HEARTLAND

CHAPTER I

THE ORIGINS OF THE "HERESY" AFFAIR AT THE UNIVERSITY OF DAYTON

1961–1964

It is easy to begin a controversy—and difficult to end it.
—John Henry Cardinal Newman to Friedrich von Hügel, July 21, 1884

The 1966–67 controversy did not just erupt without warning. As with most disputes, the signs of a developing conflict are traceable over a number of years, in this case the early 1960s—years of change in the many worlds inhabited by the University of Dayton: Roman Catholicism, the United States, American higher education, American Catholic higher education, and philosophy as taught in American Catholic colleges and universities.

In Roman Catholicism, Pope John XXIII "threw open the windows of the Church" when, on January 25, 1959, he announced the Second Vatican Council, which began in 1962 and closed in 1965 after four ten-week sessions during the fall of each year. The changes called for were sweeping— mass in the vernacular with the priest facing the people, affirmation of lay leadership within the church, freedom of conscience in matters of religion, and emphasis on the pastoral role of bishops and priests, to name a few. In many parts of the church, the changes were imposed over a short period without sufficient preparation for the laity. The very fact that the church made such changes was jarring to many Catholics. Looking back, a noted Catholic scholar described the time as one of "seismic upheaval."[1]

Within American culture, the early 1960s saw the expansion of the civil rights movement, the beginnings of the women's movement and the sexual revolution, and, by the late 1960s, escalation of the Vietnam War. Higher education underwent a period of tremendous growth in enrollment, change in academic emphases, and increased involvement with the federal government. With the number of students rapidly increasing, the numbers of faculty and administrators necessarily increased, as did the size of the physical plants of most colleges and universities.

American Catholic higher education, experiencing the same growth as secular institutions, also had problems uniquely its own. In 1955, John Tracy Ellis published a strong criticism of American Catholic intellectual life. He pointed out the lack of intellectual leadership among American Catholics and criticized Catholic institutions for being mediocre. Ellis's words were a challenge to colleges and universities to tighten standards and emphasize quality if they were going to compare favorably with secular institutions. Similar criticisms of inferiority, especially on the graduate level, were echoed in the Danforth Commission and the American Council on Education reports in 1966. As the decade unfolded, other factors such as financial limitations, the changing role of sponsoring religious orders,[2] and the meaning of Catholic identity became important issues.[3]

For the University of Dayton, undergraduate enrollment rose dramatically in the late forties, fifties, and early sixties. In 1944, there were 900

1. Philip Gleason, *Keeping the Faith: American Catholicism Past and Present* (Notre Dame, Ind.: University of Notre Dame Press, 1987), 84.

2. Reexamination of the role of religious occurred in "the context of questions of control, internal relationships between religious and lay personnel, and relationships between the Catholic colleges and universities and the hierarchy"; Charles E. Ford and Edgar L. Roy Jr., *The Renewal of Catholic Higher Education* (Washington, D.C.: National Catholic Educational Association, 1968), 7.

3. "The need for a precise and operative definition comes from the documents of the Second Vatican Council, the financial situation of most Catholic colleges and universities, misunderstandings among the American public and even among professional educators, internally from the students and faculty in the American institutions, and finally from demands of intelligent long-range planning"; Ford and Roy, *Renewal of Catholic Higher Education*, 24.

students. By 1950, with an influx of veterans studying on the G.I. Bill, there were 3,500 full-time undergraduates, 85 percent of whom were male, 83 percent from the State of Ohio, 65 percent Catholic, and 15 percent residential. By 1960, there were 4,000 full-time undergraduates who were 81 percent male, 62 percent from Ohio, 81 percent Catholic, and 21 percent housed in dormitories. Six years later, when the "Heresy" Affair reached crisis stage, the undergraduate population had nearly doubled, to 7,062 students. By then, 69 percent of the students were male, 48 percent were from Ohio, nearly 91 percent were Catholic, and 36 percent lived on campus.[4] The university had developed a reputation as a regional Catholic university.

The surge in Dayton's enrollment led to rapid growth in the faculty and in the physical plant, including new classroom and laboratory facilities, new dormitories, and the John F. Kennedy Memorial Union dedicated in 1965. Academic advances included the reorganization of the academic structure into a College of Arts and Sciences and schools of Business Administration, Education, and Engineering; the inauguration of a trimester academic program; the reinauguration of graduate programs closed during World War II; pressure on the faculty to complete doctoral and terminal degrees, including a program to pay faculty to work on their degrees; an increased emphasis on scholarly productivity, research, and professional activities; and an in-depth review of faculty policies and the tightening of expectations, including those for promotion.

THOMISM

From the mid-1920s until the mid-1960s, Thomistic philosophy was the "crucial element in integrating Catholic higher education."[5] Thomas Aquinas, an Italian Dominican priest and scholastic who lived from 1225 to 1274, was canonized a saint and named a Doctor of the Church, a title given to those who make significant contributions to the development of church teachings. Drawing upon Greek, Muslim, and Jewish thinkers, Thomas developed a dialectic approach; namely, he asked ques-

4. These statistics were calculated by the author using data from the Office of the Registrar for the fall terms of 1950, 1960, and 1966; AUD.

5. Gleason, *Keeping the Faith*, 142.

tions, made an argument, and reached a conclusion using human reason.

Since Thomas's death, there have been various periods in church history when Thomism was the dominant philosophy within the church. During the most recent period (the Thomistic Revival, 1860–1960), Pope Leo XIII issued the 1879 papal encyclical *Aeterni Patris* that claimed Thomism as the best philosophy for organizing theology and required it to be taught in seminaries. Implementation of the encyclical resulted in Thomism becoming the philosophy of the church and therefore an important part of modern Catholic higher education until the late 1960s.

By the 1950s, Thomism was taught in Catholic universities as if it had all the answers rather than as a method of philosophical inquiry. It was based on the manuals of moral theology taught to priests in seminaries; hence the approach was labeled manualist. This approach led to growing dissatisfaction among students and younger philosophy faculty. Nevertheless, philosophy continued to be a required subject for most undergraduates in American Catholic colleges and universities. The University of Dayton was no exception: the philosophy requirement in the mid-1960s for all undergraduates was a minimum of twelve semester hours: Introduction to Philosophy and Logic, Philosophical Psychology (the philosophy of human nature), Epistemology (the theory of knowledge), and General Metaphysics (the nature of reality and being). If students took eighteen hours of philosophy, as did all bachelor of arts students, they graduated with a minor in philosophy. The requirement for theology was also twelve semester hours: Introduction to Sacred Scripture, Theology of Christ, and two additional electives. Together, philosophy and theology composed nearly 20 percent of a student's curriculum at the University of Dayton. To put this requirement in perspective, a 1965–66 undergraduate in a bachelor of arts program at the Ohio State University, the foremost public university in the state of Ohio, was required to take only six hours of philosophy—PHL 551: Points of View in Ancient Philosophy, and PHL 552: Points of View in Modern Philosophy. Of course, the Ohio State University had no theology requirement.[6]

6. "Curriculum Leading to the Degree Bachelor of Arts," *College of Arts and Sciences Undergraduate Bulletin 1965–66*, 139, accessed May 28, 2017, http://kb.osu.edu/dspace/bitstream/handle/1811/62029/ARV_UREG_College_Of_Arts_And_Sciences_1965-1966.pdf?sequence=2.

The administrators at the University of Dayton during these changing times were all vowed religious, members of the founding religious order the Society of Mary, also known as the Marianists.[7] The president beginning in 1959 was Father Raymond A. Roesch. A native of Jenkintown, Pennsylvania, Roesch joined the Marianists in 1933 and earned a bachelor of arts degree with majors in English and Latin from the University of Dayton (1936). Ordained a priest in 1944, he earned a master's degree in psychology from the Catholic University of America (1945) and a Ph.D. in psychology from Fordham University (1954). Beginning in 1951, prior to his appointment as president, Roesch was a faculty member in the university's Psychology Department and served as chair of the department from 1952 to 1959.

Father Thomas A. Stanley, a native of Cleveland, Ohio, became Dayton's academic leader beginning in 1961, serving first as dean of the university and then as provost. Stanley joined the Marianists in high school and earned a bachelor of arts degree in philosophy from the University of Dayton (1943). He taught high school in New York before entering the seminary in Fribourg, Switzerland. He was ordained in 1950, earned bachelor, licentiate, and doctorate (1952) of sacred theology degrees from the University of Fribourg, and completed advanced studies at the Athenaeum Pontificium Angelicum in Rome (1953). For five years prior to coming to the University of Dayton, Stanley served as rector (president) of the Catholic University of Puerto Rico in Ponce. Rector was an appointed position serving at the pleasure of the university's founding bishop and chancellor, James E. McManus, CSsR. Stanley had a difficult time as rector, in part because the vice rector was Ivan Illich, then a young priest on loan from the diocese of New York, appointed in 1956 to the vice rector position by Stanley's predecessor, Marianist father William J. Ferree. Illich supported liberal political movements on the island and backed the first governor of Puerto Rico, Luis Muñoz Marin. Bishop McManus and Bish-

---

7. There were only two lay upper-level administrators: the deans of Business Administration and of Engineering.

op James Davis of San Juan were also involved politically, but on the other side because they opposed the government's birth control programs. Ultimately, the bishops created their own political party, urged Catholics to vote against the governor, and went so far as to say that Catholics who supported the governor's administration could be excommunicated.[8] Illich was dismissed from the diocese in 1961.[9] The Marianists relocated Stanley to the University of Dayton to serve as chief academic officer and teach theology; Illich went on to found the Centro Intercultural de Documentación (CIDOC, or Intercultural Documentation Center), a language institute for missionaries now known as the Cuernavaca Language School at Cuernavaca, Mexico.

ACADEMIC YEAR 1961–1962

The beginning of the "Heresy" Affair can be traced to the hiring of Philosophy faculty who were not Thomists, the first being John Chrisman, hired as an instructor in the fall of 1961. Having earned an undergraduate degree in philosophy (1956) at the University of Portland (Oregon), a Catholic institution run by the Congregation of the Holy Cross, Chrisman then went to the University of Toronto because one of his Portland professors told him that it was the best place to do graduate work in philosophy. Both Étienne Gilson and Jacques Maritain, two well-known Thomists, taught at Toronto. Chrisman soon discovered, however, that the philosophy at the University of Toronto was not exclusively Thomist. Other philosophers, particularly Leslie Dewart,[10] "ripped minds like [his]

8. "James EManus (sic), A Retired Bishop," New York Times, July 3, 1976, New York edition, 19, http://www.nytimes.com/1976/07/03/archives/james-mmanus-a-retired-bishop-prelate-once-led-opposition-to-puerto.html?_r=0.

9. Joseph P. Fitzpatrick, SJ., The Stranger Is Our Own: Reflections on the Journey of Puerto Rican Migrants (Kansas City, Mo.: Sheed and Ward, 1996), 29. There is no evidence that Stanley was dismissed by Bishop McManus, but, in 1966–67, local Dayton pastors wrote to the Cincinnati archbishop claiming Stanley was removed from his position in Puerto Rico. Stanley himself told the archbishop's fact-finding committee that he did not know if he was removed by Bishop McManus.

10. Leslie Dewart was born in Spain and raised in Cuba. He emigrated to Canada in 1942. After serving in the Royal Canadian Air Force, he earned a bachelor's degree in psychology in 1951 and a master's in philosophy in 1952. Both degrees were from the University of Toronto. From 1952 to 1954, he was a teaching fellow at St. Michael's College, University of Toronto. Dewart earned his Ph.D. in philosophy from Toronto in 1954. After teaching at the University

wide open." Chrisman loved the new approach to the study of philosophy. Upon finishing his master's degree in 1960, Chrisman immediately began working on his doctorate at the University of Toronto.[11]

In the spring of 1961, Chrisman took a break from his studies. He was married with three children and needed to support his family. A fellow graduate student told him of a teaching opportunity in philosophy at the University of Dayton. Chrisman applied to Dayton and several other universities. The chair of UD's Philosophy Department, Marianist father Edmund Rhodes,[12] interviewed Chrisman in person but did not ask about Chrisman's personal philosophy. Rhodes hired him to teach courses that resembled those he took as a student at Portland—namely, courses in Thomistic philosophy. Chrisman did not realize at the time that he was the first non-Thomist hired by the University of Dayton. He settled into teaching the first-year Aristotelian logic course and the required junior-level epistemology course. He taught both courses in a way that allowed him to introduce students to a different worldview than that of Thomistic philosophy. He quickly became a popular teacher in the Philosophy Department and very involved in the campus intellectual life.

Early in 1962, provost Marianist father Thomas Stanley inaugurated the Intellectual Frontiers Series to replace the Cultural Lecture Series. The series was run by a faculty committee chaired by a young biologist, James A. MacMahon. Its purpose was to provide a new and wider audience "for the professor who [had] found something, who [was] excited

of Detroit for two years, he returned to the University of Toronto. Dewart is primarily known for his 1966 book *The Future of Belief: Theism in a World Come of Age* (New York: Herder and Herder). In 1969 he was investigated by the Vatican Congregation for the Doctrine of the Faith for the "theological implications of [his] writings." No condemnation was issued.

11. Chrisman's doctoral dissertation, under the director of Leslie Dewart, is entitled, "A Study of Two Major Thomistic Attempts to Reconcile Stable Intelligibility with Evolutionary Change." It dealt with the works of Maritain, Gilson, and Henri Bergson. Chrisman's Ph.D. was awarded in 1971 from the University of Toronto, St. Michael's College.

12. Father Edmund Rhodes had degrees from the University of Dayton (bachelor's in philosophy, 1932), the Catholic University of America (S.T.L. with an emphasis in philosophy), Lateran Law School in Rome, and the University of Louvain in Belgium. He was a philosophy professor at the University of Dayton from 1947 to 1983 and was chair from 1951 to 1964. He died in 2007 at the age of 98.

about it, and who [wanted] to talk about it."[13] Speakers—from the faculty or invited from off-campus—were chosen by the faculty committee with no control by the administration. MacMahon and the committee took to heart the title of "intellectual frontiers." They tried for balance but still provoked many heated discussions, which was also their goal. If the discussion was not heated, the topic was not on a frontier.[14]

In the second lecture in the series, at the suggestion of the provost Father Stanley, John Chrisman spoke on Teilhard de Chardin's *The Phenomenon of Man*.[15] The topic was timely but also controversial, as Teilhard's works were under examination by the Vatican. A few months after Chrisman's lecture, the Supreme Sacred Congregation of the Holy Office issued a *monitum* that warned of the errors in Teilhard's works.[16] The June 30, 1962, *monitum*, enclosed with the November 16, 1962, letter to rectors from Msgr. Paul F. Tanner, general secretary of the National Catholic Welfare Conference, exhorted all ordinaries, superiors of religious institutes, rectors of seminaries, and *presidents of universities* (emphasis added) to protect minds against the dangers presented by the works of Teilhard and his followers.[17] The *monitum* against Teilhard is still in place, despite a November 17, 2017, proposal passed by the Pontifical Council for Culture urging Pope Francis to rescind it.[18]

13. Brochure of 1963 Intellectual Frontiers Series, series 7JD, box 26, folder 5, "Intellectual Frontiers," AUD.

14. James A. MacMahon, telephone interview with the author, March 2002. MacMahon grew up two blocks from the University of Dayton. He earned a bachelor's degree in zoology (1960) from Michigan State University and a Ph.D. in biology (1964) from the University of Notre Dame. He taught at Dayton from 1963 to 1971 and then continued his academic career at Utah State University, where he is Trustee Professor Emeritus of biology, served as head of the Department of Biology from 1985 to 1989, dean of the College of Science in two separate terms (1989–2000 and 2009–14), vice president of university advancement (2000–02), director of USU's Ecology Center (2005–11), and as the first chairman of the board of directors of the National Ecological Observatory Network, known as NEON.

15. *Monday Morning Memo*, April 5, 1962, 1, series 3N (3), AUD.

16. A *monitum* is an official warning given by the church when a particular teaching or author is suspected of error on matters of doctrine; Richard P. McBrien, "Monitum," in *The HarperCollins Encyclopedia of Catholicism*, ed. Richard P. McBrien et al. (San Francisco: Harper San Francisco, 1995), 882.

17. Msgr. Paul F. Tanner (General Secretary of the National Catholic Welfare Conference) to rectors, November 16, 1962, ACUA, NCWC series, education files, box 29, "Educational Institutions."

18. "Letter to the Pope to Waive the Monitum on Teilhard's Works," November 17, 2017,

Early on, Father Roesch encouraged departments to establish/reactivate graduate programs. The School of Education was the first to reactivate its programs in 1960. Education intended to use philosophy to integrate their program and included in their core curriculum nine hours of courses with a philosophical orientation. The Philosophy Department was given only a few months to prepare for the delivery of classes. Needless to say, the Philosophy faculty, overworked with their own undergraduate courses, reacted unfavorably to this demand from the School of Education.[19]

Roesch also thought it important that a Catholic university have a graduate program in philosophy.[20] In December 1960 the departmental minutes reflected the unanimous sentiment of the department: "No concrete need exists currently or will come to exist in the reasonable future for a graduate program." Despite departmental disapproval, Marianist father John Elbert submitted a proposal for a graduate program in philosophy in early 1961 to the College graduate committee. Elbert was sixty-five years old and had served as president of the University of Dayton (1938–44) and provincial of the Cincinnati province of the Marianists (1948–58) and, in 1961, was an emeritus faculty member in the Department of Philosophy.[21] When College of Arts and Sciences dean Marianist brother Leonard A. Mann asked about the discrepancy between the department minutes and the proposal, Father Elbert talked to the chair of the department, Father Rhodes, who "repudiated the minutes" and approved the graduate program.[22] The program was ultimately approved by the university's academic council with implementation scheduled for the

---

http://www.cultura.va/content/dam/cultura/docs/comunicatistampa/Letter%20to%20the%20 Pope%20to%20waive%20the%20Monitum%20on%20Teilhard%27s%20works.pdf.

19. Department of Philosophy faculty meeting minutes, February 15, 1960, 2, series 20QI (3), box 1, folder 1, AUD.

20. Edward Harkenrider, email message to the author, March 30, 1999.

21. Father Elbert held a Ph.D. in philosophy (1932) from the University of Cincinnati. Elbert's dissertation concerned John Henry Newman on the subject of faith during Newman's Anglican period. The dissertation was supervised by Robert Pierce Casey and Eleanor Bisbee. He authored six books and numerous articles. While president of the university, Father Elbert founded the Marian Library; "News from the University of Dayton, Public Relations Department," September 11, 1966, series 7J (A2), AUD.

22. College graduate committee minutes, January 4, 1961, 1, series 4EC (1), box 1, folder 2, AUD.

next summer. The reluctant faculty had no choice but to go along with the plans of the Marianist administration.

ACADEMIC YEAR 1962–1963

In the fall of 1962, days before the Cuban missile crisis, Philosophy chairman Father Rhodes announced at a department meeting that the Philosophy Club was being reactivated and appointed John Chrisman as its moderator.[23] The club was open to students and faculty "for purposes of promoting and stimulating informal discussion of philosophical topics."[24] One of the first panel discussions sponsored by the club brought together five faculty members from the sciences, English, and philosophy departments to discuss the topic "Creating Life in the Lab." While there is no record that the discussion generated controversy, the topic shows that students and faculty were willing to plunge into potentially controversial topics.

Two spring 1963 Intellectual Frontiers Series lectures on the topic of existentialism led Thomists and non-Thomists to square off publicly against each other for the first time. On February 28, Father John Elbert gave the first lecture on the subject. The student newspaper, *Flyer News*, announced that Father Elbert would "discuss this controversial philosophy as to whether it has run its course or whether it still has a future."[25]

Elbert's lecture, published a year later in the *University of Dayton Review*, assumed that his listeners lacked a good understanding of philosophy. In a rather tedious presentation, he led his listeners through various philosophical views of reality before defining existentialism as a philosophical system that gives priority and stress to existence.

After reviewing the historical evolution of existentialism, Elbert concluded that existentialism was "the bitter dregs and lees of a humanism

23. No information is available on the club's period of inactivity, the reason for that inactivity, or what prompted its reactivation. The reactivation was simply announced at the faculty meeting.

24. Department of Philosophy faculty meeting minutes, October 11, 1962, 1, series 20QI (3), box 1, folder 1, AUD.

25. "Beatniks Are First Topic in Frontier Series," *Flyer News*, February 21, 1963, 8, accessed June 9, 2016, https://flyernews.com/wp-content/uploads/2016/03/02-21-1963.pdf.

from which has been drained every last drop of what really makes man human, namely his relation to God." It is "the philosophy of those who have lost contact with God and man." In his view, an existentialist is "a helpless victim of dread,"[26] and the "way out of an existentialist impasse" is Christ and the cross. Clearly, for Elbert, existentialism was atheistic. Although he noted that there are "claimants to the name of Christian existentialism," he did not name them or explain their views.[27]

There was no coverage of the lecture in the student newspaper, but at least one person in the audience, Marianist brother John J. Lucier, a chemistry professor, was surprised at Elbert's assessment of existentialism. Lucier knew that Elbert did his doctoral work at the University of Cincinnati, a secular university, and thought Elbert would be more open to existentialism.[28]

On April 18, Theodore Kisiel, a philosophy faculty member in his first year in the department, responded to Father Elbert. A former nuclear reactor engineer, Kisiel earned his doctorate at Duquesne University, known for its program in continental philosophies, particularly phenomenology. His dissertation, "Toward an Ontology of Crisis," was on German existentialist philosopher Martin Heidegger. Kisiel took courses in Thomistic philosophy as background for his Duquesne program and knew he would be teaching Thomism at the University of Dayton. What he did not know until he arrived was that most faculty in the Philosophy Department at Dayton were opposed to existentialism. Dayton was not a good fit for him; he stayed only one year.[29]

26. John A. Elbert, "Existentialism: Horizon or Dead End?," *University of Dayton Review* 1, no. 2 (Summer 1964): 17.

27. Elbert, "Existentialism," 18.

28. John J. Lucier, interview by the author, March 12, 1999. Lucier graduated from the University of Dayton with a bachelor's degree in chemistry (1937) and received his doctorate in chemistry from Western Reserve University (now Case Western Reserve). He was a chemistry professor at the University of Dayton for forty-five years and was chairman of the department from 1964 to 1980. During his tenure, Lucier worked on a nuclear testing project with Wright-Patterson Air Force Base called Operation Upshot-Knothole, in which he devised temperature-measuring devices to gauge the effects of the atomic bomb. As a result, he was invited to witness A-bomb testing in the Nevada desert. He also required all chemistry majors to study a foreign language, a requirement still in place today.

29. Theodore J. Kisiel, email message to the author, June 11, 1999, and telephone interview with the author, June 21, 1999.

Kisiel recalls being nervous about the Intellectual Frontiers Series lecture, so much so that he practiced the lecture in order to "get it right."[30] He started his lecture by quoting Friedrich Nietzsche, "God is dead.... We *have killed him*—you and I. We are all murderers." These words "serve as a guiding clue to the immediate issue [in the lecture], namely, the extent, the significance and the challenge of atheistic existentialism."[31]

As did Elbert, Kisiel asked, "What is existentialism?" He responded that there were two versions—theistic and atheistic—and he named philosophers in both camps. Kisiel claimed that existence "has nothing to do with the Scholastic [Thomistic] notion of *existential*," things that exist. For existentialists, existence refers to "the manner of being which is proper to man, and to man alone."

Kisiel explained what existence meant to Kierkegaard, Edmund Husserl, and, ultimately, Martin Heidegger, "the greatest of the existentialist philosophers," who gave us the notion of "existence as being-in-the-world and openness to Being."[32] Kisiel explored Heidegger's four dimensions of existence and eventually determined that Heidegger and St. Thomas, among other philosophers, are relative atheists, atheists of a certain type who negate "all counterfeit gods."[33] Kisiel claimed they must be relative atheists if they are to be authentic theists.

Kisiel continued that "we must be a little more discriminate in our charges of atheism and negativism" and then asked if "philosophy can hope to bring men closer to the divine God by means of the traditional [Thomistic] Five Ways."[34] He answered that "philosophy today needs a much more personal category of causality, a category in which the divine creativity and human freedom can be reconciled."[35] This led to a critique of Thomism and recommendation that Thomism must "dialogue with existential phenomenology" in order to be "a living contemporary philosophy capable of supplying an answer to the problems of our time."[36]

30. Kisiel, telephone interview, June 21, 1999.

31. Theodore J. Kisiel, "The Atheism of Heidegger, Sartre, and St. Thomas," *University of Dayton Review* 1, no. 2 (Summer 1964): 19.

32. Kisiel, "Atheism," 21.

33. Kisiel, "Atheism," 28.

34. Kisiel, "Atheism."

35. Kisiel, "Atheism," 29.

36. Kisiel, "Atheism," 30.

His criticism of Thomism would have been enough to irritate most of the Dayton philosophers in attendance. Kisiel, however, went further than a criticism; he leveled an indictment on the way philosophy was taught at the University of Dayton and other Catholic universities:

> I mean real dialogue, and not the approach of the Scholastic manual, which sets up straw men of everyone except Aristotle and Aquinas, and then proceeds to mow them down like badmen in a Western movie. Such an approach can hardly be called dialogue.
>
> And so we casually dismiss a philosophy that holds the promise of bringing philosophy closer to the burning issues of human existence, something that the scholastic manual sorely needs. For the typical textbook now in use in Catholic universities reduces philosophy to a verbal game with stock formulas, a game that only serves to convince the student of the sterility of philosophy. Instead of presenting philosophy as an adventure of the human spirit, instead of raising the basic issues of existence, instead of opening up the world in all of its excitement and anguish, grandeur and misery, we offer our students a few exercises in logic-chopping, which they commit to memory for a short time and then forget as quickly as possible. And so philosophy in Catholic schools has become notorious for its dull and sterile courses which are the butt of standard jokes even on our own campuses. And so our students graduate without ever being exposed to the vital issues which are afoot in human existence, and especially in the world today. Such an approach can hardly be called education for life. In fact, it might be exactly the opposite. As Father James Royce warns us, "We cannot afford to educate students for life in a hypothetical English speaking 13th century."[37]
>
> Tonight we have not been dealing with trivial issues. Neither is this one a trivial issue. I refer now to our terrifying responsibilities as educators in a crucial twentieth century.[38]

Marianist brother John J. Lucier recalls that at this point Father Elbert was asked to comment. Lucier wanted Elbert to "stand up and say something scholarly,"[39] to refute Kisiel. Instead, Elbert declined, and Lucier was disappointed.

The Thomists in the audience must have been livid at Kisiel's critique of Thomism and their manner of teaching it. In a personal conversation,

---

37. James E. Royce, SJ, *Man and His Nature* (New York: McGraw Hill, 1961), vi.
38. Kisiel, "Atheism," 30–31.
39. John J. Lucier, interview with the author, March 12, 1999.

Father Stanley recalls asking philosophy professor Joseph Dieska to respond to Kisiel; Dieska refused.[40] Perhaps he was not comfortable with an oral presentation, since English was not his native language. Instead, Dieska replied to Kisiel in a document that his colleague, philosophy professor Marianist father Richard J. Dombro, edited.

Dieska, a native of Czechoslovakia, where he earned his bachelor's (1931), master's (1939), and doctoral (1940) degrees, began teaching at the University of Dayton in fall 1960 as an assistant professor. A former seminarian, Dieska's philosophical training was Thomistic. He taught at Slovak State University in Bratislava (1944–48), chaired the Slovak Philosophical Association (1945–48), edited the *Slovak Philosophical Revue* (1945–48), and directed the philosophical institute Slovak Matica (1945–48).[41]

In addition to his academic career, Dieska was involved in politics. He served as a member of the Slovak National Parliament[42] and was president of the Slovak Christian Democratic Party of Freedom.[43] In February 1948, when the communists took control of the government, he was forced to flee for his life, leaving behind his wife and two small children.[44] Dieska continued his political activity abroad as one of twelve board members of the Council of Free Czechoslovakia representing Czechoslovak exiles in their efforts to restore democracy to Czechoslovakia.[45]

40. Thomas E. Stanley, Summary testimony before the archbishop's fact-finding committee, December 31, 1966, 4, University of Dayton, Unorthodox Teaching Investigation, 1967, RG1.6, Abp Alter, AAC.

41. "L. Joseph Dieska," in *Gale Literary Databases, Contemporary Authors* [database-online]; accessed March 30, 1999, http://www.galenet.com.

42. Slovakia declared its independence in March 1939 after the combined Czecho-Slovak government collapsed under pressure from Adolf Hitler. Josef Tiso, a Roman Catholic priest, became president of the Slovak Republic and placed the country under German protection. Starting in August 1944, Slovak democrats and communists revolted against Tiso's government, and by April 1945, Soviet troops occupied the country. In April 1947, Tiso was hanged as a collaborator. In February 1948, the communists took control of the restored Czecho-Slovak state and began ruling it as a dictatorship; "20th Century History," Slovakia.org: *Guide to the Slovak Republic*, accessed November 11, 2019, http://www.slovakia.org/history6.htm.

43. "Meet the New Faculty," *Monday Morning Memo*, September 26, 1960, 3, series 3N (3), AUD.

44. Dennis Bonnette reports that the communist government sentenced Dieska to death in absentia. When the Czechoslovakian government granted a universal amnesty in the early 1960s, Dieska was one of thirteen not granted amnesty; Bonnette, email message to the author, June 4, 1999.

45. "The Council of Free Czechoslovakia," Wikipedia, accessed June 10, 2016.

Upon making his way to the United States through Canada, Dieska taught languages at Georgetown Institute of Languages and Linguistics (1951–53), languages and sociology at St. Joseph's High School in Cleveland, Ohio, where he came into contact with the Marianists (1956–60), and philosophy at Borromeo College in Cleveland (1959–60).[46]

Dieska passionately loved the church and just as passionately hated communism. He was a man with deep beliefs, willing to challenge those with whom he disagreed, and willing to support church leadership in their conflicts with the modern world. He was up to any fight with other faculty over Thomism and doctrine.

Marianist father Richard Dombro was also willing to enter the fight. With degrees from the University of Dayton (bachelor's in 1929) and Fordham University (master's degree in 1952 and Ph.D. in 1958), Dombro was appointed to the University of Dayton Philosophy Department in 1952. Although his background was in Thomistic philosophy, Dombro's dissertation, under leading Roman Catholic philosopher and theologian Dietrich von Hildebrand, offered "an exposition of Cardinal Newman's philosophy of religion through a concrete analysis of his two supreme realities, God and myself."[47]

Dieska's twenty-two-page (eleven pages of text and eleven pages of footnotes) reply to Kisiel's Intellectual Frontiers Series lecture was reproduced on bright pink paper and distributed campus-wide. This was probably the first such "open letter" between the Dayton philosophers, a method used to debate with each other in the early years of the "Heresy" Affair. Dieska always put his letters on bright pink paper. The responses were generally on yellow paper. The faculty involved do not recall how the color-coded paper concept originated, but the method ensured that the entire campus was aware of the controversy and which side they were reading.

---

46. Dieska retired from the University of Dayton in 1978 and died in Dayton on March 15, 1995. Although in later years he was able to visit his family in Slovakia, they never joined him in Dayton.

47. Richard J. Dombro, "The Two Supreme Newmanic Realities" (PhD diss., Fordham University, 1958), ASM(CIN).

Dieska objected to Kisiel's "general attitude" of contrasting the philosophy of Heidegger and Sartre with "the profoundly traditional Christian thinking of Thomism." He quoted extensively from authors who disagreed with Heidegger's philosophical position. Dieska's purpose was to refute "Kisiel's hope that Heidegger, or for that matter any of the existentialists, could contribute significantly to the growth and improvement of Thomism,... the *philosophia perennis*."[48] Dieska quoted Pius XII's 1950 encyclical *Humani generis*,[49] which described itself as "a paternal exhortation to all teachers entrusted with the formation of the minds eager for knowledge and wisdom." The paragraphs in question, addressed to teachers in ecclesiastical institutions, remind them that "due reverence and submission" must be professed toward the teaching authority of the church.[50]

Kisiel "did not want to continue the battle," since he knew he was leaving Dayton to accept a position at Canisius College. Others, however, prompted him to respond.[51] So, on May 27, 1963, he published a six-page essay reproduced on yellow paper and distributed across campus. Kisiel defended his definition of atheism and suggested that Dieska should "try to control [his] pious indignation and apologetic fervor" in order to study more carefully the atheists he rejects. Kisiel was confident that his "approach will no doubt tax the univocal minds of decadent scholastics, but it certainly should be no problem for those versed in the analogical thinking of authentic Thomism."[52]

Kisiel said that it is easy to compile a list of authorities opposed to Heidegger, but Dieska's "selective nature" of quoting from "secondary sources is reminiscent of a 1950 Senate investigation." He pointed out that

48. Joseph Dieska, "A Reply: Some Observations on Dr. R. Kisiel's "Atheism of Heidegger, Sartre and St. Thomas," n.d., 18, Roesch papers, series 91–35, box 5, AUD.

49. Pius XII, *Humani generis*, August 12, 1950, http://www.vatican.va/holy_father/pius_xii/encyclicals/documents/hf_p-xii_enc_12081950_humani-generis_en.html.

50. Dieska, "A Reply," n.d., 20.

51. Theodore J. Kisiel, telephone conversation with the author, June 21, 1999. Kisiel does not recall who prompted him to respond.

52. This comment was a critique of the philosophy being taught, based on Thomas Aquinas's commentators, not Aquinas's actual works, at Catholic colleges, including the University of Dayton; Theodore J. Kisiel, "The Sphinx of Atheism," May 27, 1963, 1, Roesch papers, series 91–35, box 5 of 6, AUD.

Dieska used sources from 1929, but that Heidegger's thought had evolved since then. As might be expected, Kisiel claimed that Heidegger's existentialism was not the type condemned in *Humani generis*. This familiar argument ("what was condemned is not what I teach") has been invoked by many philosophers and theologians.

Dieska did not let Kisiel have the last word. Four days later, he replied in another open letter, again reproduced on bright pink paper and distributed campus-wide. Dieska stated that his initial response to Kisiel's lecture was "exclusively polemical." He took issue with Kisiel's comment on "secondary sources," adding that Kisiel's lecture, "as [he] remembered it, was based on very little source material, if any at all."[53]

Dieska said that his first reply was meant for the campus and the audience in attendance at the lecture. He was concerned Kisiel misled them and felt they needed to know "the other side of the coin." Dieska wrote:

> Nowhere in your lecture did you mention a single word about the papal encyclical's alarming concern in respect to existentialism. I could then conclude from this that you were not aware that such a solemn utterance had been made. Consequently, it became my concern to let this campus know that, as Catholic teachers, such an important document deserves our meditative consideration. That much at least I feel I have achieved, for your reply says nothing to gainsay it."[54]

The concerns expressed by Dieska were particularly important, as they would be frequently repeated as tensions continued to escalate in the Philosophy Department: (1) concern that the audience, especially the student audience, was misled; (2) concern that the church's position on the issue was never mentioned; (3) the responsibility that Dieska felt as a Catholic philosopher to publicly correct Kisiel and others; and (4) a sense of loyalty in standing up for the church and making its teachings known.

53. Joseph Dieska, "An Open Letter on the Heidegger Issue," May 31, 1963, 1, Roesch papers, series 91–35, box 5 of 6, AUD.
54. Dieska, "An Open Letter," 2.

Philosophy Club meetings provided the venue for the controversy in the fall semester of 1963. At the September 23 club meeting, Dr. Eulalio R. Baltazar, the second non-Thomist in the Philosophy Department, asked, "Is Thomism right enough?"[55] He argued that Thomism was good for a medieval world but not for the present world. Instead, reality needs to be viewed as a process rather than a substance. *Flyer News* reporter Steve Bickham called Baltazar's lecture "a serious indictment of Thomism, charging [Thomism] with being irreconcilably out of step with the times."[56] He went on, "A speech differing so much from the general Philosophical (*sic*) trend at UD did not receive 100 per cent approval. Comments varied from straight out praise to definite displeasure." In fact, a number of "Heresy" Affair participants cite this lecture as the origin of the controversy.

Baltazar, a native of the Philippines, arrived in the United States in July 1955 as a Jesuit seminarian with undergraduate degrees in agriculture (1945) and philosophy (1949) and a master of arts in philosophy (1952). As a seminarian, Baltazar studied theology at Woodstock College in Maryland, where he came into contact with Jesuits John Courtney Murray and Gustave Weigel, whom Baltazar thought were "two of the greatest theologians" at that time.[57] He also read the banned works of Teilhard de Chardin that were then circulating among the Jesuits. Teilhard's writing resonated with Baltazar's background in science. Baltazar became convinced that Thomas Aquinas's "religious explanations were inadequate for a modern world of social progress, ferment, science, and change."[58] Baltazar left the Jesuits just prior to ordination and began doctoral work in philosophy at Georgetown University. There he developed a friendship with two Marianist brothers, Joseph Walsh and Gerald Bettice, who were working on their doctoral degrees. These Marianists knew the University

55. Eulalio Baltazar provided the author with a poster advertising the event. The title of the lecture was advertised as, "Is Thomism right enough?" The headline of the *Flyer News* article reporting on the meeting was "Ideas in Our University: Is Thomism Enough for Us?"; Steve Bickham, *Flyer News*, September 27, 1963, 4.

56. Bickham, "Ideas in Our University: Is Thomism Enough for Us?," 4.

57. Gabrielle Smith, "Religious Controversy Today," *Dayton Daily News*, January 2, 1967, 20.

58. Smith, "Religious Controversy Today."

of Dayton needed philosophy instructors and encouraged Baltazar to apply. He completed his Ph.D. at Georgetown University (1962) and began teaching at the University of Dayton in the fall of 1962.[59]

Shortly after the address to the Philosophy Club, dean of the university Father Thomas Stanley asked Baltazar to write an article on this topic. The following spring, "Re-examination of the Philosophy Curriculum in Catholic Higher Education" appeared in the inaugural issue of the *University of Dayton Review*.

Baltazar began by stating that "at no time in our modern era have philosophy and theology in our Catholic Colleges been in a state of greater ill-repute than at the present." Philosophy is the paramount problem because

> the students abhor philosophy and would have nothing to do with it if left to their own choice of courses. Those students who have gone through the curriculum consider it abstract, arid, academic, even pedantic and out of touch with reality. But the bigger student complaint is that Catholic schools present only one philosophy—the Thomistic. The students are not so undiscerning as to miss the obvious purpose of this so-called Catholic philosophy, which is to indoctrinate, to save souls by keeping Catholics in the Faith and perhaps win others to it. Philosophy is used for an apologetic purpose rather than as a liberalizing discipline; it produces a ghetto mentality rather than an openness of mind, which is one of the main purposes of education. The non-philosophy professors are cold, even frankly hostile towards philosophy. It is considered as so much wasted time which could have been devoted to more useful subjects.[60]

How do the philosophers themselves deal with this criticism?

> We have exculpated ourselves by explaining this antagonism in terms of the positivistic, materialistic and pragmatic attitude of modern society—attitudes which are radically opposed to philosophic thinking. There are those among us who look back nostalgically to the Middle Ages in which philosophy was supreme.[61]

59. Baltazar's dissertation title was, "A Critical Examination of the Methodology of [Teilhard de Chardin's] *The Phenomenon of Man*" under dissertation director Wilfrid Desan.

60. Eulalio R. Baltazar, "Re-examination of the Philosophy Curriculum in Catholic Higher Education," *University of Dayton Review* 1, no. 1 (Spring 1964): 27.

61. Baltazar, "Re-examination," 27.

"In the interest of truth," philosophers need to reexamine their field, the philosophic premises underlying the curriculum and the teaching method. Baltazar wanted

> a radical departure from that followed in departmental meetings where Thomistic philosophy and theology are taken for granted, unquestioned and treated as sacred cows such that whatever changes and recommendations are made are done within the context of Thomism itself. Freedom of inquiry and research are thus curtailed by an authoritative fiat.[62]

Baltazar reexamines the nature of Catholic education, questioning the traditional philosophy of man. He faults Thomism because it places human nature as an essential being outside history and temporality. Baltazar proposes a view of man that goes "back to the Scriptures, formulated by St. Paul and St. John, expressed by St. Augustine in his *City of God*, confirmed by the best modern thought in psychology, anthropology, and existential philosophy, and freshly formulated by Teilhard de Chardin in his book *The Phenomenon of Man*."[63] These thinkers view man as historical and temporal. Education, therefore, is "*incarnational, historical*," as well as "*unitive, catholic*." Its purpose is to form "a man who, in the words of St. Paul, is all things to all men."[64]

Baltazar argues that "the ghetto policy of Catholic Higher Education is based on an individualistic notion of man" that goes back to the ancient Greek and medieval times. In the 1960s, however, Catholics are beginning to see themselves not as individuals but as part of the Mystical Body, a theme the Second Vatican Council espoused. "The notion of the Mystical Body, of corporate personality, of apostolicity and the priesthood of the laity have not yet influenced our Catholic universities and their curricula."[65]

According to Baltazar, the Thomists claim that "Thomism is the one and only true philosophy,... [so] the absolutist approach must necessarily be followed."[66] Baltazar argues that if man "attains his fulness historically,"

62. Baltazar, "Re-examination."
63. Baltazar, "Re-examination," 29.
64. Baltazar, "Re-examination," 29–30.
65. Baltazar, "Re-examination," 31.
66. Baltazar, "Re-examination," 32.

then education, including philosophy, must be historical; "there is need to know thoroughly past philosophical systems, not only to understand the spirit of the past, but more importantly, to know our present and direct it with greater sureness towards its proper goal."[67]

Baltazar argues, finally, that teaching only Thomism is untenable. First, he quotes various theologians, including Joseph Ratzinger [later Pope Benedict XVI], who say that Leo XIII did not intend for Thomism to be "the official philosophy of the Church for all times." Second, Baltazar argues that the laity do not need to be protected and treated as children. Catholics must know more than Thomism in order to be apostles in the world. Third, Baltazar says that the theology and philosophy of Catholics are not better than those of others. His examples are the advances made by Protestant scripture scholars and the church's opposition to Galileo and Darwin—"sad and embarrassing consequences."[68]

Baltazar calls for philosophy and all of Catholic higher education to adopt a historical perspective and move away from an "absolutizing instinct." He backs up his conclusion with quotes from the German Julius Cardinal Döpfner, Jesuit father William Lynch, Leslie Dewart, and Pope John XXIII, "the man whom God chose to be Pope for our time and to open the Council, precisely because he had a keen historical sense." Alas, Baltazar knows "this educational change will not be in the near future."[69]

The day after Baltazar's lecture to the Philosophy Club, the philosophy faculty began reviewing the undergraduate curriculum and teaching methodologies. Obviously, the Thomists knew how Baltazar and Chrisman felt about Thomism. It was provost Father Stanley who, in October 1962, called for this review.[70] Moreover, Stanley told the department "not to overlook" Dr. Edward Harkenrider's proposal that had been submitted in response to Father Roesch's 1960 $20,000 challenge to the faculty.[71]

67. Baltazar, "Re-examination," 36.
68. Baltazar, "Re-examination," 36–37.
69. Baltazar, "Re-examination," 39.
70. Stanley's request was contained in a response he wrote to departmental minutes that were sent to him for information and review purposes. The university had a form for the purpose of review of minutes.
71. At the first faculty meeting of the 1960–61 academic year, Father Roesch stated that he would give $20,000 to the academic department that "would devise some program to 'guarantee a sound breakthrough in its academic area.'" The purpose of the challenge was to

In response to Stanley's request, Harkenrider reworked his proposal and submitted it to the department for this review.

Edward Harkenrider was hired at the University of Dayton in 1952 with bachelor's (1944), master's (1945), and Ph.D. (1952) degrees from the Catholic University of America. By the late fifties, he noticed that too often students failed to grasp the unity and integrity of philosophy, and, as a result, philosophy was "largely meaningless" to them. He therefore recommended that all philosophy courses focus on a common theme, the dignity of man, "his worthwhileness," to give students a "unified and meaningful grasp of philosophy." Students would be placed in a group and remain with that group and the same instructor for the required five semesters of courses.[72] The discussion of Harkenrider's proposal opened the door to wider discussions on the undergraduate curriculum. However, changes to the entire philosophy curriculum took another four years to implement.

A week after Baltazar's lecture, there was another Philosophy Club meeting. Approximately one hundred people attended as Father Richard Dombro lectured on the modernity of St. Thomas Aquinas and the relationship of Thomism to contemporary problems. Dombro claimed that the existentialisms were not philosophical syntheses and needed to be evaluated in a Thomistic framework. Only Thomism has, he claimed, the "basic principles for the interpretation of all reality and the relational situations of reality."[73]

An unnamed *Flyer News* reporter interviewed a number of people who attended Dombro's lecture. Dr. Francis R. Kendziorski,[74] assistant

---

encourage excellence and "significant" contributions to the educational world; "Father Roesch Offers Challenge," *Flyer News*, September 20, 1960, 1. Harkenrider's proposal came in second when the proposals were judged in May 1961; Edward Harkenrider, personal history written for his granddaughter, 104. A copy of the personal history was given to the author by Harkenrider.

72. Edward Harkenrider, "A Proposal to the $20,000 Challenge: A New Procedure in the Teaching of Philosophy," n.d. A copy of the proposal was given to the author by Harkenrider.

73. "Philosophy Club Lecture: Modernity of Aquinas Known," *Flyer News*, October 18, 1963, 8.

74. Francis R. Kendziorski is a Michigan native who received his bachelor's degree from the University of Detroit and his Ph.D. at Cornell University. He remained at the University of Dayton until 1967. The remainder of his career was spent at Western Connecticut State University in Danbury, Connecticut, where he is an emeritus professor of physics.

professor of physics and a graduate of the University of Detroit, also a Catholic university, was quoted in the student newspaper as saying, "I thought it was a great sermon. I wonder what would happen to Thomistic philosophy if its theology were removed?"[75] That comment led to a public debate through open letters between Father Dombro and Kendziorski that were reprinted in the *Flyer News*.

Kendziorski's former girlfriend Patricia, also a physics graduate from the University of Detroit and then employed by NASA, recalls that Kendziorski contacted her when he became embroiled in the controversy with Father Dombro. He needed help composing his response to Dombro and knew she was thinking about graduate study in Thomism. The communication over the response to Dombro led to a rekindling of their romance and ultimate marriage on February 29, 1964.[76]

Father Dombro's initial response to Kendziorski's question was that he would have welcomed Kendziorski's question the night of the lecture if it had been asked then. Dombro pointed out that "*all philosophy, all philosophies and all philosophers* encounter the problem of God; one needs, of course, to make the distinction between sacred and natural theology. There is one exception, the PURELY atheistic approach."

According to the report in the *Flyer News*, Dombro added

1. When argument fails, sarcasm takes over. Yet sarcasm is no argument, and more, especially, if what is expressed through it, is not TRUE.
2. Sarcasm does not foster open-minded dialogue, nor interdisciplinary communication.
3. And finally, a man who patters out a question with no concern for the answer is far from WISDOM and KNOWLEDGE.[77]

Dieska also answered Kendziorski's question, which Dombro attached to his own:

75. "Philosophy Club Lecture," *Flyer News*, 8.
76. Patricia Kendziorski to the author, March 8, 2017.
77. "Lecture Sparks Letters," *Flyer News*, November 15, 1963, 4.

If theology were removed from Thomistic philosophy absolutely nothing would happen because there is no Theology revealed, or Sacred Science included.

However, if Natural Theology or Philosophy of God were removed the same thing would happen to Thomism as to any other philosophical system past or present. We just would not have any philosophical knowledge about God.

However, the question is whether any philosophy other than the philosophy of St. Thomas is more able to support certain theological doctrines.

Philosophy, in supporting certain theological truths, does not deprive itself of its philosophical character, just as biology is not less an empirical science because some of its discoveries are in support of certain theological doctrines.[78]

Kendziorski replied in an open letter, printed side by side with Dombro's letter in the *Flyer News*, pointing out that the quote printed in the newspaper was "an abbreviation of what I said to the reporter" and that "there is a difference between sarcasm for its own sake and the making of a critical statement." Kendziorski thought that approaching Thomism through theology was a weakness from the philosophical viewpoint. Philosophical errors should be refuted with reasons from other philosophers, not using documents of faith. Indeed, one of the critiques of the Thomists during the "Heresy" Affair is that their arguments were based on papal documents rather than philosophy. Kendziorski claimed that Catholic universities had so little faith in Thomism "that students are permitted a minimum amount of contact with other philosophies under unrealistic laboratory conditions." This leads to philosophy becoming "the thinking man's theology," which is not good for philosophy or for sacred theology. Kendziorski continued, "What is there to fear by allowing [Thomism] to face other philosophies on their own terms?" He ended by calling for a public debate by "qualified philosophers."[79]

Father Dombro responded to Dr. Kendziorski in an open letter dated November 21, 1963, the day before President John F. Kennedy's assassination, which was distributed campus-wide. His letter indicates that a philosophical controversy exists on campus:

78. "Lecture Sparks Letters."
79. "Lecture Sparks Letters."

The kind of ferment that is now stirring in some places on this campus has now come into the clear. Your open letter of November 4 is an evidence of this type of thinking. Textually one might suspect that the document is a compilation of unsupported opinions from several quarters.

Dombro points out that Kendziorski missed the most important point in his letter, the distinction between natural and sacred theology. If Kendziorski understood the difference, he would not be confused about theological and philosophical approaches.

Dombro states that Kendziorski allows "a commitment to every philosophy, except the Christian philosophy of St. Thomas." He quotes Thomas saying that we should be open to the truth of all things and says this quote is evidence that "there is (and always has been) an open tradition in our Christian philosophical heritage together 'with a critical yet generous response to modern thought.'"

Dombro concludes by saying that before students can explore other philosophies, they "must be equipped first with a thorough understanding of the truth of fundamental concepts and principles.... [A] reason for emphasizing the philosophy of St. Thomas over 'other philosophies' is: this philosophy is rooted in a soil in which religious convictions are formed."[80]

Regarding the debate proposed by Kendziorski, Dombro thinks the idea does not go far enough. He would like a "DISCIPLINED DEBATE carried out within the framework of the university between individuals and among the faculties, where there is a dedication to an integrated truth."[81] There is no evidence that a debate as described by Dombro occurred on the UD campus. Baltazar's and Dombro's talks at the Philosophy Club meetings led the *Flyer News* to editorialize:

> Exciting—is the best term to describe the recent lectures which took place under the auspices of the Philosophy Club. A university should be the home of ideas, and in sponsoring such dialogues and lectures, the Philosophy Club is doing a great service for UD. We'd like to see more dialogues and discussions of this sort by other groups on campus; such things are what a true university is made of.[82]

80. Richard J. Dombro to Francis Kendziorski, November 21, 1963.
81. Dombro to Kendziorski, November 21, 1963.
82. Editorials, *Flyer News*, October 18, 1963, 2.

Several students contributed to the campus conversation by writing columns for the *Flyer News*. Senior philosophy major Robert Baumgartner, writing to Kendziorski, clearly saw the issues in late fall 1963 when he pointed out in his "Be It Resolved" column that three correlations must be kept in mind: "the attitude toward truth, the question of academic freedom, and the fact that UD is a Catholic university."[83] Senior German major Ed Esch, responding to Baumgartner in his "The Eschtray" column, accepted Thomism but also wanted to examine it, "see where it is lacking, and try to fill in the gaps with those systems which can offer us newly found truths."[84]

Baumgartner replied to Esch in the January 10, 1964, issue. His column is worthy of review because he unwittingly predicts future occurrences. He pointed out the dangers inherent in a public dialogue without guidelines and noted that "if there has been no prior general agreement about guidelines, highly personalized presentations, although not wrong, will tend to predominate, opening the door for an extended clash of personalities rather than ideas." Possible results include loss of respect for professors and a "mockery of perennial acknowledged thought."[85] Baumgartner correctly identified that there were strong personalities on both sides of this issue, that the discussion was getting out of hand, and that guidelines were needed. Unfortunately, Baumgartner's warnings were not heeded, and an "extended clash" ensued. His suggested committee to develop guidelines only became a reality in 1967 when it was part of the resolution of the controversy.

In the middle of the 1963–64 academic year, Lawrence Ulrich was hired as a philosophy faculty member to replace a faculty member on medical leave. Ulrich entered St. Gregory's Seminary in Cincinnati at the age of fourteen. He earned bachelor's (1961) and master's (1962) degrees from the Catholic University of America and was working on a master's degree in education from Xavier University. After much soul searching, Ulrich decided not to return to the seminary after Christmas break.

---

83. Robert Baumgartner, "Be It Resolved: A Real Issue?," *Flyer News*, November 22, 1963, 3.
84. Ed Esch, "The Eschtray: A Real Issue," *Flyer News*, December 6, 1963, 5.
85. Robert Baumgartner, "Be It Resolved: An Approach to Truth," *Flyer News*, January 10, 1964, 3.

About the same time, he met Father Raymond Roesch at a funeral he attended in Dayton. Ulrich asked Roesch about the possibility of obtaining a teaching position. Upon learning Ulrich's academic background, Roesch suggested Ulrich contact the University of Dayton provost, Father Thomas Stanley. Ulrich did so and was hired over the telephone.

Both the students and the Marianist administration kept alive the campus controversy during the spring semester of 1964. Senior Steve Bickham was one of the most vocal critics of Thomism and the way it was taught. A Dayton native, Bickham entered UD as an English major. In his junior year, he took John Chrisman's philosophical psychology course as his third required philosophy course. Chrisman taught philosophy as open and "wrestling with exciting stuff" versus "closed with the death of Thomas." Bickham saw that "philosophy [was] not what [he] thought it was" and asked himself, "If this is philosophy, why don't others teach it?" After the course ended, Bickham changed his major to philosophy, hung out with Chrisman and Baltazar, and ultimately earned a doctorate in philosophy (1970) from Southern Illinois University. He devoted his thirty-three-year career to teaching philosophy at Mansfield University in Pennsylvania, "trying to embody Chrisman's spirit and approach to philosophy."[86]

Throughout February and March 1964, Bickham wrote columns in *Flyer News*. In the Valentine's Day special issue, he took on the legend that a four-headed monster lived on the second floor of St. Mary's Hall (the administration building) and ate "boys not signed with the sign of Thomas." To find out if the monster was real, he wrote "a nasty, bitter, underhanded and satirical attack on the system of Thomistic philosophy" and held his breath.

> Rumors to the contrary, I was not eaten. No thunderbolt flashed from the hand of Jove, no yawning chasm opened itself to swallow me, and I saw no apparition saying, "Stephen, thou hast written poorly of me." Now I believe I am safe in concluding that the halls of St. Mary's are once again safe for the freshmen to wander in peace, and that the myth administration has been exposed as a myth.

86. Stephen H. Bickham, email message to the author, August 21, 2000, and telephone interview with the author, February 4, 2003. Bickham's dissertation title was "Moore, Ayer, and Austin on Sense-Data."

Bickham emphasized that the students are free:

> The administration of this school administrates; they run the school, they make the policy. And since the administration is wise it is not the policy of the University that the student must believe in anything. He does not have to be a Catholic, he does not have to be a Thomist, he does not have to believe in the equality of man. There are certain things he must not attack, such as the Divine Trinity and the Blessed Virgin, and this is the way it should be. But there is a lot of difference between the Blessed Virgin and the system called Thomism.
>
> In the past there have been discussions on campus about academic or intellectual freedom and some people have wondered if it exists here at UD. The doubting of this freedom was caused by the myth of the administration, but now that myth has been exposed. We have been crying for freedom and all the while we have had it. The administration knows that I do not accept the system of Thomism and yet this column still retains its little corner in the paper. If anyone thinks he is not free at this University, he has only himself to blame, because he is still holding on to the old myth.[87]

Although Bickham stated that he had not heard from the administration, at some point the university provost, Father Thomas Stanley, reached out to him. Bickham recalls that Stanley did not say anything negative to him or make any veiled threats. Rather, Stanley wanted to hear Bickham's take on the controversy. Thomists Dombro and Dieska, on the other hand, were enraged at being challenged by a student. Father Dombro, according to Bickham, refused to speak to him when he ran into him on campus, and, a year after Bickham graduated, Dieska was still ranting in class about the "horrible person who wrote columns" criticizing Thomism.[88]

At least one person wondered in a letter to the editor, "Who is Bickham?"[89] Another *Flyer News* columnist, Jim Cain, replied that Bickham is a student who does not agree with Thomas. Cain challenged Bickham for not saying why he disagrees with Thomas. After pointing out that with

---

87. Stephen H. Bickham, "You and I: Myth of the Administration," *Flyer News*, February 14, 1964, 4.

88. Bickham, telephone interview with the author, February 4, 2003. Bickham's wife, Nancy Orazio Bickham, took a class with Dieska a year after Bickham graduated. She is the source of the information that Dieska was still upset with Bickham a year after he graduated.

89. Kathie Pfefferle, "Letters to the Editor: Box 8: A Thinker," *Flyer News*, February 14, 1964, 2.

freedom comes responsibility, Cain stated that in order to disagree with someone, you must have views of your own. Cain realized he did not know enough philosophy to refute Thomas. He knew that there were other students with greater proficiency in philosophy than his own. His point, however, was that other philosophers know enough to challenge Thomas, and yet exposure to them is limited.[90] Cain's column evidently elicited responses, because his next column was entitled, "The Rocket's Red Glare." He notes that "polemics have become pyrotechnics" and that his argument for teaching the thought of other philosophers has become for others a "let's cut Thomas" campaign.[91]

Opposite Cain's column in the February 28, 1964, issue of *Flyer News* was a news report of a Philosophy Club student discussion held the previous week. More than one hundred people attended to hear four students, including Bickham and Baumgartner,[92] discuss Thomistic philosophy and its place in the curriculum. Each speaker was given ten minutes to express his opinions. Questions from the audience followed. Two students were against Thomism, one supported it, and Baumgartner, also a philosophy major, called for stronger faculty guidance on basic philosophical issues.

The *Flyer News* lists Baltazar and Chrisman as faculty attendees. Baltazar, pleased that students were getting involved, is quoted as saying that the first step toward philosophical growth at the university is for professors to realize that "a student is not obliged to passively accept a professor's lecture without question." Chrisman, too, encouraged students to question but "expressed some misgiving about the campus discussion; that the negativity of the approach may convey to some a feeling of antagonism." A "static type of Thomism," not Thomas, is what needed to be attacked.[93]

Chrisman's reported comments make more sense when read along with his letter to the editor in the same issue of the *Flyer News*. There, he

90. Jim Cain, "Right Here: Cato," *Flyer News*, February 20, 1964, 2.
91. Jim Cain, "Right Here: The Rocket's Red Glare," *Flyer News*, February 28, 1964, 3.
92. The other two students were Roland Wagner and Thomas Mappes.
93. "After Student Discussion: 'Thomistic' Question Unresolved," *Flyer News*, February 28, 1964, 3.

acknowledges complaints that Bickham's attack on Thomism "undercuts Catholic education" and oversteps his position as a student." Chrisman indicates that personally he is "a little uneasy" about some of Bickham's expressions because they appear to attack St. Thomas himself, "a great saint and a great thinker." Nevertheless, Chrisman supports his protégé in that Bickham "seems aware that if one is to be heard, one must speak strongly. In order to go far enough, one must sometimes go too far." Further, Bickham has the right to be wrong, and he does not need a "diploma in hand to begin to think for himself and to express his own opinions."[94]

While the students were having their discussions, the faculty continued their conversation with public lectures. Both Harkenrider and Dr. Richard Baker lectured as part of the Intellectual Frontiers Series. Harkenrider spoke on the significance of philosophy,[95] while Baker reviewed the controversy surrounding C. P. Snow's views on science and humanism.[96] Richard R. Baker was the first lay faculty member hired in philosophy at the University of Dayton in 1947 with bachelor's (1931), master's (1934), and Ph.D. (1941) degrees from the University of Notre Dame. Like Harkenrider, Baker was trained as a Thomist. There is no news coverage of either lecture.

At the March 18, 1964, Philosophy Club meeting, Baltazar spoke on the topic "A Philosophy for the Age of Anxiety." Although no news report of the event is available, some general ideas of the substance of Baltazar's lecture can be filtered through Dieska's five-page public response entitled, "Six Questions to Dr. Eulalio Baltazar." According to Dieska, Baltazar suggested we

> do away with Thomism because it is neither adequate nor timely to our needs and demands... and accept the views of Fr. Pierre Teilhard de Chardin, whose evolutionism offers more acceptable solutions to certain philosophical and theological problems.[97]

94. John Chrisman, "Letters to the Editor: Box 8; Right of Expression," *Flyer News*, February 28, 1964, 2.

95. "Faculty Lecture Series to Feature Dr. Harkenrider," *Flyer News*, February 28, 1964, 1.

96. "Intellectual Frontiers Features Dr. Baker," *Flyer News*, March 13, 1964, 8.

97. Joseph Dieska, "Six Questions to Dr. Eulalio Baltazar," n.d., 1, "Heresy File," ASM(CIN).

In response, Dieska asks whether Baltazar's "personal views on Thomism and [Teilhard] de Chardin's cosmic evolution were compatible with Catholic teaching on Thomism as expressed in papal documents (notably since 1879), and particularly as voiced in the Canon Law of the Church." Dieska then quotes Canon 1366, §2, which states that rational philosophy and theology must be "conducted entirely according to the method, doctrines, and principles of the Angelic Doctor."[98]

Question two asks whether the University of Dayton "in its teaching and educational activities" is to "acknowledge and give consent to the exposition of the ordinary teaching authority of the church as expressed in papal decision and decrees." Dieska refers to a 1959 declaration that a university falls under the jurisdiction of the Sacred Congregation of Seminaries and Universities "as long as such a university is under the control in any way of the secular clergy or a religious society."[99]

In question three, Dieska asks Baltazar whether he is familiar with the 1962 *monitum* on Teilhard de Chardin that exhorts presidents of universities, among others, to protect minds, particularly of the youth, against the dangers presented by the works of Father Teilhard and his followers. Question four quotes Aristotle and Thomas and asks Baltazar how to explain these passages "if the Aristotelico-Thomistic mind is as static and anti-evolutionistic" as Baltazar says it is. Dieska notes that Teilhard de Chardin used the same Thomistic quote to support his evolutionistic theory.

Dieska, in question five, asks for an explanation of how the church, "consistently promoting and defending the primacy of St. Thomas," is able to "admit" certain theories of evolution. Dieska clarifies that he is not opposing evolution as a "valid scientific theory." He is opposing anyone who says that Thomistic philosophy is "contrary to the phenomena of evolution."[100]

Question six refers to a point made in Baltazar's lecture that the "ar-

98. Dieska, "Six Questions."

99. Dieska, "Six Questions," 2. For further information on the Sacred Congregation of Seminaries and Universities, see James Tunstead Burtchaell, CSC, *The Dying of the Light: The Disengagement of College and Universities from Their Christian Churches* (Grand Rapids, Mich.: William B. Eerdmans, 1998), 587–89.

100. Dieska, "Six Questions," 4.

ticle of faith formulated by Vatican Council I (1869–70) concerning the possibility of proving God's existence" by human reason "has no reference [to] and does not involve" Thomistic proofs. If Baltazar's point is correct, how is one to understand Pius X's (1910) statement quoted by Pius XI (1923) that "the certain knowledge of God as the first principle of creation... can be inferred, like the knowledge of a cause from its effect, by the light of the natural reason."[101]

In summary, Dieska believed Baltazar's views were in opposition to the teachings of the church. Dieska quoted the appropriate supporting evidence primarily from papal sources. There is no record of a public response by Baltazar, nor does Baltazar recall ever seeing Dieska's document.[102]

During the 1964 spring term, fall teaching assignments were given to the Philosophy faculty by the chair, Father Edmund Rhodes. Dr. Edward Harkenrider was assigned to teach a graduate-level course in existentialism along with his undergraduate courses. Harkenrider had opposed adding the graduate program. Now the course in existentialism was being offered for the first time, and Harkenrider was assigned to teach it. Harkenrider had never even taken a course in existentialism, so much preparation was required. He began preparing almost immediately, certain that he did not look forward to teaching the course.

The stress from the tensions in the Philosophy Department and the extra work of preparing for the new course affected Harkenrider's health.[103] He saw an opportunity to get a "respite from the philosophy department" when Marianist brother George Nagel became ill and was unable to perform his duties as director of student aid and scholarships.[104] Harkenrider asked to replace Brother Nagel during academic year 1964–65. Eventually, Father Roesch agreed but he cut Harkenrider's

101. Pius X, *Motu Proprio* "Sacrorum Antistitum," September 1, 1910, quoted in Pius XI, *Studiorum Ducem*, June 29, 1923, quoted by Dieska, "Six Questions," 5.

102. Eulalio R. Baltazar, telephone interview by author, May 23, 1999.

103. At the time, he suffered from a severe nervous condition resulting in sleeplessness and constant tenseness in his legs; Edward Harkenrider, personal history written for his granddaughter, 199.

104. Brother Nagel died on September 2, 1964. He had been ill for three months; "Bro. Nagel, Head of Student Aid, Dies in Hospital after Three Month Illness," *Flyer News*, September 11, 1964, 1.

salary for the year and still required him to teach the course in existentialism. Harkenrider accepted Roesch's terms, although he felt betrayed and angry over the reduction in pay and the requirement to teach existentialism. These festering emotions and the valuable experience he gained as director of the university's student aid office later prove to be critical to Harkenrider's actions as the controversy unfolded.

The university administration fueled the flames of the controversy with publication of articles in the *University of Dayton Review*, a journal created by the provost, Father Thomas Stanley, for publication of faculty research. The chair of the eight-person editorial board was Stanley; the remaining board members included faculty, four of whom were Marianists. The inaugural issue, published in spring 1964, featured Baltazar's critique of Thomism. The Elbert-Kisiel lectures were published in the second issue in summer 1964. In both issues, the progressive faculty, Baltazar and Kisiel, appeared to be more scholarly than the Thomists. To the Thomists, it seemed that the administration sided with the non-Thomists in the controversy.

The end of the term brought the announcement that Father Edmund Rhodes was stepping down as chair of the Philosophy Department. Father Stanley was not happy with the way Rhodes was handling the conflict in the department. Earlier, Rhodes had reported to Stanley that he had received student complaints that Baltazar was advocating relativism. Rhodes wanted to investigate further and mentioned this again in his faculty evaluation in reference to preparing contracts for the upcoming year. He recommended not renewing the contracts of Baltazar and Chrisman. Stanley did not approve terminating them; he deemed them valuable to the university.[105] Following the then-current process for removing a Marianist from his position at the university, Father Roesch wrote a January 1964 letter to the provincial, Father James Darby, requesting that Father Rhodes be removed. The reason given for removal was that Rhodes was a "poor administrator." Darby approved the request in April 1964, and Rhodes was given an unrequested one-year sabbatical at the University of

105. Father Edmund Rhodes and Edward Harkenrider, Summary of testimonies to archbishop's fact-finding commission, December 20 and 23, 1966, University of Dayton, Unorthodox Teaching Investigation, 1967, RG1.6, Abp Alter, AAC.

Louvain.[106] Dr. Harkenrider said that the "general impression of many in the philosophy dept. [was] that Fr. Stanley removed Fr. Rhodes…because of his expressed opposition to Baltazar and Chrisman."[107] With Rhodes gone, Dr. Richard Baker was appointed acting chair.

In summary, the academic years 1961 to 1964 were a period of change for Catholic colleges and universities in the United States, including the University of Dayton. The university had a new academic leader, Father Thomas Stanley, and new philosophy faculty, several of whom had backgrounds that varied from the traditional Thomism taught in Catholic colleges and universities. These faculty were young and dynamic in the classroom. Not surprisingly, they attracted students and challenged the Thomists, who responded by quoting papal documents rather than engaging in philosophic discussions. It was obvious that Father Thomas Stanley supported the non-Thomist faculty. This emboldened them as the fight continued to escalate for the next two academic years, leading to a full-blown crisis in the fall semester of 1966.

106. James M. Darby to Raymond A. Roesch, April 5, 1964. Darby's letter was a response to a letter from Roesch in January 1964; National Archives of the Marianist Province of the United States.

107. Harkenrider, Summary of testimonies.

CHAPTER 2

ESCALATION

1964–1966

Catholics generally take one of two lines: there are the bold, and these are sometimes rash; and the cautious, who are sometimes reactionary.

— Monsignor Maurice d'Hulst, as quoted in Albert Houtin, *La question biblique chez les catholiques de France au XIXe siècle*

The tumult in Dayton's Philosophy Department continued to escalate in academic years 1964–65 and 1965–66. The administration appointed a new chair of the department, additional faculty were hired, and the issues expanded from the inadequacies of Thomism to moral issues such as situation ethics, contraception, and abortion. The Thomists became more and more convinced that the non-Thomistic faculty were teaching and advocating things contrary to the church. They actively tried to counter the false teachings, mostly by appealing to authorities within and outside the university.

Albert Houtin, *La question biblique chez les catholiques de France au XIXe siècle* (Paris, 1902), 129–34, quoted in Marvin R. O'Connell, *Critics on Trial: An Introduction to the Catholic Modernist Crisis* (Washington, D.C.: The Catholic University Press, 1994), 115.

The academic year 1964–65 began with John Chrisman and Lawrence Ulrich benefitting from Father Thomas Stanley's effort to raise the standards of the faculty; that is, they were on leave for the entire year, with full pay from the university, continuing their doctoral education at the University of Toronto. With Chrisman and Ulrich on leave and the student body growing, five new philosophy faculty were hired for the fall semester. Two got directly involved in the "Heresy" Affair—Hugo A. Barbic and Thomas J. Casaletto. Barbic had a bachelor's degree from the University of San Francisco (1961) and a master's from the University of Toronto (1963).[1] Casaletto arrived at Dayton with a bachelor's degree from Aquinas College in Grand Rapids, Michigan (1960) and a master's degree from the University of Notre Dame (1963).

Theology faculty were also needed. Prior to 1964, Marianist priests were the only faculty in the Theology Department. In addition to teaching, these same Marianists performed other assigned duties such as celebrating mass on campus, hearing confessions, counseling students, performing dorm duty (living in the dorms), teaching at the Marianist Scholasticate at Mount St. John's, and participating in Sunday mass assignments in Dayton area parishes.[2] The first four lay faculty members were hired in the Theology Department in 1964 when it became apparent that there were not enough Marianists to cover the classes for the increased number of undergraduates. Two of the new hires were a husband-and-wife team, Thomas and Dorothy (Irvin) Thompson. In addition to being among the first lay faculty hired to teach theological studies at the University of Dayton, Dorothy Thompson was the first woman hired to teach in the department. The Thompsons stayed at Dayton only one year. Their contracts were not renewed when Mr. Thompson clashed with his chair over class scheduling and the required textbook for a course on the concept of God and the divine in Old Testament literature. For Thompson, the neo-Thomistic textbook proposed by the chair was "quite irrelevant." Thompson was "very pleased" to leave Dayton, as

---

1. Chrisman and Barbic did not know each other at the University of Toronto.
2. Matthew F. Kohmescher, telephone interview with the author, March 10, 1999.

he "found little respect there for either scholarship or teaching and an almost complete lack of any respect for academic freedom."[3]

In the Philosophy Department, a decision needed to be made on a new chair to lead the department during this time of change and to pursue development of the graduate program. All previous chairs had been Marianists, chosen by the university and provincial administrations. In the mid-1960s, choosing a chair for a department was the responsibility of the university administration—namely, the provost, then Father Stanley, with little or no faculty input. Father Stanley believed it would be best to have a layman as chair. He felt that there was also a need for faculty to carry on discussion in an intelligent and scholarly manner.[4] He therefore invited Dr. Anthony A. Nemetz, a Catholic philosopher at the University of Georgia and formerly at the Ohio State University, to lecture on January 26, 1965, as part of the Intellectual Frontiers Series. Nemetz's lecture, "Memory of Things Future," dealt with "time and change in a universal objective way," an aspect of contemporary philosophy touching on Thomism. In addition to the lecture, the purpose of Nemetz's visit was a mutual "look-see." The administration wanted to see if Nemetz was a possible candidate for the chair of Philosophy. Nemetz, for his part, needed to ascertain his own interest in the position. After meeting with the Philosophy faculty, Nemetz made suggestions to the administration for strengthening the department. He also decided that he was not interested in the chair position. He preferred a department with a graduate program

---

3. Thomas L. Thompson, email message to the author, June 11, 2017. Prior to arriving at the University of Dayton, Thomas L. Thompson was a graduate student at the University of Tübingen. After leaving Dayton, Thompson continued his doctoral work at Tübingen. Ultimately, his dissertation, "The Historicity of the Patriarchal Narratives: The Quest for the Historical Abraham," was rejected by Joseph Ratzinger as not fitting for a Catholic theologian, and Thompson left Tübingen without a degree. (Thompson's memoir published online in April 2011 can be found at http://www.bibleinterp.com/opeds/critscho358014.shtml.) Thompson spent much of his career at the University of Copenhagen and is closely associated with the biblical minimalist movement known as the Copenhagen School. Dorothy Irvin has an S.T.D. and Ph.D. in Catholic theology from Tübingen. In addition to teaching theology at several Catholic universities, she is a field archaeologist in Jordan. She is a frequent lecturer on the archaeological sources for women's ministries in the early church. The couple divorced in 1980.

4. Thomas A. Stanley, Summary of testimony to archbishop's fact-finding commission, December 31, 1966, University of Dayton, Unorthodox Teaching Investigation, 1967, RG1.6, Abp Alter, AAC.

already developed rather than one in the process of building a program.[5]

Also in early 1965, senior English major Bob Killian picked up Bickham's *Flyer News* debate on the teaching of Thomistic philosophy through his weekly column "Down Here." Killian "lamented the fact that UD [did] not teach philosophy in a historical context." He claimed to be "abysmally ignorant of the great thinkers of the past six centuries" and "put a great deal of the blame on the philosophy curriculum at UD." His four years of philosophy were a "colossal bore" and "wasted time." He dubbed UD's system of teaching philosophy a "failure" because "philosophy failed to stimulate the student to think for himself" and "failed to generate thought."[6] Killian continued "grinding his ax" in two more columns.[7] Finally, Dr. Richard Baker, the acting chair of Philosophy, responded in a letter to the editor of *Flyer News*. Baker told the story of a young man who bought a spade and used it to try to chop down a tree. When the spade did not work for this purpose, the young man "cursed the person who sold it to him, complained to the Better Business Bureau and even wrote a letter to the editor of the local paper." The young man's twin brother enrolled in a Catholic university and took a course in Christian philosophy. After he graduated, he tried to use his philosophy as a debating tool with "various neo-positivists, phenomenologists and existentialists." Upon losing every debate, "he cursed his alma mater, his old philosophy professors and even wrote [a] letter to the school paper."[8]

Claiming that "it ran in the family," Baker said that neither twin brother learned the purpose of their tools: a spade or a course in Christian philosophy.

> Christian philosophy is studied primarily to acquire a genuine insight into those natural truths accessible by rational methods whereby a student can appreciate the meaning and significance of the truths of divine revelation. A course in Christian philosophy… is a presentation of the basic truths about God, man, and the world, truths which, up to now, have been best expressed among others by such giants as Augustine, Aquinas, and Maritain.

5. Stanley, telephone interview by author, April 10, 1999. Nemetz remained at the University of Georgia throughout his career. He died on February 17, 1989.

6. Bob Killian, "Down Here: Troublemaker," *Flyer News*, January 22, 1965, 5.

7. Bob Killian, "Down Here: Angry Week," *Flyer News*, March 12, 1965, 5.

8. Richard R. Baker, "Box 8: Letters to the Editor: A Spade Is a Spade," *Flyer News*, March 19, 1965, 2.

Dr. Baker concluded that the moral of this story is "find out the purpose of a tool before crying about its inefficiency."[9]

Bob Killian, indicating his respect for Dr. Baker, responded two pages later in the same issue of *Flyer News*, pointing out three things:

1. Implied in a definition of Thomism as "Christian philosophy" is the rather dubious thesis that other philosophies are somehow non-Christian or anti-Christian. [Killian] could name any number of good Christians who are not Thomists and see[s] no contradiction inherent in such a combination.

2. Philosophy was not born nor did it die in the thirteenth century. Thomism is one philosophy among many, and to pretend that the questions of philosophy have all been answered is naïve insularity at best, and self deception at worst.

3. By claiming to have arrived at the "correct answers" Thomism turns doctrine into dogma, reducing the teaching of philosophy from a search for truth to an indoctrination session where the student is force-fed pre-packaged "correct" answers to be memorized and repeated.[10]

Killian "reserves the right to object" because he feels he got "the short end of the stick" when he was required to spend his tuition dollars on philosophy courses: "Are we in an institution of higher learning only to be handed a set of correct answers, pointed in the right direction, and turned loose? Is education that dangerous that it must be replaced by training?"[11]

Baker's letter also generated a response from theology instructors Thomas and Dorothy Thompson. Granted that the purpose of Christian philosophy is as stated by Baker and that the purpose of the university's philosophy courses is to teach a Christian philosophy, the Thompsons questioned whether Baker's three "giants" are adequate to express a Christian philosophy today. They pointed out that defining "Christian

9. Baker, "A Spade Is a Spade."
10. Bob Killian, "Down Here: Reply, with Questions," *Flyer News*, March 19, 1965, 4.
11. Killian, "Down Here: Reply, with Questions."

philosophy as Aristotelian Thomism" also "seems open to the accusation of indoctrination." The Thompsons listed a number of recent Christian philosophers whom Baker forgot to mention. They also pointed out that "if one wanted to limit himself to medieval philosophy, one could hardly reasonably exclude such outstanding Christians as Boethius, Albertus Magnus, Duns Scotus, Pseudo-Dionysius, Peter Lombard, Bonaventure, and William of Occam."[12]

Ironically, on the same page as Thompson's letter to the editor, Dr. Baker announced a change in the philosophy curriculum for incoming freshmen in fall 1965. An "Introduction to Philosophy" course was to replace the freshman Logic course. The new course was "a basic introduction to the problems of philosophy with reference to the Greek philosophers," mainly Plato and Aristotle. Baker indicated that changes to the rest of the philosophy curriculum were "contemplated in the future."[13]

The April Fools' Day 1965 edition of *Flyer News* came out the next week. Alumnus Steve "Bigham" and senior Robert "Killhand" were elected co-chairmen of a revamped Philosophy Department that taught Miscellanism rather than Thomism.[14] No reaction by the Philosophy Department is documented.

ACADEMIC YEAR 1965–1966

The fall semester of 1965 began with the appointment of Marianist father Charles J. Lees as provost. Earlier in 1965, the Marianist provincial, Father James Darby, gave Father Stanley his choice of continuing in the position of provost or becoming the "religious superior at Mount St. John, overseeing the activities and personnel at the busy Scholasticate (the college-level school for men preparing to be Marianists), retreat house and Marianist community."[15] Father Darby preferred that Stanley

---

12. Thomas Thompson and Dorothy Thompson, "Box 8: Letters to the Editor: Philosophy Giants," *Flyer News*, March 26, 1965, 2.

13. "Announce Philosophy Change," *Flyer News*, March 26, 1965, 2.

14. "Thomistic Philosophy Nixed, Philosophy Dept. Revamped," *Flyer News*, April 2, 1965, 5.

15. Death Notice for Thomas Stanley, November 20, 2013, accessed June 10, 2017, https://www.marianist.com/files/2013/11/TomStanleyObit.pdf.

take the superior position, so that is what Stanley did. Stanley, however, continued to work at the University of Dayton as a chaplain, a faculty member in theology, and in the newly created institutional studies office. This allowed Father Roesch to appoint him to key positions on the administrative council and the faculty forum and to continue to seek his counsel.

The appointment of Father Lees as provost was made by Father Darby, presumably with Father Roesch's approval. Lees had a bachelor's degree in philosophy from the University of Dayton (1943), a master's degree in English from the University of Pittsburgh (1952), and a Ph.D. in English from the Ohio State University (1962). He was ordained a priest in 1946. Prior to being named provost, he was a faculty member in the university's English Department for one year. Needless to say, Lees did not have the academic or leadership experience to be chair of a department, let alone provost of the university.

In the Philosophy Department, Dr. Richard Baker, the senior lay person in the department, was appointed chair by the university administration. Although the faculty were not consulted, they "were all delighted because [they] regarded Dr. Baker with respect and esteem and ability."[16] Chrisman returned to the faculty from his studies, while Ulrich remained in Toronto. Five additional Philosophy faculty were hired that year. Two became involved in the "Heresy" Affair—Paul I. Seman and Dennis Bonnette. Seman, a former seminarian hired at the rank of instructor, earned a Ph.B. (Bachelor of Philosophy degree) from Borromeo Seminary in Cleveland (1957) and a master's from the Catholic University of America (1962).[17] By the time he arrived at Dayton, he had completed his doctoral coursework at the Catholic University of America and taught at St. Leo's College in Florida. Seman knew of the Marianists from his high school days at Cleveland Cathedral Latin High School.

Bonnette came to the University of Dayton as an assistant professor. His degrees included a bachelor's from the University of Detroit (1960) and a master's from the University of Notre Dame (1962). By 1963, he had

16. Edward J. Harkenrider, email message to the author, April 1, 1999.

17. Although Seman's transcript reads "Borromeo Seminary," he attended classes at Catonsville in Maryland. Seman was in the seminary for eight years.

completed his doctoral coursework in philosophy at Notre Dame.[18] Prior to arriving at the University of Dayton, Bonnette taught a year at San Diego College for Women (1963–64) and one year at Loyola University in New Orleans (1964–65).[19] He heard about the University of Dayton from a New Orleans friend, Dr. Joseph J. Cooney, a biologist who had been hired by Dayton for the fall of 1965.[20] Bonnette and his family did not like living in the South because of the racial injustices he witnessed and the church's apparent indifference to them. The situation bothered Bonnette so much that he wrote an article, "Race: The Failure of the Church," which was the cover story for the October 23, 1965, issue of the national weekly magazine *Ave Maria*. Bonnette wrote to the University of Dayton and was hired "sight unseen."[21]

In the Theological Studies Department, seven new faculty—one Marianist priest and six laypersons—were hired for the 1965–66 academic year. Among them was Randolph F. Lumpp, who earned his bachelor's degree in philosophy from Seattle University (1963). Lumpp then entered Marquette University's new Ph.D. program in religious studies, which was, according to Marquette University president Jesuit William F. Kelley, the "only program in [the U.S.] situated in a Catholic university and directed towards the scholarly training of men and women in the field of religious studies."[22] Bernard J. Cooke, then still a Jesuit, founded and headed the program.

By spring 1965, Lumpp completed the master's level coursework and one year of doctoral work and was president of Marquette's graduate stu-

---

18. In 1970 Bonnette completed his dissertation, "St. Thomas Aquinas on: 'The *Per Accidens* Necessarily Implies the *Per Se*,'" under director Joseph Bobik (Ph.D. diss., University of Notre Dame). Bonnette's dissertation was later published under the title *Aquinas' Proofs for God's Existence: St. Thomas Aquinas on "The Per Accidens Necessarily Implies the Per Se"* (The Hague: Martinus Nijhoff, 1972).

19. Ironically, Bonnette was hired at Loyola University to replace Joseph Kunkel, who left Loyola to go to the University of Dayton; Kunkel, personal interview with the author, June 3, 1999.

20. Dennis Bonnette, email message to the author, April 10, 1999.

21. Bonnette, email message to the author, April 9, 1999.

22. William F. Kelley, SJ, president, to Members of the [Marquette] University Council, March 18, 1963, quoted in Pamela C. Young, CSJ, "Theological Education in American Catholic Higher Education, 1939–1973" (Ph.D. diss., Marquette University, 1995), 47–48.

dent association. His roommate, Richard G. Otto, was offered a job teaching theology at the University of Dayton. When Lumpp heard that UD was hiring additional faculty, he applied and subsequently was hired by department chair Marianist father Matthew F. Kohmescher.

Kohmescher joined the Marianists in 1938 and received a bachelor's degree in philosophy from the University of Dayton in 1942. After teaching high school for several years, he went to the Marianist seminary at St. Meinrad in Indiana and then to the Marianist seminary at the University of Fribourg in Switzerland, where he was ordained in 1948 and received three degrees: bachelor (1948), licentiate (1949), and doctorate (1950), all in sacred theology. His S.T.D. thesis topic was "Additional Vows of Religion and in Particular the Vow of Stability in the Society of Mary." Kohmescher was appointed *censor deputatus* by the Marianist provincial after returning to Dayton from his S.T.D. studies.[23] Later, he earned a master's degree (1956) in education from Western Reserve University (now Case Western Reserve University) in Cleveland.

In 1960, following ten years of teaching in a high school and at the Marianist Scholasticate, Kohmescher was named associate dean in the University of Dayton's College of Arts and Sciences and a faculty member in theological studies. He was named acting department chair in January 1962 and department chair in fall 1962, a position he held for twenty-one years. Under his leadership, the department name changed from Theology to Theological Studies to Religious Studies, and the first laypersons, including Protestants and Jews, were hired.[24]

It did not take long for philosophy to become once again a topic in the *Flyer News* in the fall term of 1965. Columnist Bob Veries resurrected the debate by supporting Thomism in the September 24, 1965, issue. A news story on the five new faculty in Philosophy appeared in the Octo-

23. A *censor deputatus* is a person who is appointed to review Catholic documents related to faith and morals and approve them for publication. The approval is known as *Nihil Obstat*; John A. Hardon, SJ, *Catholic Dictionary: An Abridged and Updated Edition of Modern Catholic Dictionary* (New York: Image, 2013), 333.

24. After stepping down as chairperson, Father Kohmescher continued to teach full-time for another ten years. He then became the unofficial "UD greeter" in the admission office and welcomed thousands of prospective students and their families. He died on May 5, 2007, at the age of eighty-six.

ber 1, 1965, paper. The reporter asked the faculty for their views on the teaching of philosophy in a Catholic university. Only one, Daniel Hoy, was outspoken against Thomism when he said that Heidegger's "method of presenting this material is much better suited to the twentieth century than is St. Thomas." Seman felt the need to bring Thomism into contact with "the contemporary sciences without relinquishing our grasp of basic, unchanging truths." The *Flyer News* reporter did not quote Bonnette. Rather, he mentioned the publication of Bonnette's upcoming article on race relations and the church.[25]

The main topic of discussion in the fall semester was contraception. It began with the *Flyer News* reporting on the October 1964 publication of Eulalio Baltazar's chapter in *Contraception and Holiness: The Catholic Predicament*, a compilation of articles by contributors such as Gregory Baum, OSA; Leslie Dewart; Justus George Lawler; former Archbishop Thomas D. Roberts, SJ; and Rosemary Ruether. The text, published after Pope Paul VI issued his June 23, 1964, statement that was sometimes interpreted as a termination of the discussion on contraception, called on the bishops at the Second Vatican Council to reexamine the relationship of natural law to contraception.[26]

The news story was the prelude to an October 19 Philosophy Club meeting on the topic of "Birth Control—A Time to Re-evaluate." The discussion was to begin with the statement: "The question of birth control is not a theological one since the reasoning is based on natural law." In other words, contraception was framed as a philosophical issue. Since Eulalio Baltazar made this argument in his book chapter, it made sense that he was listed as the discussion leader.

On the afternoon of the scheduled meeting, Father Richard Dombro met with university president Father Roesch and reported that the majority of the Philosophy Department did not want the discussion to be held.[27] They were concerned about "the damage that could be done

25. "Five Newcomers Join Philosophy Department," *Flyer News*, October 1, 1965, 3.

26. "Dr. Baltazar Gives Views in 'Contraception and Holiness,'" *Flyer News*, October 15, 1965, 3.

27. Richard J. Dombro, memo to Raymond A. Roesch, n.d., 1. Dombro does not name the faculty members who oppose the meeting, but one can assume they are the Thomists.

to the students." Although the exact details of the conversation remain unknown, according to a memo Father Dombro wrote later to Father Roesch, Roesch did not object to contraception being discussed at the Philosophy Club meeting. Roesch referred to Sabin's solution[28] and Pope Paul's remarks at the United Nations[29] that implied that food—not contraception—was the answer to the population problem and stated that "birth control was not a *theological* question." Roesch also justified the discussion at the University of Dayton by appealing to similar discussions that had occurred at neighboring Antioch College, a non-Catholic campus in Yellow Springs, Ohio.[30] Clearly, Roesch was comfortable with campus dialogues even though the topics were controversial.

Dombro disagreed "in conscience" with the points made by Roesch, but he did not say so during their meeting. In his memo to Roesch after the meeting, he reported on the meeting and "revisited" their conversation. Dombro indicated the view of the Thomists that

> The position of true Christianity is not pluralistic. There are not many possible Christian philosophies for a Catholic. A Catholic does not have the liberty to chose [*sic*] or to evolve for himself a philosophy that is not subject to the jurisdiction of Catholic theology. Our Christian theology and Christian dogma contain a philosophical structure that is uniquely ONE. And it is the dutiful task of a Catholic institution to see to it that this philosophy is explained thoroughly and unswervingly to its students.[31]

28. The author assumes that this reference is to Albert B. Sabin, the developer of the oral live-virus polio vaccine (administered on a sugar cube) who was associated with the University of Cincinnati. There is no indication that Sabin was involved in issues of population growth or birth control. On the other hand, Jonas Salk, the developer of the first vaccine against polio, was involved in discussions on population problems. Perhaps Roesch or Dombro mistakenly referred to Sabin.

29. At the United Nations, Paul VI stated that "you must strive to multiply bread so that it suffices for the tables of mankind, and not rather *favor* an artificial control of birth" (Vatican translation). The United Nations translation reads, "Your task is to ensure that there is enough bread on the tables of mankind, and not to *encourage* an artificial birth control, which would be irrational, in order to diminish the number of guests at the banquet of life" [emphasis added]; "What Did the Pope Say?," *National Catholic Reporter*, October 20, 1965, 7.

30. Richard J. Dombro, memo to Raymond A. Roesch, n.d., 5. A copy of Dombro's memo was given to the author by Dennis Bonnette.

31. Dombro, memo to Roesch, n.d.

Father Dombro's memo provided a "cross section" of the discussion at the Philosophy Club meeting, including the false ideas presented. He began with the surprising statement that, at the request of Chrisman, the club's moderator, Baltazar, did not attend the meeting.[32] In Baltazar's absence, students attempted to explain his viewpoint; after the students' explanation, a discussion followed.

Dombro's "cross section" is valuable because it identifies the speakers, including four Philosophy faculty: Barbic, Bonnette, Chrisman, and Dombro. Bonnette spoke up early in the meeting, recalling Paul VI's statement that "no one should ... pronounce himself in terms differing from the norm in force." Chrisman reportedly answered that he had authorized the discussion and stated that the club had the "full right to debate it regardless of the Pope's words."[33] Chrisman suggested that Bonnette leave the meeting if his conscience did not permit him to discuss birth control so that the rest of the participants could follow their "consciences by continuing the discussion."[34]

Barbic asked Chrisman if he had any theological training, since the debate was about whether birth control was a theological or philosophical topic. Recall that Baltazar had theological training and, if he had been present, could be considered competent to discuss the topic. Chrisman replied that he had no theological training but that Barbic did. Barbic responded that if Chrisman had theological training, he would understand Bonnette's question about the legitimacy of the discussion.[35]

Dombro recalled that a student suggested that the conditions of poverty and crime in "highly populated slum areas" are a "legitimate reason for enforced birth control." Dombro replied that John XXIII's encyclical *Mater et Magistra* addressed "these very sociological and economic aspects of procreation," to which the student replied that encyclicals are "just one man's opinion" and "not infallible." Dombro countered that encyclicals

32. Dombro, memo to Roesch, n.d., 1. Joseph Quinn, the Philosophy Club president, does not recall the specific event nor its circumstances; Quinn, email message to the author, June 24, 1999.

33. Dombro, memo to Roesch, n.d., 2.

34. John Chrisman, "Box 8, Letters to the Editor: Some Corrections," *Flyer News*, November 18, 1966, 2.

35. Dombro, memo to Roesch, n.d.

are part of the "infallible magisterium" when they "treat of faith and morals." He referred to *Humani generis* as support that this was not just his interpretation.[36]

At this point, Chrisman ruled the discussion "irrelevant" because popes contradict one another and change the statements of their predecessors. Chrisman continued that "Father knows this too." Dombro responded that he was "ignorant of a single change or contradiction" in matters of faith and morals. An unnamed person then asked whether birth control was a matter of personal conscience. Before anyone could answer, Dombro reported that, "out of the clear blue," the student president abruptly adjourned the meeting, presumably because the meeting was getting out of hand. Dombro's report to Father Roesch lists the following as "frightening facts and flagrant failures in Catholic Marianist education" that occurred during the discussion: (1) the belittling of the popes; (2) the end justifies the means; (3) a situation ethics approach that endorsed relativism; (4) expressions of "pure naturalism" that discarded man's need for any supernatural order; and (5) "scornfully casting aside as unworthy of a hearing" the church's traditional position in philosophy and theology.[37] Bonnette would later list these points, along with their defense of birth control, as evidence of teachings contrary to the magisterium that were occurring at the University of Dayton.

Dombro's report to Roesch shows that both sides were equally passionate about their beliefs. It also shows that the public debate was intense, antagonistic, and, at times, sarcastic. In a letter to the editor of *Flyer News*, student James Wade expressed disappointment. He hoped to have the "subject aired congenially and objectively," but "this was not the case."[38]

Dombro's memo is also valuable because it shows how he and the Thomists tried to resolve the debate. Dombro went to the highest level of the university administration when he and others were concerned about the church's teachings not being presented accurately. In addition

36. Dombro, memo to Roesch, n.d., 2–3.
37. Dombro, memo to Roesch, n.d., 3–4.
38. James Wade, "Box 8, Letters to the Editor: Debate Dissent," *Flyer News*, October 29, 1965, 2.

to reporting on the Philosophy Club meeting, Father Dombro gave Father Roesch some "points for [his] sincere meditation"—quotations from the encyclicals *Ecclesiam Suam* ("Paths of the Church," Paul VI [August 6, 1964]) and *Divini illius magistri* ("The Christian Education of Youth," Pius XI [December 31, 1929]), and from the Constitutions of the Society of Mary. These texts call for fidelity to the church and the pope and a commitment to the true meaning of education from the Catholic and Marianist perspectives.

Finally, Dombro recommended some "practical steps" for Father Roesch. These recommendations provide insight into the issues Dombro, and presumably others in the department, perceived to be problematic. The first recommendation was that the Philosophy Club not debate issues the church asks its members to refrain from discussing. Dombro was concerned that these discussions were confusing to students. He suggested that the moderator of the club be nominated and elected by members of the department and that discussion topics be presented to the department for approval "on the basis of the conformity or non-conformity of the topic with the policy of the department committed to a Catholic Marianist education." Dombro specifically stated that a topic should be avoided if it "could cause a 'split' among the members of the department."[39] He observed that the topics discussed through the previous few years increasingly polarized the department. Given the number of Thomists in the department, the Thomists would control the club and the discussion topics if Dombro's suggestions were accepted.

Dombro concluded his memo to Father Roesch by reminding the president of his address to the faculty less than two months prior to the memo. At that time, Roesch stated that the University of Dayton was a Catholic, Marianist university. Dombro again quoted *Ecclesiam Suam*, referring to the dangers of reform, particularly in conforming to the secular world. Dombro noted that it takes courage to follow the church "regardless of the 'public image'" and that Roesch needed to do so if he wants the University of Dayton to be "an outstanding Catholic Marianist university."[40]

39. Dombro, memo to Roesch, n.d., 7.
40. Dombro, memo to Roesch, n.d.

Winter term 1966 began with Dr. Harkenrider appointed acting chair while Dr. Baker took a sabbatical to the University of Texas at Austin, where he worked with Dr. John Silber[41] for the purpose of gaining a perspective on modern philosophical trends.[42] Silber, later president and chancellor of Boston University, was known for giving a "place of honor to scholastic philosophy in a state university."[43] Since Baker's background was strictly Thomistic, the administration felt that experience in modern philosophies would enable him to provide leadership as the department underwent change.[44]

In early 1966, mainstream America was talking about Joseph Fletcher's controversial book *Situation Ethics: The New Morality*. Situation ethics is, in Fletcher's words, a method (rather than a system) of making moral decisions.[45] One comes to decision-making with the "ethical maxims of [the] community and its heritage." Reason is used as "the instrument of moral judgment," and scripture is accepted as "the source of the norm ... to love God in the neighbor."[46] In making a decision, acts are judged according to the situation or context and then Christian love, *agape*, is used as the "binding and unexceptional" norm for behavior.[47] All other rules, maxims, and principles are guides in the decision-making process, but they are expendable in any given situation. To put it in simpler terms, Fletcher urges doing the most loving thing in all situations. He admits that "its thesis was set forward within the context of Christian rhetoric, but situation ethics as a theory of moral action is ... utterly independent of Christian presuppositions or beliefs."[48]

41. At the time, Silber was the chairperson of the Department of Philosophy. He later became the dean of the College of Arts and Sciences at the University of Texas at Austin. In 1971, Silber was appointed the seventh president of Boston University, and in 1996 he became chancellor; "John Silber," in *Boston University, Philosophy Department, Faculty*; accessed July 7, 1999, http://www.bu.edu/philo/faculty/silber.html.

42. Administrative council minutes, March 16, 1965, 3, series 87–3, box 3, AUD.

43. Thomas A. Stanley, telephone interview with the author, April 10, 1999.

44. Administrative council minutes, March 16, 1965.

45. Joseph Fletcher, *Situation Ethics: The New Morality*, ed. Robin W. Lovin, Douglas F. Ottati, and William Schweiker, Library of Theological Ethics (Louisville, Ky.: Westminster/John Knox Press, 1966), 11.

46. Fletcher, *Situation Ethics*, 26.

47. Fletcher, *Situation Ethics*, 30.

48. Joseph Fletcher, "Memoir of an Ex-Radical," in *Joseph Fletcher: Memoir of an Ex-Radical: Reminiscence and Reappraisal*, ed. Kenneth Vaux (Louisville, Ky.: Westminster/John Knox Press, 1993), 82.

At the University of Dayton, faculty and students became part of the national conversation, talking about situation ethics, love, and sexuality. A Religion in Life Series panel discussion was held on February 15, 1966, to discuss "Love between Man and Woman: Contemporary Views." John Chrisman was the moderator and Randolph Lumpp a panelist discussing the "historical development" of love from "ancient times until the present."[49] The annual St. Thomas Aquinas Day Honors Convocation on March 9, 1966, included a speech entitled, "Contemporary Thoughts and Situation Ethics," by Dr. Vernon J. Bourke, a philosophy professor from St. Louis University and noted authority on Thomas Aquinas.[50]

The Religious Activities committee sponsored a lecture on situation ethics in March 1966 with presenters Eulalio Baltazar and John Chrisman. In attendance was Marianist father Francis Langhirt, a chaplain at the university, who—having heard disturbing reports about Baltazar and Chrisman—wanted to get firsthand information. The presentation upset him so much that he wrote a letter to Monsignor Henry S. Vogelpohl, the archbishop's chancellor, reporting that Baltazar and Chrisman did not just review situation ethics, they advocated it strongly.[51] He also quoted Chrisman saying, "No act is intrinsically evil; in particular, contraception and therapeutic abortion are not wrong in themselves." Langhirt went on to report that the "authorities here are aware of their questionable principles and teaching, but they fail to do anything about it."[52] Vogelpohl responded that the archbishop would study the letter and that Father Langhirt should inform the president of the university and the Marianist provincial of his concerns.[53] Evidently, Langhirt did so, because Father Dombro reported that Father Roesch said he was "actively studying the problem."[54]

49. UD Press Release, February 9, 1966, 1, series 7J (A2), AUD.

50. "Dr. Bourke Speaks at Assembly," *Flyer News*, March 11, 1966, 4.

51. Francis Langhirt, Summary of testimony to archbishop's fact-finding commission, December 19, 1966, University of Dayton, Unorthodox Teaching Investigation, 1967, RG1.6 Abp Alter, AAC.

52. Francis Langhirt, to Henry J. Vogelpohl, March 30, 1966, 1–2, "Controversy 'Academic Freedom, Etc.,' 1966–67," Belmont Ave., general files, 1.6 Abp. Alter, AAC.

53. Msgr. Henry J. Vogelpohl to Francis Langhirt, April 4, 1966, University of Dayton, general correspondence, 1963–66, RG1.6 Abp Alter, AAC.

54. Richard J. Dombro, Summary of testimony to archbishop's fact-finding commission, December 20, 1966, 7, University of Dayton, Unorthodox Teaching Investigation, 1967, RG1.6 Abp Alter, AAC.

Additional particulars on the lecture can be extracted from letters to the university president by Bonnette, Baltazar, and Chrisman. Bonnette's letter, written on October 28, 1966, seven months later, listed himself, fellow Philosophy faculty members Barbic and Gonzalo Cartagenova, and Father Langhirt among other attendees. His letter states

> Baltazar eloquently defended situation ethics in precisely that form which has been condemned by the Holy Father. Both [Baltazar and Chrisman] insisted that *their* form of situation ethics was not the target of the condemnation since their's [*sic*] was "Christian" in that it was "Theistic," rather than "Atheistic."… [Dr. Baltazar] also said, "If the Church does not take a positive attitude toward situation ethics, then she will fail to influence modern morality (or man?) [*sic*]."[55]

Baltazar, in his undated response to Father Roesch, stated that he could not answer this accusation because Bonnette did not define the "condemned" situation ethics, nor did Bonnette show how Baltazar's ethics were the same as the condemned ethics. Baltazar clarified that

> I expressly stated in my talk that the situation ethics I accept is that based on the interpersonal encounter between Yahweh and Israel and between Christ and His Church. This view is not new. It is the view of Father Bernard Häring, Herbert McCabe, OP, Schilleebeeckx, [*sic*] etc. and more recently expressed by Father Charles Curran of Catholic University when he stated that the experience of the Christian people is the norm of morality. Thus, an objective norm of morality is not denied.[56]

Regarding Bonnette's objection to Baltazar's statement about the church's influence on morality, Baltazar suggested that Bonnette read any current works on moral theology and Christian ethics and he will see that "the orientation of Christian renewal in moral theology is towards an emphasis of the situation and of the subjective dimension of morality."[57]

Bonnette claimed that Chrisman publicly endorsed all that Baltazar had said and then "proceed[ed] to insist that 'Man must lovingly create. I don't mean that man discovers the moral law, he creates it. That is, based on

55. Bonnette to Raymond A. Roesch, October 28, 1966, 1–2.
56. Eulalio R. Baltazar to Raymond A. Roesch, n.d., 6–7.
57. Baltazar to Roesch, n.d., 7.

my metaphysics.'" Bonnette said that Chrisman then defined and defended the following definition of situation ethics: "Man has no right to hide under *a priori* and abstract decisions handed down from extrinsic authorities, e.g., (and he points to the words 'self-mutilation' and 'abortion' written on the blackboard)." Chrisman then used the example of Sherri Finkbine—an American actress on the children's television show *Romper Room*, who went to Sweden for an abortion rather than give birth to a deformed baby—as a morally justified abortion.[58] Chrisman described Mrs. Finkbine's baby as "a jelly bean with eyes," a crude description that he later regrets using.[59]

Chrisman's response to Bonnette's charges stressed that "situation ethics is a label attached to a broad range of ethical positions." He then listed Catholic theologians, mostly at the University of Toronto, and their varying interpretations of "situation." Chrisman also quoted a *National Catholic Reporter* interview where Father Charles Curran called for the "Church to stop handing down *a priori* decrees and to start listening to the whole Church so that Christians will have to rely more on their own decisions while the magisterium will 'always be a little bit behind the times.'"[60]

Chrisman continued, using a quotation from his lecture notes to explain his own situation ethics:

> If situation ethics meant that there is no right and wrong, that in fact there is no morality, then I would be against it. But if it means that man must lovingly create the right action according to the requirements of the total situation, and that man has no right to evade self-responsibility by hiding under *a priori* and abstract decisions handed down from an extrinsic authority, then I see nothing un-Christian about it.[61]

Chrisman stated that he did not advocate abortion because "to advocate an abstraction is as irrelevant as to condemn an abstraction." He used

---

58. Bonnette to Roesch, October 28, 1966, 2.

59. Chrisman, telephone interview with the author, January 25, 1999. At least one female student was upset because she interpreted the "jelly bean" description to be Chrisman's view of *all* fetuses. Since the expression was misinterpreted, Chrisman says now that it was not a good expression. At the time, Chrisman was trying to make a "strong case" for abortion to be a woman's right; Chrisman, telephone interview with the author, June 21, 1999.

60. *National Catholic Reporter*, September 21, 1966, quoted in John Chrisman to Father Raymond A. Roesch, n.d., 5.

61. John Chrisman to Raymond A. Roesch, n.d., 6.

Mrs. Finkbine's "situation to exemplify the agony faced by a moral agent who must choose" and noted that "no person not in her position could condemn her."[62]

Chrisman also stated that he "stressed the communal and cultural character of our developing morality" in his lecture "as opposed to an individualistic and subjective origin" of morality. He "emphasized the requirement of considering the total situation rather than merely picking out the aspects one wished to emphasize." He also dwelt on the "difficulty encountered in finding an adequate criterion of morality." Chrisman concluded his letter to Father Roesch by stating that Dr. Baltazar and he were "philosophizing about a crucial human problem."[63]

This event was critical in the ongoing escalation of the "Heresy" Affair. After previous lectures questioning Thomism and the church's teachings on contraception, Baltazar and Chrisman now appeared to be directly attacking the church's foundational principles on moral issues. In the wake of this lecture and knowing that the department was moving to "greater freedom [in] teaching techniques within the curriculum," Bonnette drafted a "Statement of Departmental Conviction," which he distributed to the Philosophy faculty on March 21, 1966.[64] He intended to move to adopt the proposal at the March 25, 1966, departmental meeting.

The proposed statement begins by quoting Paul VI in his September 1965 address to the Sixth International Thomistic Congress. The pontiff noted the role of the philosopher in the modern world and warned against the two extremes, atheism and fideism.[65] Paul VI reiterated the importance of St. Thomas. The draft then states that since the Department of Philosophy is moving to "greater freedom in teaching tech-

62. Chrisman to Roesch, n.d.

63. Chrisman to Roesch, n.d.

64. Bonnette does not recall how the idea of a statement materialized, but it was not unique to Dayton's Philosophy Department. Leslie Dewart recalls that prior to Vatican II, the Philosophy Department at the University of Toronto tried to get its faculty to "sign a document 'clarifying' the position of Catholic philosophers in Catholic institutions towards Thomism." Dewart and two others resisted, and the eventual outcome was a draw; Leslie Dewart, email message to the author, June 16, 1999, 3.

65. Fideism is the "view that religious knowledge is an act of faith alone and not at all an act of the human intellect"; Nancy Dallavalle, "Fideism," in *The HarperCollins Encyclopedia of Catholicism*, ed. Richard P. McBrien et al. (San Francisco: Harper San Francisco, 1995), 528.

niques," the department "wishes to express the nature of its philosophical commitment... so that no one will misinterpret our convictions."[66] Although the definition of the term "no one" was not clarified, the linkage with "teaching techniques" implied that students were the intended audience. The audience, however, could also possibly include parents, the administration, other faculty, or the church hierarchy. There could conceivably be other uses for a statement of conviction—that is, bringing faculty in error into line if they transgressed official policy.

Anticipating an objection that a statement of conviction hinders pursuit of truth, Bonnette quoted Paul VI and the Second Vatican Council's Declaration on Christian Education on the value of Thomas. Bonnette was careful to point out Paul VI's statement that the church's use of Thomistic philosophy did not preclude "interest in the positive contributions of the great minds of all ages."[67] In the same statement, Paul VI quoted Pius XII saying the church accorded "preference and not exclusivity" to Thomas.[68] While Bonnette included these references in the draft, his actions—as evidenced by the fact that five of the six individual convictions were Thomistic—seem to indicate his unwillingness to include philosophies other than Thomism. The statement reads:

> As a department of the faculty of a Catholic institution... and acting in virtue of a rational evaluation of the foregoing illuminating statements of the Church, the Department of Philosophy of the University of Dayton emphatically rejects the errors of atheism and fideism, and positively asserts its commitment to the following philosophical convictions:
>
> 1. We hold that the existence of God can be known through the proper exercise of unaided human reason.
> 2. We hold that far from being mutually contradictory, faith and reason are, in reality, complementary to one another.
> 3. We hold that the extramental world has an intelligible structure which, in its broadest outlines, can be grasped with objective certitude by the human mind.

66. Dennis Bonnette, "A Statement of Departmental Conviction," March 21, 1966, 1.

67. Bonnette, "Statement of Departmental Conviction," 2.

68. Bonnette, "Statement of Departmental Conviction," 3. The Pius XII quotation is from "Allocution to the Gregorian University," Discourse XV, 409–10.

4. We hold that the abiding formal elements of a dynamic reality can be validly described through the analogous application of the primary principles of a realistic metaphysics.
5. We hold that an outstanding example of a philosophy consonant with the "preambles of faith" is to be found in the writings of St. Thomas Aquinas.
6. We hold that any philosophy, to the extent that it is compatible with the above-stated principles, and makes a positive contribution to man's understanding of himself in his relation to the world and to God, is to be welcomed and its development is to be encouraged.[69]

The final page of the proposed statement called for a roll call vote and included a caveat that passage of the resolution constituted "a formal request by the members that this document be promulgated in such manner that a copy of it shall, henceforth, be placed in the hands of every student enrolled in a philosophy course at the University of Dayton."[70]

The department met on March 25, 1966. As expected, Bonnette made the motion to adopt the proposal, and it was seconded. In the discussion that followed, Chrisman objected on the grounds that he had insufficient time to consider the proposal. He questioned Bonnette on the "purpose and intent" of the proposal. Bonnette replied that the purpose and intent were "fully disclosed in the two-page preamble." Chrisman "countered" that the preamble was ambiguous and unsatisfactory.[71]

Baltazar suggested that any proposal on the "purposes and goals" of the department should have "emanated" from the departmental Purposes and Goals Committee. Bonnette countered that since the committee "had not been able to meet this year,"[72] it was proper to bring the proposal to the whole department, which was ultimately necessary "regardless of its place of origin."[73]

Since the addition of the caveat complicated the vote, Bonnette proposed an amendment to his original proposal. The amendment called for

69. Bonnette, "Statement of Departmental Conviction."

70. Bonnette, "Statement of Departmental Conviction," 4.

71. Department of Philosophy faculty meeting minutes, March 25, 1966, 3, series 20QI (3), box 1, folder 1, AUD.

72. No reason is given for the purposes and goals committee not meeting. The wording of the minutes, however, suggests some reason other than not having any items of business.

73. Philosophy faculty meeting minutes, March 25, 1966, 3.

a roll call vote on the statement with the meaning of the vote being approval or disapproval of the principles involved. Abstention from voting was also an acceptable option. In other words, Bonnette eliminated from the vote the promulgation aspect of the statement. Bonnette's amendment was seconded and passed.

At this point Chrisman inquired if the secretary (Seman) was "carefully" recording the discussion and an "exact count" of the votes. Seman retorted that "he was recording the present discussion with the same degree of thoroughness (or lack thereof) as he has used regarding all previous meetings and asked whether his previous efforts had met with Mr. Chrisman's approval."[74] No response by Chrisman was recorded.

As the discussion returned to the issue at hand, Chrisman "conceded that the overall intent" was "definitely NOT to force Thomism on all the members of the department." He objected, however, that students might think this was the case. Daniel Hoy disagreed and stated that he interpreted the document as a statement of minimal propositions that all agreed upon.[75]

Casaletto stated that "he [did] not recognize the authority of any encyclical governing or determining his philosophy." Seman responded by questioning "whether, in the light of our Catholic faith, we could be entirely 'free' in our approach to philosophy." To Seman, "certain truths of Christianity" such as the "existence of God, the divinity and historicity of Christ, and the infallibility of the Church" must be accepted. Debates on these matters were "academic questions" and not "valid questions open to unrestricted philosophical scrutiny."[76]

Dombro apparently anticipated that the discussion would involve adherence to church teachings and that *Humani generis* would be needed. He entered the discussion by reading a passage from *Humani generis* that stated that the ordinary magisterium [teaching authority] of the church was exercised in encyclicals. The minutes record that Dombro concluded "in the light of this passage" that "teaching *as a Catholic* and in

---

74. Philosophy faculty meeting minutes March 25, 1966.
75. Philosophy faculty meeting minutes, March 25, 1966, 4.
76. Philosophy faculty meeting minutes, March 25, 1966.

a CATHOLIC school necessarily demands a commitment to Catholicism."[77] It follows that Casaletto as a Catholic teaching in a Catholic school must accept the authority of the encyclicals as issued.

At this point, Hoy moved that the consideration of Bonnette's six points be postponed until a later date. Bonnette objected by pointing out that the proposal called for a vote at *this* meeting [emphasis added]. Not surprisingly, the vote to postpone the discussion resulted in a split department—six yea and six nay.[78] Evidently the discussion was postponed, because the minutes record the next action as a motion for adjournment, which passed after unrecorded discussion.[79]

The next meeting called for the purpose of discussing the proposal was scheduled for a week and a half later.[80] One day prior to the meeting, Baltazar gave a letter entitled, "Concerning the Statement of Departmental Conviction" to Acting Chair Harkenrider and distributed copies to the faculty. Baltazar indicated that the apparent purpose of Bonnette's statement was to make sure students do not get the "wrong impression" that "one philosophy is just as good as another."[81] Baltazar opposed the statement on the grounds that students will not "mistake ecumenism for relativism." He pointed out that the real danger is in students rebelling against an imposed philosophy and against the department. Baltazar suggested that students be told that the department is "going to be ecumenical" and that the attitude is one of "dialogue and aggiornamento." The term "aggiornamento," meaning a bringing up to date, was used often in connection with the Second Vatican Council. Baltazar noted the importance of showing that a

> spirit of dialogue exists among members of the department, that plurality is not necessarily a split but the sign of health, that inspite [*sic*] of differences of opinion and philosophic views, we are able to respect one another with-

77. Philosophy faculty meeting minutes, March 25, 1966.
78. Philosophy faculty meeting minutes, March 25, 1966.
79. Philosophy faculty meeting minutes, March 25, 1966.
80. A faculty meeting was held on March 31, 1966, for the purpose of reviewing curriculum changes; Philosophy faculty meeting minutes, March 31, 1966, 2, series 20QI (3), box 1, folder 1, AUD.
81. Eulalio R. Baltazar, "Concerning the Statement of Departmental Conviction," n.d., 1. A copy of the statement was given to the author by Baltazar.

out denouncing, villifying, and condemning one another in our respective classes—acts which are totally unprofessional and against the declaration of the Vatican Council on religious liberty and freedom of conscience.[82]

Baltazar's stated opposition to the document is of an entirely different nature than previously, when he objected to the *process* in which the document was presented. In this letter, Baltazar disagreed with the *purpose* of the document and ultimately relayed his vision for the department: dialogue and respect for one another in the midst of philosophical pluralism.

In his letter, Baltazar quoted "Marianist" father Maurice Villain as a supporter of ecumenism. Perhaps he thought that quoting a Marianist would be advantageous in a Marianist university. Villain, however, while a supporter of ecumenism, was not a Marianist. Rather, he was a Marist. There is no indication that anyone noticed this error.[83] Baltazar also noted the recent positive experiences of DePaul's Philosophical Horizons Program.[84] He concluded that Bonnette's proposal was "sadly behind the times" and suggested a "more timely" statement of conviction:

1. The spirit of aggiornamento and ecumenism motivates the department.
2. In conformity with the declaration on religious liberty the department safeguards freedom of speech and intellectual and scientific research as long as these are done responsibly.
3. The department holds that religious liberty is founded on the very nature of the human person, therefore we affirm the right

82. Baltazar, "Concerning the Statement of Departmental Conviction."

83. Father Maurice Villain was a Marist, not a Marianist. Baltazar apparently picked up the misinformation on Villain from the German-language issue of *Concilium* 2 (1966): 287–97, where Villain was listed as a Marianist who studied at San Anselmo; see Alois Greiler, "Marists at Vatican II," at *MaristStudies.org*, 20n99, accessed August 1, 2016, http://www.mariststudies.org/w/images/8/81/5FN11Greiler.pdf.

84. The Philosophical Horizons Program was an experimental philosophy curriculum developed by Gerald F. Kreyche at DePaul University in Chicago. Offered to students in 1964–65, the program included four new courses to explore "man's encounter" with man, the world, God, and morality. Students also took a fifth course from any area of the history of philosophy. Although the initial proposal "violently divided" the DePaul Philosophy Department, the experiment was ultimately deemed a success; Gerald F. Kreyche, "The Philosophical Horizons Program at DePaul University," *New Scholasticism* 39 (1965): 524.

of the person to immunity from coercion, indoctrination in religious and philosophic matters.

4. The department assures the freedom of conscience of all students and difference in philosophic and religious matters be not the basis for grading or passing a student.

When the departmental meeting began,[85] Harkenrider, as acting department chair, read his own statement on Bonnette's proposal, noting that its context caused him "a great deal of anxiety." Harkenrider stated that he anticipated "strong opposition" to Bonnette's proposal from within the department. After the previous meeting, faculty from other departments, administrators (including the dean of the College of Arts and Sciences),[86] and students questioned him about the need for this statement. Baltazar's letter also made Harkenrider consider the impact of such a statement on the relations between Catholics and others. Harkenrider pondered whether it was prudent to pass the proposal at that time. A rift already existed in the department; would passing the proposal make it wider? Would passage of the proposal give the impression that only Thomism is to be taught? Would passage of the document "undermine the spirit of charity"?[87]

Harkenrider stated that he did not solicit Bonnette's proposal, nor did he know of its formulation until ten faculty members submitted it with their signatures attached. He indicated that he had prayed over what to do and decided that since a large majority had requested that the proposal be considered, it should be brought before the department. Harkenrider then laid out the procedure for the remainder of the meeting: ten minutes of discussion on the introductory paragraph and ten minutes on each of the individual numbered points of the proposal. A vote would be taken on each item.

The proposal being discussed was a slight revision of the original

85. Chrisman did not attend this meeting. The minutes record that he was excused. No reason is given; Department of Philosophy faculty meeting minutes, April 5, 1966, 1, series 20QI (3), box 1, folder 1, AUD.

86. Edward Harkenrider, Summary of testimony to archbishop's fact-finding commission, December 20, 1966, University of Dayton, Unorthodox Teaching Investigation, 1967, RG1.6 Abp Alter, AAC.

87. Philosophy faculty meeting minutes, April 5, 1966, appendix I, 1.

proposal. In the interval between meetings, Bonnette and his supporters removed the two-page preamble and dropped the objectionable wording "foregoing illuminating" from the paragraph preceding the numbered points. At first glance, these deletions seem to be an improvement. However, the revised opening paragraph now included "rational evaluation" of *all* the statements of the church rather than only those listed in the preamble. The revision also includes the addition of "relativism" to the rejected errors of atheism and fideism and an additional numbered point:

> We hold that, based upon the firm foundation of man's common nature, a general science direction of moral conduct can be derived; we reject any ethical system which implies complete moral relativism, such as certain forms of "situation ethics."[88]

The remainder of the points remained the same.

The minutes of the April 5, 1966, meeting record much discussion. Of particular concern was the meaning of fideism. Eventually, the faculty voted 11 to 4 in favor of changing the word "reject" to "does not accept" fideism. At this point, Baltazar interjected that it was pointless to continue the discussion. Even if he endorsed each point individually, he would vote against the entire proposal because he felt it was "contrary to the spirit of aggiornamento and renewal urged by Vatican II." Dieska wanted a vote on the entire proposal. Seman countered that perhaps by voting on individual items, a statement acceptable to all might be crafted.

Ultimately, Joseph Kunkel stated the obvious—any further discussion was pointless because there was an 11 to 4 split in the department. The majority would always win. Kunkel reminded the faculty that the same thing happened the previous year when the "conservative majority" voted for logic to be included in the introductory course even though all those teaching the course objected. Kunkel noted that this was an example of why the "liberal minority" felt discriminated against. He wondered why the minority were not included in the original attempt to formulate the proposal. This was a return to Baltazar's original point at the previous meeting—the origination process was flawed.

88. Philosophy faculty meeting minutes, April 5, 1966, appendix II, 1.

Since the development of the proposal appeared to be the issue, Bonnette acknowledged that he authored the document and then asked others for comments. Those he consulted agreed with the contents of the proposal and with his intent to present it to the department.[89] Harkenrider then suggested that a committee be formed to develop a statement acceptable to all. Dieska objected because a proposal was already being considered. Bonnette then moved "the previous question," presumably his proposal already under consideration; a vote was taken, and the issue passed 8–6. Since four faculty were absent, their votes were solicited after the meeting, with the final result of 11 yeas, 7 nays.[90]

Cartagenova, one of the "yea" votes, tried to end the meeting on a positive note by proposing that each faculty member try to understand the views of the others. He denounced unprofessional conduct such as "spreading rumors" that Thomism is being forced on the department.[91] Casaletto immediately remarked that the proposal seemed to be doing just that. After a few volleying shots, Dieska made the final recorded remarks when he affirmed "his adherence to Thomism stressing that it was precisely in this capacity that he was originally hired." Dieska continued that "in a [recent] private conversation ... Father Stanley, [the] former provost of the University, had stated his wish that the philosophy department would be committed to Thomism and would openly reaffirm this conviction."[92]

In looking back, what Harkenrider worried would happen did happen: the creation of a wider rift, the impression that Thomism is the only philosophy, and the undermining of charity. The exchange appears to have been very blunt. Both sides stated their beliefs. Baltazar and Cart-

89. If Bonnette named those he consulted, the minutes do not record their names.

90. The minutes do not indicate what passed. If the vote was to form a committee, there is no record of a committee being formed. There is also no record of a later vote on the full proposal. The fact that the votes of those not in attendance were solicited indicates that the item being voted on was important. It is logical, therefore, to assume that the issue was Bonnette's proposal.

91. Philosophy faculty meeting minutes, April 5, 1966, 4.

92. Philosophy faculty meeting minutes, April 5, 1966. Father Stanley does not recall this specific conversation with Dieska. Stanley states that he was trained in Thomism and has great regard for it. He also believes that Thomism can "hold its own in any dialogue" and that it has "lasting value." In the 1960s, Stanley believed that Thomism should be taught at a Catholic university but "not exclusively"; Stanley, telephone conversation with the author, July 7, 1999.

agenova addressed unprofessional conduct. The non-Thomists expressed their frustrations with majority rule. In the end, however, neither side was willing to concede. Baltazar refused to discuss individual items. Dieska rejected the opportunity for compromise proposed by Harkenrider. Ultimately, the majority ruled, and the Department of Philosophy had a Statement of Departmental Conviction. The statement, however, was simply paper. In essence, the department's conviction was, "We agree to disagree."

In late March, while the departmental discussion was ongoing, Bonnette, Harkenrider, Cartegenova, and Seman paid a visit to the provost, Marianist father Charles J. Lees. They evidently asked that Baltazar and Chrisman be fired because Lees told them it was too late to fire them for the following year. Bonnette met again with Lees in April. At that time, Lees asked Bonnette for a summary of the teachings of Baltazar and Chrisman.[93]

Father Dombro also reached out to the Marianist administration. On May 8, 1966, he sent a note to Father Roesch and Brother Leonard A. Mann, SM, the dean of the College of Arts and Sciences. Attached to the note was a two-page editorial, "A Teaching Church," from the May 1966 issue of *Catholic Mind*. Dombro wanted Roesch and Mann to "see the problematic situation as our Holy Father sees it… because of [their] responsibility of 'correcting defects of the church's members.'" Dombro feared that Roesch and Mann would "fall into a purely pragmatic approach of expediency which leads to the dethronement of objective truth natural and supernatural."[94]

Brother Mann, a physicist by discipline, responded to Father Dombro in a three-page, single-spaced letter. He assumed that Dombro sent the editorial to him because of the "lively dialogue currently in progress" in the Philosophy Department. On the one hand, he is

93. Dennis Bonnette, Summary of testimony to archbishop's fact-finding commission, December 19, 1966, 3, University of Dayton, Unorthodox Teaching Investigation, 1967, RG1.6 Abp Alter, AAC. Assuming such a summary was prepared, no copy exists.

94. Richard J. Dombro, note to Raymond A. Roesch, and Leonard A. Mann, with attachment, May 8, 1966.

delighted that there is dialogue that has the campus buzzing, and which has brought a faculty to a keen edge in formulating convictions.... On the other hand, [he] nurture[s] a deep concern lest this freedom of dialogue might lead some to believe that permissiveness of thought and latitude of belief have no bounds, and that our theological or moral convictions have no absolute basis. The balance is a delicate one, but it must be maintained if [the university is] to preserve [its] precious heritage of truth, and also encourage scholarly discussion so necessary in an institution of higher learning.[95]

Mann continued that his public silence on the situation should not be interpreted as "weak convictions, or a deviation from our traditional purposes, or worse, an abandonment of the precious tenets that have always been an essential part of the heritage that we have received from our Holy Faith through the Church." He explained he was not "adverse to the teaching authority of the Church. Any commitment to pragmatic philosophies, or to pure expedience, would be most unworthy of anyone in a Catholic institution of higher learning."[96]

Mann indicated that the administration had made "probings and inquiries" into the situation: "It would be a dereliction not to be alert during these times or on these issues." However,

it would be delightful and most appropriate in a university if inadvertent errors, or statements of position that appear contrary to the purposes of the institution were recognized and handily dispatched in disputation by the faculty itself, rather than by administrative directive.[97]

Mann had confidence in the faculty that "they have the right philosophy and also the skill and competence to defend the truth." If

administrative directive were invoked quickly and easily, [he feared the university] would soon lose [its] identity as an institution of higher learning, and [it] would not be able to justify a faculty of scholars whose role and responsibility is to promote the truth, both in defense and in research.[98]

Mann indicates concern for the students before he concludes:

95. Leonard A. Mann, to Richard J. Dombro, May 16, 1966, 1.
96. Mann to Dombro, May 16, 1966, 2.
97. Mann to Dombro, May 16, 1966.
98. Mann to Dombro, May 16, 1966.

It did not seem necessary to assure the faculty that I have not been passive in the activity that is in progress, or that I seek prudent counsel from others, with still higher responsibilities for the future of the University of Dayton, on all matters that touch the heart of our mission. I had assumed that the faculty would have expected me to recognize these grave responsibilities, and with the best wisdom, prudence and courage at my command assume the role proper to a Dean.[99]

This is hardly the response Dombro had in mind. He wanted Mann to intervene.

The discussions of controversial issues were not limited to the academic year. On the evening of June 7, 1966, the Union Activities Organization experimented with a unique program on the topic "God is Dead."[100] If there ever was an event truly symbolic of the 1960s, this was it. Faculty members, including John Chrisman and Dennis Bonnette, participated in discussions that were interspersed with folk singing and poetry reading. The event was held on the rooftop terrace of the student union with beverages and peanuts in the shell served as refreshments.[101] More than two hundred students and faculty attended.

During the discussion, Chrisman denounced the "tyrant concept of God" even if God is a "benevolent tyrant." Richard Otto, an instructor in Theological Studies, noted that the existence of evil causes some to conclude that God is dead. According to the *Dayton Daily News*, Bonnette suggested that it was "man—not God—who was dead" because man is trying to reshape God to his own uses.[102]

Chrisman got a number of laughs from the audience. He said he "deplored the idea of a 'string-pulling' God" and thought "Christians had carried this idea too far." He mocked the basketball player who made the

---

99. Mann to Dombro, May 16, 1966, 3.

100. The theme listed in the press release was the "Missing Link," since answers to difficult questions were sought during the discussions; press release, University of Dayton Public Relations Department, June 3, 1966, series 7J (A2), AUD. The *Dayton Daily News* reporter stated, however, that the programs were called "Missing Link" because they were "aimed at bridging the communication gap between instructors and students"; Julie Leader, "Bury Tyrant Idea of God," *Dayton Daily News*, June 8, 1966.

101. UD press release, University of Dayton Public Relations Department, June 3, 1966, series 7J (A2), AUD.

102. Leader, "Bury Tyrant Idea of God."

sign of the cross before shooting a free throw. Chrisman parodied: "Bless us oh Lord and these thy two points, which we are about to receive." He also told the story of his grandmother the day an apricot fell from a tree into her lap. "Thank you, God," she said. Minutes later, a robin's droppings landed on her head. This time, his grandmother blamed the bird. Her lack of consistency shows why "believers have a hard time explaining away evil in the world."[103]

The day after the discussion, Bonnette publicly challenged Chrisman, in the form of a letter distributed to faculty and students, to a timed debate on the concept of God held by Chrisman "as opposed to the 'traditional view' which [Chrisman] opposed" and "ridiculed."[104] Bonnette "demanded" that Chrisman "assert the position" he held rather than give "negative remarks" about what he opposed. Chrisman recalls that he toyed with the idea of debating Bonnette. However, since Chrisman's ideas about God deviated from traditional Catholic teaching, he realized it could be a problem if he debated Bonnette. Upon the advice of faculty leader and friend Rocco Donatelli—who suggested that this contest was not one Chrisman should get into—Chrisman simply ignored Bonnette's challenge.[105]

Although it was apparent in the discussion that Chrisman's views about God were not traditional, he made an additional remark during the program that proved to be even more problematic. Bonnette reports that someone asked Chrisman about his position on heaven, hell, purgatory, and the immortality of the soul. Chrisman refrained from commenting on heaven, hell, and immortality but stated that he did not believe in purgatory.

The issue of purgatory was problematic because Bonnette understood purgatory to be a dogma of the Catholic Church.[106] The issue of whether

103. Leader, "Bury Tyrant Idea of God."

104. Bonnette allowed Chrisman to speak first and last and choose the referee; Dennis Bonnette to John Chrisman, June 9, 1966, 1.

105. John Chrisman, telephone interview with the author, January 25, 1999.

106. "A doctrine is an official teaching of the Church. A doctrine that is taught definitively, that is, infallibly, is called a dogma. Every dogma is a doctrine but not every doctrine is a dogma"; McBrien, "Doctrine," in *The HarperCollins Encyclopedia of Catholicism*, 424–25. Bonnette labeled purgatory a dogma in his letter to Roesch, October 28, 1966, 3.

it was or was not a dogma then had to be sorted out.[107] Denouncing a dogma is a more serious matter than denouncing a less central issue of the faith. For a Catholic to persistently reject a dogma is a matter that could be heretical and lead to excommunication. Therefore, Chrisman elevated the conflict to another level when he stated that he did not believe in purgatory.

Word of Chrisman's denial of purgatory reached the provost's office the next day. The provost, Father Lees, wrote to Chrisman and asked him to discuss the matter.[108] At that meeting, Chrisman defended himself by saying he meant to deny the "notion of fire" in purgatory. The provost evidently was satisfied with the explanation, because no disciplinary action resulted from the discussion. Chrisman held to the "notion of fire" defense throughout the remainder of the "Heresy" Affair. Only in 1999 did he admit that the statement he gave was not the complete truth—in reality, he questioned whether purgatory existed at all.[109]

After the "God is Dead" program, Bonnette and his supporters discussed what to do about the situation. The statements against church teachings and the lack of respect toward the leadership of the church became more blatant with each presentation. Bonnette recalls that he met with the provost about the false teachings, and Lees suggested consulting several well-known theologians and eliciting their advice.[110] Bonnette wrote letters to Father John Courtney Murray, SJ, on June 28, 1966,[111] and to Father Joseph Gallen, SJ, on July 14, 1966.[112] He personal-

107. Purgatory was doctrinally defined in an official letter (*sub catholicae*) dated March 6, 1254, from Pope Innocent IV to his legate to the Greeks on Cyprus. Purgatory was later affirmed at the Second Council of Lyons (1274) and the councils of Florence (1439), Trent (1563), and Vatican II (1965); Joseph A. Dinoia, "Purgatory," in *HarperCollins Encyclopedia of Catholicism*, 1,070.

108. Charles J. Lees to John Chrisman, June 23, 1966.

109. John Chrisman, telephone interview by the author, January 25, 1999.

110. Dennis Bonnette, email message to the author, May 13, 1999.

111. John Courtney Murray, SJ, was a professor of theology at Woodstock College in Woodstock, Maryland. He edited *Theological Studies* and contributed to *Thought*. He was one of the chief writers of the Second Vatican Council's Declaration on Religious Freedom. Murray died on August 16, 1967; "John Courtney Murray," *Gale Literary Databases, Contemporary Authors* [database-on-line]; accessed May 28, 1999, http:// www. galenet. com.

112. Joseph Gallen, SJ, was a professor of canon law at Woodstock College in Woodstock, Maryland. Gonzalo Cartagenova, an instructor in philosophy at the University of Dayton, was

ly consulted French Mariologist Father Rene Laurentin when Laurentin was on the Dayton campus for a summer program.[113] Paul Seman visited Father Francis J. Connell, CSsR, in Washington, D.C., and then wrote a follow-up letter on July 21, 1966.[114]

While the particulars of the letters vary, the substance remains essentially the same: a "hypothetical" moral case is explored.

> What is the moral responsibility of an American Catholic university administrator who has in his charge a Catholic teacher of philosophy who participates in public talks and discussions held on campus before students, faculty, and others and insists that his views, as given below, represent the positions that the Church either now holds or ought to hold in the future?

The views listed in the letters included a defense of situation ethics, moral justification of abortion, disbelief in purgatory, belittlement of papal statements, and denial of the traditional concept of God. The letters closed with a request for general guidelines for administrative action regarding this type of problem.

Although a copy of the letter sent to John Courtney Murray no longer exists, Murray's response indicates that its content was similar to the other letters. Written on the letterhead of the John LaFarge Institute in New York City on August 30, 1966, Murray responded.

> Do forgive my long delay in answering your letter of June 28th. Even at the moment I am afraid that I hardly know what to say about your "hypothetical" moral case. Your professor of philosophy does indeed seem to entertain some strange ideas. However, all the subjects mentioned in your letter are

a former student of Gallen's. Gallen also wrote the column "Questions and Answers" for the periodical *Review for Religious*.

113. At the time, Father Laurentin was a professor at Catholic University, Angers, France. He is a renowned Mariologist and was a *peritus* at the Second Vatican Council. He was instrumental in forming the final chapter of *Lumen gentium*; brochure from Religion in Life 1966 Summer Lecture Series, series 7JD, box 23, folder 6, "Religion in Life," AUD.

114. Francis J. Connell was a Redemptorist priest who contributed articles to *Angelicum, American Ecclesiastical Review* (from 1943 to 1967), *Clergy Review, Thought,* and *Homiletic and Pastoral Review.* He was a professor of dogmatics and moral theology at several seminaries and universities and eventually served as dean of the school of Sacred Theology at the Catholic University of America. He was a charter member and the first president of the Catholic Theological Society of America; Patrick J. Hayes, "Redemptorists and Vatican II: Two American Contributions," accessed at https://books.openedition.org/larhra/5694?lang=en.

being discussed actively today and might indeed be called controversial in some sense. I should hesitate to say anything about his position unless it were more adequately described. It is always perilous to judge a man on such a brief account.

I fear this will not be useful to you and I am sorry. But it is about the best that I can do.[115]

Murray's response is obviously cautious, and is understandable in light of his own earlier difficulties with the church hierarchy. Perhaps Murray was getting many requests for expert advice following the adoption of his Declaration on Religious Liberty at the Second Vatican Council on December 7, 1965, and, therefore, graciously declined many of them. Nevertheless, since it was obvious that the example was not a hypothetical case, it was disappointing that Murray did not offer some advice.

There is no record of a response by Gallen, nor does Bonnette recall how Laurentin responded. Laurentin does not recall being asked about the controversy.[116] Connell responded in writing and in a column in the *American Ecclesiastical Review*. In his letter, dated July 25, 1966, he states emphatically that any professor of philosophy in a Catholic university who proposes or defends such "doctrines" as described should not be permitted to teach. Having such a person on the faculty is a "scandal." Connell is using "scandal" in its technical sense—that is, the faculty member is a stumbling block to the faith of others.[117] Connell went on to state that he would discuss the problem in the *American Ecclesiastical Review* but would not mention any names. He concluded his letter with the statement, "Stick to your Catholic principles."[118] Obviously, Connell supported the position of Bonnette and the other Thomists. His response was distributed by Father Richard Dombro to the president, the provost, the dean of the College of Arts and Sciences (Brother Leonard Mann), and the chair of Philosophy.[119]

---

115. John Courtney Murray, SJ, to Dennis Bonnette, August 30, 1966.

116. Rene Laurentin to the author, June 6, 1999.

117. Daniel Kroger, "Scandal," in *The HarperCollins Encyclopedia of Catholicism*, 1,165.

118. Francis J. Connell, CSsR, to Paul I. Seman, July 25, 1966.

119. Dennis Bonnette, Summary of Testimony to archbishop's fact-finding commission, December 19, 1966, 3, University of Dayton, Unorthodox Teaching Investigation, 1967, RG1.6 Abp Alter, AAC.

Connell discussed the "hypothetical" case in his column "Answers to Questions" in the November 1966 issue of *American Ecclesiastical Review*. He titled the question "Academic Freedom in a Catholic College" and restated his views presented previously. He also stated that "academic freedom does not permit" a Catholic professor to propose as "tenable" views that are contrary to the teaching of the church. Connell continued, "The objective of every Catholic educational institution is to propose the truth as it is taught by the Catholic Church. If a college does not measure up to this standard, it should close its doors."[120] By the time Connell's column appeared, it was too late to be useful for Bonnette and his supporters. One wonders what would have happened had Connell's column been available prior to the eruption of the controversy.

In addition to appealing to the university's administrators and outside theologians, the Thomists consulted their local pastors. Father Arnold F. Witzman, the pastor at Ascension Parish, was especially supportive of Edward Harkenrider during the crisis. Monsignor James E. Sherman, the pastor of Immaculate Conception in Dayton from 1956 to 1976, was Dennis Bonnette's pastor. Bonnette knew Sherman as his pastor; only later did he find out Sherman's academic background, which qualified him to judge the teachings occurring at the University of Dayton: a 1928 graduate of the University of Dayton, doctorate in theology from the University of Fribourg in Switzerland, faculty at St. Gregory and Mount St. Mary seminaries in Cincinnati, organizer of the Philosophy Department at Our Lady of Cincinnati College, and a judge in the Archdiocesan Tribunal.[121] These priests, along with the St. Helen's pastor, Father James L. Krusling, were the pastoral leaders in the Dayton region. If they saw something unorthodox, they were prepared to act in the name of the church.

As academic year 1965–66 ended, the new Philosophy chairperson had his hands full dealing with a department split down the middle.

---

120. "Answers to Questions: Academic Freedom in a Catholic College," *American Ecclesiastical Review* (November 1966): 349.

121. "Msgr. James E. Sherman," Class Notes, *University of Dayton Alumnus*, 16, accessed June 18, 2017, https://issuu.com/ecommons/docs/1966_fall_uda.

The controversy expanded from philosophy to moral issues that had potential for a negative impact on the spiritual life of undergraduates. The
non-Thomist faculty were bold and flippant as the controversy escalated.
The Thomists reacted by appealing, to no avail, to authority figures within and outside the University of Dayton. The conduct on the part of the
Philosophy faculty became increasingly unprofessional and uncharitable.
With no end in sight, the stage was set for the controversy to become a
crisis that spread beyond the university.

CHAPTER 3

CRISIS

Fall 1966

In an age like ours, when development and change are necessary and desirable, it is inevitable that doctrinal controversies—some of them violent—should break out on various campuses. [The University of Dayton] gives us an early-warning flash that comes through loud and clear.
—Thurston N. Davis, *America*, November 26, 1966

What began in fall 1961 as academic presentations on controversial topics became by fall 1966 a religious dispute over the proper teachings of, and respect for, the magisterium of the Roman Catholic Church. Both sides were so entrenched in their positions that newly hired philosophy faculty recall being asked, "Which side are you on?"[1] As tensions built, the Thomists tried one approach after another to stop the controversial teachings. The administration hoped for a resolution without their direct intervention. Settling the dispute was no easy matter for a Catholic university trying to achieve academic legitimacy in the higher education community while at the same time remaining true to its Catholic identity.

1. Both Dennis Bonnette and Xavier Monasterio reported being asked this question by the accused.

As academic year 1966–67 began, Marianist father John A. Elbert, an elderly former president of the university and professor emeritus of philosophy, was very upset over the situation in the Philosophy Department. He knew the Thomists had talked to the university's president and provost and that they had written to theologians about the situation. He decided to bring the matter to the attention of the university's all-Marianist board of trustees, of which he was a member.[2] Before he could do so, however, Elbert died on September 11, 1966, while preparing to distribute communion during his mass at the University of Dayton Health Center chapel.

Elbert's death must have been a blow to Bonnette and his supporters, who hoped the board of trustees would do something about the situation in the Philosophy Department. With that out of the question, the day after Elbert's death, Bonnette wrote a letter to Giuseppe Cardinal Pizzardo, prefect of the Sacred Congregation of Seminaries and Universities in the Vatican, asking for guidance for the university's academic council, which reported to the provost.[3] The letter was sent to Monsignor Egidio Vagnozzi, the apostolic delegate (the Vatican's representative) in Washington, D.C., to be forwarded to Rome. Vagnozzi's September 19 response to Bonnette indicates that Vagnozzi already knew the contents of the letter to Cardinal Pizzardo.[4] By mid-September, before the controversy reached crisis stage, Vagnozzi knew about the situation at the University of Dayton.

On the day of Father Elbert's funeral, the Philosophy Department held its first meeting of the academic year. After the typical welcoming remarks and a few announcements, the chair, Dr. Richard Baker, began the meeting by pointing out that pluralism is a fact within the department and the entire university. The minutes indicate he continued:

> Each of us has, therefore, the perfect right to express his own views and convictions provided this is done in a responsible and professional manner.

2. Dennis Bonnette, telephone interview with the author, April 10, 1997.

3. Dennis Bonnette, Summary of testimony to archbishop's fact-finding commission, December 19, 1966, 3, University of Dayton, Unorthodox Teaching Investigation, 1967, RG1.6 Abp Alter, AAC.

4. Egidio Vagnozzi to Dennis Bonnette, September 19, 1966.

Snide remarks, cute comments, and sneering jests made at the expense of another member of the department are certainly unprofessional. Honest differences of opinion must be handled professionally. He stressed that we must resist the temptation of simply playing to a crowd of impressionable nineteen-year-old kids and suggested as final guidelines that we never attack the views of another derogatorily. He lamented the fact that some members of the department seem to have been guilty of such unprofessional conduct.[5]

Baker stressed "two obligations incumbent on each faculty member": (1) to identify their own philosophical position; and (2) "to present other philosophical positions fairly and refute them *philosophically* [*sic*]."[6]

In the discussion that followed, Professor Dieska asked,

"Is the range of philosophical inquiry to be limited by dogma?" He noted that five years ago the signing of a contract at this University constituted a tacit agreement not to teach anything contradictory to dogma. He queried whether... philosophers can legitimately bring new approaches to dogma; and asked what the official position of the University [was] on this question.[7]

Baker responded that he "had no knowledge of an official position." He pointed out that theological statements by the philosophers are "private opinions," and "ill-considered and not really our business as philosophers." Bonnette asked whether Baker's recognition of pluralism was "purely pragmatic or whether it was also Dr. Baker's own opinion." Baker said it existed and had to be accepted as fact. "Whether such a fact ought to be, he declined to answer."[8]

At that point in the meeting, the discussion moved on to reports by faculty members. Mr. Seman reported on his attendance at a summer workshop on teaching philosophy held at the Catholic University of America. He indicated that there was "a great deal of confusion and no general agreement as to solutions" in other philosophy departments. Dr.

5. Department of Philosophy faculty meeting minutes, September 14, 1966, 3, series 20QI (3), box 1, folder 1, AUD.

6. Philosophy faculty meeting minutes, September 14, 1966.

7. Philosophy faculty meeting minutes, September 14, 1966, 4.

8. Philosophy faculty meeting minutes, September 14, 1966.

Harkenrider agreed, having attended a Notre Dame symposium entitled, "The Place of Philosophy in an Age of Christian Renewal."

The department minutes indicate that the Thomists communicated with faculty at other universities and were aware that their internal disagreements were not unusual. The minutes also show that some members of the department were not acting in a professional manner. The controversy had become mean-spirited. A graduate student with an office in the department recalls that the two sides labeled each other "the idiots" and "the heretics."[9] Baker warned the faculty to stop playing to their audience, trying to get the students on "their" side by cutting down the views of the opposing faculty.

On October 11, 1966, the Philosophy Club, under the guidance of faculty member Daniel Hoy, met for presentations on situation ethics by philosopher Lawrence Ulrich and theologian Randolph F. Lumpp. John Chrisman moderated the discussion that followed. The *Flyer News* reported that nearly one hundred fifty people attended,[10] including Bonnette and Barbic.[11] This meeting was the "last straw" for Bonnette—four days later he wrote to his local archbishop, Karl J. Alter of Cincinnati, reporting on the situation at the University of Dayton. Fortunately, the texts of both lectures are available for review.[12]

Ulrich opened the meeting with his presentation entitled, "Some Basic Concepts and Principles for a Situation Ethics." He began by acknowledging some of the difficulties in using the phrase "situation ethics," including the fact that anyone defending situation ethics is thought to be "advocating moral irresponsibility." His lecture, however, attempted to "set forth a few [basic] concepts [which lead a man to such an ethical position] with the hope that [these concepts] will lead to understanding,

9. Robert Eramian, telephone interviews with the author, January 22, 1999, and June 27, 1999.

10. "Situation Ethics," *Flyer News*, October 28, 1966.

11. Dennis Bonnette to Raymond A. Roesch, October 28, 1966, 5.

12. Lawrence Ulrich, "Some Basic Concepts and Principles for a Situation Ethics," Lecture notes dated October 1966; Randolph F. Lumpp, "A Theological Perspective on 'Situation Ethics,'" University of Dayton Philosophy Controversy, 1966, ASM(E). Neither Ulrich nor Lumpp cited situation ethicists or other authorities in their presentations. Lumpp recalls, however, that he drew upon Bernard Cooke's biblical theology of person; Lumpp, email message to the author, April 20, 1999.

and if not this, at least to questions which will clarify some of the issues involved."[13]

Ulrich stated that the "basic point of view in this discussion" could be expressed by the word "experience." Man is a being in relationship with other conscious beings in a world in space and time; that is, man is historical and evolutionary.[14] Man reflects on his human situation both "as it is" and "as it ought to be," a realization that leads man to be aware that "his actions are adequate or inadequate to his situation or possible situation."[15] This awareness leads to an understanding that the "human situation is an ethical situation." Ulrich stated that because man's situation is temporal, his ethics must be temporal, and since man is in relationship with others, his ethics must be on the "level of a conscious community."[16] Going "outside of the spatio-temporal world" to solve ethical problems, (i.e., to God), is "an attempt by man to escape from the experience of his situation… and is a shirking of his responsibility as a moral agent."[17] Ulrich reviewed man's evolution in thinking to show that "it was man who formed the system and man who judged the action. In other words, morality was created by man."[18]

Ulrich explained man's common moral awareness as the result of sharing a common history. This explanation led to a discussion of ethics as subjective-temporal-particular versus objective-atemporal-universal. Ulrich proposed a level of intersubjectivity between the aforementioned two poles that is temporal and maintains universality conditioned by time.[19] Two questions then arise: (1) When can an individual morally act contrary to society?; and (2) How can universality be extended on an intersubjective level? Ulrich responded to the first by taking a consequentialist approach; that is, an individual should analyze the circumstances, consider the consequences, and if the act is "productive of good, i.e., is helping in the development of the process," then it is morally good.

13. Ulrich, "Some Basic Concepts," 1.
14. Ulrich, "Some Basic Concepts," 2.
15. Ulrich, "Some Basic Concepts," 3.
16. Ulrich, "Some Basic Concepts."
17. Ulrich, "Some Basic Concepts," 4.
18. Ulrich, "Some Basic Concepts," 4–5.
19. Ulrich, "Some Basic Concepts," 6–7.

Obviously, this approach leads to difficulties regarding unforeseen circumstances and consequences. The best one can say about "a past action which seemed good at the time but which failed to produce good" is "if the past action were to be performed in the light of the present experience, it would be a morally bad act."[20] In discussing the second difficulty, Ulrich noted that universality cannot be discussed in the sense of the totality of human experience because that experience is still evolving; that is, "the future is [being] made by man." Situation ethics, then, "presents no pat answers to ethical problems. Instead it presents man with the responsibility for creating his own answers and his own ethical criterion in the light of his consciousness of himself as an historical reality."[21]

Bonnette's critique of both Ulrich's presentation and Lumpp's—whose presentation follows—is found in his October 28, 1966, letter to Father Roesch. Bonnette reported that

> the impression given to many students and professors present was that universal immutable moral norms were either being denied or ignored. Despite the condemnation by the Magisterium, no attempt was made by either speaker to show how either the title of the talk or its contents could be made to harmonize with recent Church teaching. During the entire talk neither speaker presented in a positive manner the traditional teaching on the natural law.[22]

Ulrich responded to Bonnette in a letter to Father Roesch dated November 22, 1966. Ulrich acknowledged that "two officials of the Church who could share in the Magisterium" had spoken on the topic of situation ethics: Cardinal Ottaviani and Pius XII. After naming and dating these references, Ulrich stated that to his knowledge, these are not infallible teachings.[23] Presumably, that means the teachings were open to debate. In regard to Bonnette's complaint that the traditional teaching on natural law was not presented during the lecture, Ulrich stated that the topic of the lecture was situation ethics and that he was permitted only fifteen minutes for presentation.

20. Ulrich, "Some Basic Concepts," 8.
21. Ulrich, "Some Basic Concepts." 9.
22. Dennis Bonnette to Raymond A. Roesch, October 28, 1966, 4.
23. Lawrence Ulrich to Raymond A. Roesch, November 22, 1966, 1.

This response indicates that, at the time it was written, Ulrich was aware of the church communications on situation ethics. He correctly listed Ottaviani and Pius XII and the dates of their communications, but mistakenly attributed to the pope the decree that was issued by the Holy Office in 1956.[24] Ulrich called these communications "references" to situation ethics and stated that they were made in a letter, an instruction, and an allocution.[25] Ulrich did not acknowledge that the church condemned situation ethics, which the decree, issued by the Holy Office, did in no uncertain terms. Also, by referring to them as a letter, an instruction, and an allocution, he is able to call them "documents" and avoid calling them church teachings.

Lumpp's presentation was entitled, "A Theological Perspective on 'Situation Ethics.'" His key idea was that "theologically based ethics has different sources from philosophical ethics," and therefore, "Christian behavior is motivated by factors that come from faith and may not be obvious to reason."[26] He began by concurring with Ulrich that those supporting and opposing situation ethics generally misunderstand it. He explained that ethics or morality has to do with values concerning the relation of the individual human to other humans. After explaining the Aristotelian and Stoic approaches, Lumpp turned to his topic, the biblical approach. He intended to develop three points: (1) The history of God's self-revelation to man makes situation ethics possible; (2) The revealed notion of history makes classical ethics unfeasible and obsolete; and (3) The Incarnation makes man's ethics and morality not more universal, but more particular and concrete.[27]

In order to arrive at a definition of situation ethics, Lumpp reviewed salvation history, noting that it is "a history of a gradual development of man's self understanding." He began with the pre-Exodus period when humans thought of themselves and God in physical terms. The emphasis was on physical life, and God was understood through creation. The next stage begins with the departure of the Hebrews from Egypt. Their under-

24. Ulrich, "Some Basic Concepts," 1. This error would have been easy to make. The decree was issued by the Holy Office on February 2, 1956, but published in *Acta Sanctae Sedis* (*AAS*) on March 24, 1956, 144–45. Ulrich quotes the *AAS* source, which is published in Latin.
25. Ulrich, "Some Basic Concepts."
26. Randolph F. Lumpp, email message to the author, January 14, 1999.
27. Lumpp, "Theological Perspective," 2.

standing of themselves changes from the physical to the social level. They become God's people. Their understanding of God also changes through the covenant expressed in terms of the law. The third stage of salvation history occurs in Jesus Christ. The development of humans continues from the physical and social levels to the personal level. God reveals himself through Jesus as a personal God offering humans everlasting life.[28]

The relationship between humanity and God changes throughout salvation history, as does the nature of ethics. At first, ethics were "primarily physical and concerned with the preservation of physical life." As the Hebrews became God's people, their ethics became concerned with the preservation of Israel as a society, and the law became a way of life. Under Jesus, the law is fulfilled on a personal level. Lumpp used examples from Christian scripture to show the limitations of the law. He pointed out that Jesus did not give universal moral principles such as "love all mankind." Rather, he stated, "Concretely and personally: Love one another as I have loved you." In 1 Corinthians 10, Paul discusses the question of meat sacrificed to pagan idols. The proper response for Christians is to "respond to the situation of the person involved." This approach, Lumpp believed, is the "ethics of the situation"; that, is situation ethics.[29] It is the very basis of Christianity—confronting each person in each situation and asking whether an action is "an expression of true personal life" based on honesty and love.[30]

Lumpp's second point is that the "revealed notion of history makes universal ethics unfeasible" because of differences in "psychological time." On a practical level, Lumpp explains that "presenting a person of primitive understanding with universal moral principles will not lead necessarily to [that person's] development." What is needed is a "person-to-person encounter" where "one treats this individual personally" and confronts him in his situation.[31] In other words, Christian ethics is much more than universal law. Humans fully develop and experience salvation through contact with each other.[32]

28. Lumpp, "Theological Perspective," 2–3.
29. Lumpp, "Theological Perspective," 4.
30. Lumpp, "Theological Perspective," 5.
31. Lumpp, "Theological Perspective," 6.
32. Lumpp, "Theological Perspective."

Lumpp's third point draws on the second—living a Christian life is not based on "abstract universality," but on "concrete particularity." The true Christian does not respond to others because of laws and principles. Lumpp notes that laws do not disappear but that the Christian's attitude toward law is different. The true Christian responds "in honesty and love to each and every person" confronted in each and every moment of life.[33]

Lumpp concluded by restating that situation ethics is a possibility because Christians have stressed the "interpersonal encounter as the basis of moral behavior." In dealing with each other, each person must be encountered where they are and led "through personal self-dedication to a realization of full humanity." That full humanity is concretely realized in the person of Jesus Christ.[34]

Lumpp responded to Bonnette's criticism by reporting that he believed, as stated in his lecture and in the discussion that followed, that

> we obviously can formulate and teach [universal immutable moral] norms.... It is an historical fact. The question remains, however, as to how one proceeds from such norms to the immediate application in the concrete moral instance.... Are the formulation and application of universal moral norms (and *norms* they are) sufficient for the Christian?

Lumpp did not think so, and he used remarks from Karl Rahner as supporting evidence.[35] Lumpp did not use the term "universal immutable moral norms" in his lecture, but instead referred to "laws and principles."

Lumpp also discussed the term "situation ethics" in his response to Bonnette. He stated that he "dislikes the term intensely" because it is "vague and represents a wide variety of opinions and speculations, some more acceptable and some more objectionable than others."[36] He ac-

33. Lumpp, "Theological Perspective."
34. Lumpp, "Theological Perspective," 6–7.
35. Randolph F. Lumpp, response to Bonnette's letter to Father Roesch, November 21, 1966, 2. Unfortunately, Rahner's remarks are not attached to the letter in the author's possession.
36. Throughout the written copy of the presentation, Lumpp placed quotation marks around the term "situation ethics." In response to a question from the author, Lumpp stated that he did not remember whether he used gestures during the lecture to indicate quotes. He often does use gestures, so it would not have been unusual for him to do so; Randolph F. Lumpp, email message to the author, May 31, 1999.

knowledged that there is a "truth contained in all these speculations," and cites Karl Rahner for authoritative support. Lumpp speculated that if the Philosophy Club had used Rahner's title, "formal existential ethics," for the discussion, perhaps the misunderstanding might have been avoided. There is a grain of truth in situation ethics, for even in traditional moral theology, circumstances mitigate culpability.

Concerning the magisterium's "condemnation," Lumpp pointed out that the two papal statements on situation ethics "do not define their terms in detail, but rather point to certain *dangers* [*sic*]." Since Lumpp does not name which papal statements he is referring to, it is difficult to assess the accuracy of this response. The Ottaviani letter referred to previously was the most recent statement issued and one in which one of the "errors and abuses" described appears to be "situation ethics."[37]

Lumpp continued, "These [papal] statements are not the last word on the subject directed toward stifling discussion but rather are, as the ordinary Magisterium is always, instructive guidance. Consequently, the question is far from closed." Lumpp described the document as "descriptive" rather than "precisely technical."[38] Lumpp believed that the response Catholics owe to the ordinary Magisterium is to (1) take it seriously, (2) study it carefully if one is going to teach about it, (3) be cautious in disagreeing with the Magisterium, and (4) if one disagrees, do not represent one's disagreement as church teaching.[39]

"Relationship" as a moral category was clearly an important component in the lectures of both Lumpp and Ulrich. The intersubjectivity espoused by Lumpp, however, differed from Ulrich's in that God and Jesus are at the center. Where Ulrich saw "man ... creating his own answers and own ethical criterion in the light of his consciousness of himself," Lumpp saw humans coming to self-understanding through God's self-revelation

---

37. One of the abuses listed by Cardinal Ottaviani is, "In moral theology, some deny any objective basis at all to morality. They do not accept natural law and hold that wrongness and righteousness are established by moral situations in which people find themselves. Bad ideas about morality and responsibility in sexual and marital matters are also heard." This description appears to refer to situation ethics; John Cogley, "Ottaviani Lists Doctrine 'Abuses,'" *New York Times*, September 20, 1966, 18.

38. Randolph F. Lumpp, email message to the author, June 19, 1999.

39. Randolph F. Lumpp, email message to the author, June 18, 1999.

in history. God's revelation included creation, the law, and Jesus Christ. In Lumpp's presentation, Jesus did not destroy the law but instead fulfilled it; that is, the law still existed as a moral norm.

Bonnette criticized Lumpp's presentation because Lumpp did not mention natural law. While Bonnette's criticism is true, it is also true that Lumpp did not deny natural law. The basic point Lumpp wanted to make was that the natural law standard is a lesser standard than the gospel. The way Lumpp made his point, however, was misinterpreted by some of the listeners.

Bonnette also criticized both Lumpp and Ulrich for not mentioning recent church teaching. In Lumpp's mind, the purpose of his lecture was to present a theological perspective on situation ethics. The title of Lumpp's lecture implies that he was offering an argument that would make situation ethics theologically plausible even though he himself did not advocate situation ethics. Lumpp also made the point that "universal ethics [was] unfeasible." Finally, Lumpp—and the other three faculty accused in the "Heresy" Affair—made presentations on controversial topics to an undergraduate audience after magisterial statements had been issued on the matter they discussed.

A discussion immediately followed the presentations by Ulrich and Lumpp. Lumpp recalls that Bonnette asked him "whether the Church would change its teaching on abortion." Lumpp answered that he believed the church already had changed its teaching when the principle of double effect was applied to the case of an ectopic pregnancy.[40] Bonnette pressed further about how the church might or might not change its position, and Lumpp recalls declining to speak for the church.[41] Bonnette was concerned about the way church teachings were being presented and taught as changeable.

Lumpp recalls a subsequent conversation with Bonnette where Lumpp quoted from paragraph 5 of *Gaudium et Spes*, Vatican II's Pastoral

40. Lumpp cites Father T. Lincoln Bouscaren, SJ. At the time, Bouscaren was a consultor to the Sacred Congregation for the Propagation of the Faith. Bouscaren was also an author of canon law books. Lumpp most likely referred to Bouscaren's work entitled, *Ethics of Ectopic Operations* (1933; repr. Milwaukee: Bruce, 1944).

41. Randolph F. Lumpp, email message to the author, January 18, 1999, 2.

Constitution on the Church in the Modern World: the human race is experiencing changes "and so mankind substitutes a dynamic and more evolutionary concept of nature for a static one."[42] Lumpp recalls Bonnette being "distressed" by this quotation.[43]

In summary, the October 11, 1966, Philosophy Club meeting dealt with a controversial topic. The teachings of the Roman Catholic Church were not explicitly stated, and, in Bonnette's opinion, the entire tone of the talks was "subjective." This meeting occurred very early in the 1966–67 academic year and was the first of a scheduled series on ethics. Bonnette had no reason to believe that the meetings to follow would be any different. Appeals had already been made in one form or another to the department, the provost, the president, and outside theologians, and the opportunity to appeal to the university's board of trustees was lost following Father Elbert's death. Bonnette felt that the time was right to appeal to the next level, the local archbishop in Cincinnati.

❦

Bonnette wrote a letter to Archbishop Karl J. Alter on October 15, 1966, with a carbon copy to apostolic delegate Egidio Vagnozzi. Bonnette stated that he was writing so that the archbishop could fulfill his duties as required by Canon 1381, §2; that is, his right and duty to be vigilant over all schools in his territory to make sure nothing contrary to faith and morals is being taught.[44] In Bonnette's opinion, a "crisis of faith" was developing at the University of Dayton, and so it became necessary to send a "second appeal" for the archbishop's intervention, following up on Father Langhirt's previous letter to the archbishop.[45]

In the letter, Bonnette listed several events that occurred on campus and named four faculty he believed were out of line with church teach-

42. Austin Flannery, OP, ed., "Pastoral Constitution on the Church in the Modern World," *Vatican Council II: The Conciliar and Post Conciliar Documents* (Collegeville, Minn.: Liturgical Press, 1979), 907.

43. Randolph F. Lumpp, email message to the author, January 18, 1999, 2.

44. "The right and duty to be vigilant over all schools in his territory is assured to the local ordinary by Can. 1381, §2. He is to see to it that nothing contrary to faith and morals is taught in the schools or that no activity in the schools is likewise a source of danger to the Catholic students there"; James Jerome Conn, SJ, *Catholic Universities in the United States and Ecclesiastical Authority* (Rome: Editrice Pontificia Universita Gregoriana, 1991), 34–35.

45. Dennis Bonnette to Karl J. Alter, October 15, 1966, 1.

ing: Eulalio Baltazar, John Chrisman, Randolph Lumpp, and Lawrence Ulrich. He singled out Chrisman for the two most serious charges: endorsement of abortion in some cases and publicly denying belief in purgatory. Bonnette asked the archbishop to intervene because the situation, in his opinion, had reached the "point of doing grave harm to the faith and morals of the entire university community."[46]

Bonnette explained that many of the "theories condemned in Cardinal Ottaviani's famous letter" of July 24, 1966, were being advocated by a "substantial number of the theology and philosophy faculty" at the University of Dayton.[47] The "influence of the erroneous teachings virtually permeates" the university, "even in some of the highest quarters."[48]

Bonnette asked the archbishop to send a "competent representative" to Dayton "for the purpose of conducting a comprehensive investigation of the grave spiritual harm" that was occurring. The matter was urgent, Bonnette said, because of the "harm to souls" that occurred daily in the classroom, and because University of Dayton regulations required notification of nonrenewal of faculty contracts by December 15. Bonnette continued, stating that "the consciences of some professors have been compromised too long already." If there is no action before the contractual deadline, Bonnette noted that some might resign in protest of the administration's "failure to fulfill its moral duty."

In conclusion, Bonnette said he was available if the archbishop needed "further evidence before taking action." He then asked Alter to keep his name "in confidence" unless the archbishop was unwilling to act, in which case, Bonnette "freely [sacrificed] the security of [his] position to the service of the cause of Christ." Bonnette appeared to be ready to resign publicly.[49]

Upon receiving Bonnette's letter and then speaking with the apostolic

46. Bonnette to Alter, October 15, 1966.

47. This letter will be discussed in detail in chapter 4.

48. Bonnette to Alter, October 15, 1966, 2.

49. One wonders what Bonnette would have done if the archbishop had chosen to do nothing. Presumably, Bonnette was prepared to resign publicly in protest of the university administration's "failure to fulfill its moral duty." Would Bonnette have included the archbishop in his public protest if the archbishop did not respond to his letter? It is an interesting question with no answer. Maybe sending the carbon copy to the apostolic delegate guaranteed that the archbishop would act.

delegate, the archbishop telephoned Father Roesch and asked him to investigate. Roesch took the call during his regular administrative council meeting. After discussing the call with the council, Roesch called a meeting of Bonnette and the four faculty members accused. At this meeting on October 24, 1966, Baltazar, Chrisman, and Ulrich first heard that they had been accused of teaching against the magisterium. Lumpp, who was unable to attend the meeting, heard about the accusation later in a private meeting with Roesch.

Bonnette, when asked to read his letter to the archbishop, gave a verbal summary. Roesch then asked Bonnette to prepare a statement detailing and substantiating his charges. This was a surprise development for Bonnette. Although he gave some specifics to the archbishop, he had not intended to charge the faculty individually. Rather, he wrote the letter to the archbishop to report a bad situation that needed action. He naively thought the archbishop would handle the situation with discretion. He also did not intend to go public with his charges, but an unknown source leaked the full story to the *National Catholic Reporter* (*NCR*) the day after the meeting, and then a reporter called Bonnette asking for his views on the situation.[50] Suddenly, he was labeled an accuser, "not a good thing in a free society."[51]

Bonnette's prepared statement, a six-page letter to Roesch dated October 28, 1966, listed the four faculty members and specific instances where each publicly "deviated from Catholic doctrine." The letter included two pages of names of persons in attendance at various events where the alleged deviations occurred. Bonnette clarified that by speaking of "deviations from Catholic doctrine," he meant "failing to be in full agreement with the mind of the Holy See and of its legitimate organs of expression, e.g., sacred congregations, papal pronouncements, speeches, allocutions, etc."[52] In addition to the substance of faculty teachings, Bonnette took issue with the way Baltazar, Chrisman, Lumpp, and Ulrich conducted themselves. For example, Bonnette stated that at one public lecture, the "general tone was to poke fun at papal directives"; at another, "great fun

50. Dennis Bonnette, telephone interview with the author, April 10, 1997.
51. Bonnette, telephone interview with the author, April 10, 1997.
52. Dennis Bonnette to Raymond A. Roesch, October 28, 1966, 1.

[was made] of the Cardinal"; and "neither speaker presented in a positive manner the traditional teaching." Baltazar, Chrisman, Lumpp, and Ulrich responded in letter form to Roesch and included the remarks that were called into question. In general, they claimed their views were "within the bounds of current Catholic speculation."[53] Their remarks included quotations from articles that supported their statements and their right to "express their difficulties with the official non-infallible positions of the magisterium."[54] They called Bonnette's views "traditional,"[55] "classical,"[56] "fundamentalist,"[57] and "static triumphalist."[58]

To assist in the investigation, Father Roesch consulted a canon lawyer, Jesuit father James I. O'Connor,[59] "on the point of whether or not there were grounds for a canonical investigation into the charges." O'Connor's finding was that the four faculty members were not guilty of heresy, a charge that would require a canonical investigation. Upon receiving O'Connor's recommendation, Roesch called Bonnette to his office and asked him to retract his charges. Roesch wanted to get the affair out of the ecclesiastical realm and keep it in the academic. Bonnette was given a few days to think about retraction. When Bonnette came in front of Roesch's administrative council on November 28, he was asked again to retract the charges. Roesch indicated that the archbishop was only concerned about abortion and purgatory. Roesch believed that he had already convinced the archbishop that these were not issues. In Roesch's opinion, "the accused faculty members [were] innocent of the charge of teaching and advocating doctrines contrary to the magisterium of the Church."[60] Roesch intended to appoint an ad hoc committee to "conduct an open discussion directed toward establishing clear directives for

53. John Chrisman to Raymond A. Roesch, n.d., 1.

54. Gregory Baum, *Search* (reprinted in *Commonweal*, November 25, 1966), typed and attached to John Chrisman's undated letter to Father Roesch.

55. Randolph F. Lumpp to Roesch, November 21, 1966, 1.

56. Eulalio R. Baltazar to Raymond A. Roesch, n.d., 11.

57. Baltazar to Roesch, n.d., 9.

58. John Chrisman to Raymond A. Roesch, n.d., 3.

59. Father O'Connor was from Bellarmine School of Theology of Loyola University in North Aurora, Illinois.

60. Raymond A. Roesch, to University of Dayton Faculty and Staff, December 3, 1966, 1.

the pursuit of truth in academic debate" on campus.[61] The composition of the committee was to include members of the faculty nominated by the faculty forum, Bonnette, and the four faculty members. This solution was not to Bonnette's liking. He did not agree that Baltazar, Chrisman, Lumpp, and Ulrich were innocent of teaching and advocating doctrines contrary to the magisterium. Therefore, he did not retract his charges, saying he was not concerned with formal heresy but with the whole situation of ignoring the ordinary teaching of the church.

Archbishop Alter relied on the university's investigation and Roesch's explanation and, on December 2, 1966, accepted Roesch's decision to appoint a committee. According to Roesch, Alter expressed "his satisfaction" with the appointment of this committee and called "attention to the care that must be taken to avoid disturbance of mind and a species of scandal, or at least, wonderment on the part of the ordinary student or hearer because of the way and/or the occasion in which one or other Catholic tenet, dogma or practice may be subjected to academic examination and discussion."[62]

Roesch wrote a December 3, 1966, letter to the faculty and staff and released it to the faculty and the press on December 5. On the day following Roesch's announcement of the results of his investigation, Bonnette and eight supporters—seven Philosophy faculty members and Father Langhirt—called the conduct of the university's administration a "classic whitewash." Dennis Bonnette and Thomas Casaletto read their statement, a "Declaration of Conscience on the Doctrinal Crisis at the University of Dayton," and discussed the controversy on Phil Donahue's local radio talk show, *Conversation Piece*.[63] The signers of the declaration were angry because six of them had been witnesses at "public talks in which teachings contrary to the magisterium [had] been *defended*," and they were not

61. Roesch to University of Dayton Faculty and Staff, December 3, 1966, 2.
62. Roesch to University of Dayton Faculty and Staff, December 3, 1966.
63. "A Declaration of Conscience on the Doctrinal Crisis at the University of Dayton," December 5, 1966, 1. Copy of the declaration given to the author by Bonnette. The faculty members who signed the declaration were: Hugo A. Barbic (instructor), Dennis Bonnette (assistant professor), Thomas J. Casaletto (assistant professor), Joseph Dieska (professor), Richard J. Dombro (assistant professor), Edward W. Harkenrider (professor), Allen V. Rinderly (instructor), and Paul I. Seman (assistant professor). Father Francis Langhirt also signed the Declaration, but he was not a full-time faculty member.

called to testify in the university's investigation.[64] They stated that the declaration was issued

> in order (1) to defend [their] integrity as to the positions which we hold in consonance with, and as declared by, the Teaching Magisterium as binding on every Catholic educator and (2) to distinguish ourselves from those colleagues on the faculty who revealed and confessed publicly their incompetence in the field of philosophy and their deviation from fundamental principles of Catholic doctrine.

The statement also declared that the university was "co-responsible for their deviations from universally held positions as declared and interpreted by the Holy Father—who is the only and ultimate interpreter of all doctrinal pronouncements of the Roman Catholic Church."[65]

The university administration's response to this charge was that no witnesses were needed because the faculty members charged did not deny that they had made the statements. That being the case, the university investigated "what [the progressives] intended to mean by using [the statements] in the context in which they were uttered." The administration admitted that "there is a problem of just how such expressions of personal cerebration should be made on a Catholic campus." Roesch hoped the ad hoc committee would solve that problem.[66]

Calling their fellow faculty incompetent was unacceptable for the faculty leaders at the University of Dayton. In a series of three special meetings held on December 9, 12, and 14, 1966, the faculty forum listened to a recording of the Phil Donahue show and then voted on a number of motions concerning this situation. After approving "the manner in which the President exercised his leadership in adjudicating the cases of the four professors recently accused,"[67] the forum voted on December 9 on the motion of former provost Father Thomas Stanley[68] to censure the eight

64. "Declaration of Conscience," 2.
65. "Declaration of Conscience."
66. "Statement given to the nine who signed Bonnette's statement," December 9, 1966, 1. Copy of the statement given to the author by Bonnette.
67. Minutes of faculty forum, December 9, 1966, 1.
68. Richard Baker, Summary of testimony to archbishop's fact-finding commission, December 30, 1966, University of Dayton, Unorthodox Teaching Investigation, 1967, RG1.6 Abp Alter, AAC.

members of the faculty who signed the "Declaration of Conscience" for "conduct unworthy of members of the University of Dayton faculty." The forum also demanded that the charge of incompetence be rescinded in a public statement or fully substantiated or "if they should fail to meet either of these alternatives, resign from their positions at the University."[69] It took the meetings of December 12 and 14 before the forum was able to resolve the details of a statement to be issued to the public. In response, the eight signed the following statement: "We withdraw the charge that colleagues on the faculty 'revealed and publicly confessed their incompetence.' It is a statement we should not have made."

About the same time, a number of local pastors, including Msgr. James L. Krusling, the dean of the Dayton deanery and founding pastor of St. Helen Church, and Msgr. James E. Sherman, pastor of Immaculate Conception Church, wrote to Father Roesch and to Archbishop Alter expressing dissatisfaction with the university's findings and with "the religious climate at the University generally."[70] The intervention of the pastors and the appeal of the nine signers of the "Declaration of Conscience" prompted the archbishop to form a fact-finding commission composed of four priests from the Archdiocese of Cincinnati: Father Donald G. McCarthy, Father Robert Hagedorn, Father W. Henry Kenney, SJ, and Father Robert Tensing, chair of the commission. Kenney was the chair of the Philosophy Department at Xavier University, while the other three priests

---

69. Faculty forum minutes, December 9, 1966, 1–2. The vote was passed by a vote of nine ayes, three nays, and four abstentions. Of particular interest is the membership on the forum of John Chrisman, one of the four accused faculty, and Richard Baker, chair of the Philosophy Department. Chrisman attended the meetings of December 9 and 14. Baker attended all three meetings. The forum chairman, Dr. Rocco Donatelli, invited five professors to the December 14 meeting: Harkenrider, Barbic, Bonnette, Casaletto, and Seman. At the beginning of that meeting, a motion was made to allow the visitors to remain at the meeting. No vote was taken, however, because the visitors indicated they were leaving. The statement the visitors intended to present was not read by the forum. The author of this report finds it interesting that Chrisman and Baker were permitted to participate in these meetings, since there appears to be a conflict of interest in their participation. It is difficult to ascertain their level of participation, since the minutes contain only the motions and votes. The author is unable to draw any conclusions from the voting records from these three meetings, since for every motion, there was at least one abstention and no consistency in the number of abstentions. In the author's conversations with members of the forum, there was no indication of a conflict of interest in Chrisman and Baker attending the meetings in which the censure was discussed.

70. "The 'Heresy' Affair," *University of Dayton Alumnus*, March 1967, 18.

were associated with Mount St. Mary's Seminary of the West in Cincinnati.[71]

The news of the formation of the commission became public on January 9, 1967, when the *Dayton Daily News* carried a front-page story with a headline stating "Alter Probing Teaching at UD."[72] This news led to (1) Baltazar challenging publicly the philosophical competence of three of the four commission members on the grounds that they were seminary professors, not university professors, (2) the university's newly formed chapter of the AAUP calling the creation of the commission "a flagrant breach of academic freedom,"[73] and (3) the student council calling the establishment of the commission an "unnecessary seizure of authority" on the part of the archbishop.[74]

In mid-February 1967, after a six-week investigation, the archbishop's commission issued a three-page summary of their report.[75] The commission found that there had been on "some specified occasions teaching contrary to Catholic faith and morals, which teachings may not have been contrary to defined doctrines but which were opposed to the teaching of the Magisterium." The summary indicated that in some lectures, a lack of respect was shown for the magisterium. The situation at the university was "more than a dispute between individual faculty members; the difficulty extend[ed] further into the University community." The report concluded by commending the university for creating the ad hoc committee to develop guidelines for the future and noted that the com-

71. All four members of the archbishop's committee were from the Archdiocese of Cincinnati. McCarthy, reportedly trained at Louvain, was chaplain of the Newman Center at the University of Cincinnati and was the brother of then-auxiliary bishop of Cincinnati and later archbishop emeritus of Miami, Florida Edward A. McCarthy. Hagedorn was associated with Mt. St. Mary's Seminary of the West in Cincinnati, as were Tensing and McCarthy. Kenney was in the Department of Philosophy at Xavier University. It is interesting to note that Lawrence Ulrich was personally acquainted with Hagedorn, Tensing, and McCarthy. Association with Mount St. Mary's Seminary of the West found in Roger Fortin, *Faith and Action: A History of the Archdiocese of Cincinnati, 1821–1996* (Columbus: Ohio State University Press, 2002), 352.

72. Doug Walker, "Alter Probing Teaching at UD: Group Seeks More Facts After Profs' Hassle," *Dayton Daily News*, January 9, 1967, 1.

73. "U.D. Dispute Still Simmers," *Catholic Telegraph Register*, January 27, 1967, 2.

74. "UD SC Resolution 16A," *Flyer News*, February 10, 1967, 3.

75. The summary states that the full report covers approximately seventy-five pages of testimony. Two copies of the full report existed. One was given to the archbishop and the other to Father James M. Darby, as chairman of the University of Dayton Board of Trustees.

mission made no suggestions about dismissals of "any professors involved in the investigation."[76]

At the same time the commission released its results, Father James M. Darby, Marianist provincial and the chair of the university's board of trustees, issued a statement on behalf of the university that stated that the commission report "reinforced the decision of the University in so far as it clear[ed] the accused professors of any charge of heresy."[77] The chair of the commission issued a counter statement that the university's press release gave an "unfortunate and wrong interpretation" of the report, since it gave the mistaken impression that the university and its faculty were cleared of all wrongdoing.[78]

With conflicting press reports issued by the archbishop's commission and the university, the University of Dayton faculty insisted on meeting with Father Roesch. They did this through a letter from Dr. Ellis A. Joseph, chairman of the Ad Hoc Committee for the Study of Academic Freedom at the University of Dayton, that was "strongly endorsed" by the presidents of the university's AAUP chapter, the student council, and the chairman of the university's faculty forum. Roesch had not issued a statement to the faculty since his December 3 letter clearing the four faculty. The faculty now wanted to know where Roesch stood on the controversy, what it meant for the University of Dayton, and more importantly, what it meant for them personally as faculty members.

76. Robert Tensing, Summary statement from archbishop's fact-finding commission, February 13, 1967, Series 91-35, AUD.

77. James M. Darby, "Statement Relative to Report of Archbishop Alter's Fact-Finding Committee," February 17, 1967, "History of U of D Heresy," 1967, D33, Day, ASM(CIN).

78. John Reedy, CSC, and James F. Andrews, "The Troubled University of Dayton," *Ave Maria*, April 1, 1967, 8, 20.

CHAPTER 4

THE HEART OF THE CONTROVERSY

The Response of Catholics to the Teaching Authority
of the Church

*In matters of faith and morals, the bishops speak in the name of Christ and the faithful are to
accept their teaching and adhere to it with a religious assent of soul.*

—Lumen Gentium ¶25

Upon receiving the letter from Ellis Joseph, Father Roesch quickly
scheduled a faculty meeting for the following Wednesday, March 1, 1967.
As the meeting started, Roesch told the faculty that his remarks would
not be duplicated or distributed at the meeting. He asked the faculty to
"listen carefully to my reading, so that you may remember a phrase, a
word, an idea which disturbs or puzzles you." He urged them to send him
their comments in written form so that ultimately, his remarks could be
put into document form and distributed to "each and every member of
the faculty and staff."[1]

Roesch intended to answer all ten questions that the faculty posed
to him, "first, by stating present university positions clearly and un-

1. Raymond A. Roesch, carbon copy of a typed manuscript of the lecture, n.d., 1, AUD,
Roesch papers, series 91–35, box 6. Future quotes from this manuscript appear parenthetically
in this chapter.

equivocally, and second, by indicating areas of policy interpretation and formulation... currently under study... by the Ad Hoc Committee for Guidelines Relative to Scholarship on our campus" (1).[2] In other words, the answers to the faculty questions would be found randomly within Roesch's remarks, not in a numbered list of responses.

Roesch began by telling the faculty that *Lumen Gentium (LG)*,[3] paragraph 25 (¶25), was the "heart of the controversy."[4] He then read the entire paragraph to the faculty:

In matters of faith and morals, the bishops speak in the name of Christ and the faithful are to accept their teaching and adhere to it with a religious assent of soul. This religious submission of mind and will must be shown in a special way to the authentic teaching authority of the Roman Pontiff, even when he is not speaking ex cathedra [*sic*]; that is, submission must be shown in such a way that his supreme Magisterium is acknowledged with reverence, the judgments made by him are sincerely adhered to, according to his manifest mind and will. His mind and will in the matter may be known chiefly either from the character of the document, from his frequent repetition of the same doctrine, or from his manner of speaking.[5]

Roesch continued that "every Catholic adheres to that pronouncement" (3) and that the university's faculty handbook implicitly contained a similar statement when it indicated that the faculty "may not advocate and disseminate doctrines that are subversive of... the aims and purposes of this Catholic institution which is committed to the upholding of the deposit of faith and Christian morality."[6] If it could be assumed that the faculty accepted that formulation of their obligation, then their behavior should reflect that acceptance. If the faculty disregarded that statement, conflict was bound to arise.

2. The name of the committee changed over time. When its final report was issued, the name of the committee was the Ad Hoc Committee for the Study of the Guidelines for Academic Freedom.

3. *Lumen Gentium (LG)*, the Second Vatican Council's Dogmatic Constitution on the Church, was released on November 21, 1964.

4. Raymond A. Roesch, "Statement Relative to the Controversy Touching Academic Freedom and the Church's Magisterium," University of Dayton, April 10, 1967, 1.

5. Roesch, "Statement Relative to the Controversy."

6. *University of Dayton Faculty Handbook*, 1966, 31. Roesch did not mention that this clause was also in the then-current faculty contract signed by each faculty member sitting in the audience.

Dennis Bonnette and his supporters agreed with Father Roesch that the primary issue in the controversy was the response of Catholic faculty to church authority. They must have been dismayed as Father Roesch continued with his lecture, reminding the faculty that a committee was currently at work reformulating the faculty handbook so that it avoided any statement that gave "a misleading emphasis on defense of doctrine and which neglects to bring to the fore the dynamic aspect of developing academic intellectual efforts on the campus" (3).

❦

Dennis Bonnette did not refer to *Lumen Gentium* ¶25 when he wrote to Archbishop Alter in October 1966. He might well have cited that paragraph, since the document, released in late 1964 and published widely in 1965, supported his charges. Bonnette's first reference to the paragraph is in an article he published in *Social Justice Review* in November 1967, six months after Roesch's lecture.[7] Since Bonnette likely would have used *LG* ¶25 to support his position if he had been aware of the existence of the paragraph, we can assume he was not aware of it when he wrote the letter to the archbishop.

Bonnette's two-page letter to the archbishop affirmed the authority of Archbishop Alter in such matters and then listed instances of heterodox teaching occurring on campus. Bonnette mentioned that "many of those theories condemned in Cardinal Ottaviani's famous letter of July 24, 1966 [were] being openly advocated by a substantial number" of the University of Dayton's Theology and Philosophy faculty.[8] It is important to explore Ottaviani's letter, what theories it condemned, and which ones matched Bonnette's charges.[9]

The letter Bonnette refers to is the "Circular Letter to the Presidents of Episcopal Conferences Regarding Some Sentences and Errors Arising

7. Dennis Bonnette, "The Doctrinal Crisis in Catholic Colleges and Universities and Its Effect upon Education," *Social Justice Review* (November 1967). By the time the article was published, slightly more than a year had passed since Bonnette's letter to the archbishop.

8. Dennis Bonnette to Archbishop Karl J. Alter, October 15, 1966, 2.

9. Alfredo Ottaviani (1890–1979) was an Italian cardinal who served as secretary of the Holy Office from 1959 to 1966, when the office was reorganized as the Congregation of the Doctrine of the Faith (CDF), and as pro-prefect of the CDF until his retirement in 1968. He was recognized then and now as the leader of the minority, conservative forces at the Second Vatican Council.

from the Interpretation of the Decrees of the Second Vatican Council."[10] Sent "at the direction of the Holy Father," it was distributed to the bishops around August 10, 1966, so that the contents of the letter could be considered at their conference meetings in November. In the letter, Ottaviani reminds the bishops that they are responsible for properly interpreting and implementing the documents of the Second Vatican Council. He "regret[s] that alarming news has come from various quarters on the subject of growing abuses in the interpretation of the Council's doctrine and with strange and audacious opinions appearing here and there greatly upsetting the minds of many faithful." He lists ten examples of such teachings:

- lack of respect for inspiration in Scripture and inerrancy in Biblical texts;
- dogmatic formulas are subject to historical evolution and their objective meaning may change;
- the ordinary magisterium is reduced to mere opinion;
- denial of the objectivity and immutability of truth;
- a Christological humanism where Jesus is human and gradually becomes aware of his divinity;
- the Real Presence is reduced to symbolism;
- the Sacrament of Penance is about reconciliation with the Church, not God, and personal confession is not necessary;
- minimization of the doctrine of original sin;
- the affirmation of situation ethics and other ideas in sexual and marital matters; and
- ecumenical action that offends the unity of faith and of the Church.[11]

10. "Circular Letter to the Presidents of Episcopal Conferences Regarding Some Sentences and Errors Arising from the Interpretation of the Decrees of the Second Vatican Council," accessed on April 6, 2014, http://www.vatican.va/roman_curia/congregations/cfaith/documents/rc_con_cfaith_doc_19660724_epistula_en.html.

11. For a detailed study on the American bishops' response to Ottaviani's letter, see Samuel J. Thomas, "After Vatican Council II: The American Catholic Bishops and the 'Syllabus' from Rome, 1966–68," *Catholic Historical Review* (April 1967): 233–57. The full English version of the errors follows.

1. In the first place it concerns sacred Revelation. There are some people, in fact, who have recourse to Holy Scripture, while deliberately leaving tradition on one side; they reduce the extent and the force of biblical inspiration and inerrancy and they do not have a correct notion of the value of the historical texts.

2. As regards the doctrine of the faith, dogmatic formulae are said to be subject to historical evolution that even their objective meaning is subject to change.

3. The ordinary magisterium of the church, especially that of the Roman pontiff, is sometimes neglected or disdained to the extent of relegating it to the field of mere opinion.

4. Some hardly recognize absolute, firm, and unchangeable objective truth; they subject everything to a certain relativism, advancing as a reason that all truth must necessarily follow the rhythm of the evolution of conscience and history.

5. Even the adorable Person of Our Lord Jesus Christ is attacked when, in rethinking Christology concepts occur on His nature and His person that are hard to reconcile with the dogmatic definitions. A certain Christological humanism is creeping in, which reduces Christ to the simple condition of a man who had little by little acquired the consciousness of His divine filiation. His virginal conception, His miracles, even His resurrection are granted in words, but are actually reduced to the purely natural order.

6. Likewise, in the theological study of the sacraments, certain elements are either ignored or else not sufficiently considered, especially where the Most Holy Eucharist is concerned. With regard to the real presence of Christ under the species of bread and wine, there are certain people who, in their dissertations, favor an exaggerated symbolism, as if the bread and the wine were not changed by transubstantiation into the body and blood of Our Lord Jesus Christ, but were simply subject to a certain change of signification. There are some, too, who on the subject of the Mass stress more than is right the idea of meal (agape), to the detriment of the idea of sacrifice.

7. Certain people prefer to explain the Sacrament of Penance as a means of reconciliation with the Church, without expressing sufficiently the reconciliation with God Himself Who is offended. They also claim that, for the celebration of this sacrament, the personal confession of sins is not necessary; they are content to set forth the social function of reconciliation with the Church.

8. There are also those who minimize the doctrine of the Council of Trent on original sin or comment on it in such a way that Adam's original fault and the transmission of his sin are at least obscured.

9. No less serious errors are spread in the field of moral theology. In fact, many people dare to reject the objective reason of morality; others do not accept natural law and affirm the legitimacy of what they call situation ethics. Pernicious opinions are spread about morality and responsibility in the matter of sex and marriage.

10. To all that, a note must be added on ecumenism. The Apostolic See assuredly approves those who, in the spirit of the conciliar decree on ecumenism, take initiatives to encourage charity with our separated brothers and draw them to the unity of the Church. But the Apostolic See deplores that there are persons who interpret the conciliar decree in their own way, advocate an ecumenical action that offends the truth regarding the unity of the faith and of the Church; in this way encouragement is given to a dangerous irenicism and indifferentism, which is completely foreign to the spirit of the Council.

English translation found in "Letter from the S. Congregation 'Pro Doctrina Fidei' on 'Strange and Audacious Opinions,'" *Christ to the World*, January 1967, 66–67.

Ottaviani asked the bishops to "arrest or prevent" these opinions and errors, to discuss them at an Episcopal Conference, and to report back to him before December 25, 1966, what might be done to curb these errors. Ottaviani states in the final paragraph of the letter that "this matter is not to be made public and the bishops may discuss [the letter] only with those whom they deem it necessary to consult *sub secreto*."[12]

Not surprisingly, there was a leak, and, six weeks later, John Cogley reported on Ottaviani's letter in the September 20, 1966, issue of the *New York Times*, listing the ten abuses. Since such a listing was reminiscent of Pius IX's Syllabus of Errors (1864) and Pius X's *Lamentabili sane exitu* (1907), Cogley and writers following him began calling the letter Ottaviani's Syllabus.

Cogley reported that a similar letter was sent to the heads of Catholic religious orders, presumably because "some of the leading theologians in the Church, especially those whom Cardinal Ottaviani's strictures might involve, are members of orders." The superiors were asked to report what they were doing to curb erroneous teaching.[13]

On October 5, 1966, several weeks after the Cogley article, the full letter appeared in the Vatican's *Acta Apostolicae Sedis* with the explanation that since the letter was published in part by certain newspapers, the full letter needed to be made available to be properly understood.

Upon reading Ottaviani's letter, Bonnette and his supporters were more assured than ever that they were right. After all, the second-highest official in the church proclaimed as errors items being taught at the University of Dayton, specifically, dogmatic formulas can change (no. 2), the ordinary magisterium is reduced to mere opinion (no. 3), truth is subject to change (no. 4), and situation ethics is affirmed (no. 9). Furthermore, these errors were influencing the minds of young Catholics in a location where their faith should be protected.

12. Archbishop Patrick A. O'Boyle to U.S. bishops, includes Ottaviani's letter as attachment, August 5, 1966, series NCWC, box 7 administration, ACUA.

13. John Cogley, "Ottaviani Lists Doctrine 'Abuses': Tells Bishops That 10 Errors Arose after Council," *New York Times*, September 20, 1966, 18.

When the university began its investigation, Father Roesch asked Bonnette to produce a detailed statement of charges because Bonnette's initial letter was sent to the archbishop. Bonnette complied and stated in his document that Baltazar, Chrisman, Lumpp, and Ulrich were "responsible for deviations from Catholic doctrine" that he described as "failing to be in full agreement with the mind of the Holy See and of its legitimate organs of expressions, e.g., sacred congregations, papal pronouncements, speeches, allocutions, etc."[14] He continued,

> I do not mean merely direct heresies, by which I understand the refusal of the declared dogmas of the Church. Rather, I refer to all such theories and doctrines which the Holy See has publicly condemned as contrary to the mind of the Church, e.g., the approval of contraception, the denial of the right of the Church to teach and guide Her faithful in matters of faith and morals, the theory of polygenism, situation ethics, abortion, etc.[15]

Bonnette's understanding of what it meant to be an orthodox Catholic required "full agreement" with every statement issued by the pope and the Vatican congregations, regardless of the level of authority at which an official statement was made.

In his *Social Justice Review* article, Bonnette claims that *LG* ¶25 is pivotal to his position.[16] His interpretation of *LG* ¶25 focuses on the sentence "the faithful... (must show)... religious submission of will and of mind... to the authentic teaching authority of the Roman Pontiff, even when he is not speaking ex cathedra (*sic*)."[17] He mentions that paragraph 25 "demands" adherence and states that a "Catholic is not free to respectfully differ from the magisterium."[18] Bonnette's "central and very concrete

14. Bonnette to Roesch, October 28, 1966, 2.

15. Bonnette to Roesch, October 28, 1966. Polygenism is the belief that there are multiple origins of the human species, as opposed to Adam and Eve being the first humans.

16. Bonnette also indicates that the First Vatican Council's teaching on papal primacy is crucial to his position. He uses papal primacy to articulate that the Roman pontiff has supreme power of jurisdiction over the universal church as well as the individual faithful in matters of faith and morals. This focus from the pope to the individual, an ultramontane reading of *Pastor Aeternus*, is not a common interpretation of papal primacy. Bonnette recollects relying on Dr. Joseph Dieska for the theological aspect of his argument. We have no way of knowing for sure why Dr. Dieska appealed to papal primacy; Bonnette, email message to the author, October 22, 2002.

17. Bonnette, "Doctrinal Crisis in Catholic Colleges," 224.

18. Bonnette, "Doctrinal Crisis in Catholic Colleges," 225. The *LG* paragraph Bonnette

point" is that "to be Catholic it is not enough merely to believe the dogma. One is also bound to accept *all* the teachings of the Church, *even those which are not solemnly defined*" [emphasis provided by Bonnette].

Bonnette interpreted *LG* ¶25 without any distinction among the levels of teaching authority that might be in play. The fact that theologians and philosophers openly questioned and advocated positions differing from church teaching authority meant, to him, that they were not adhering with religious obedience of mind and will.[19]

Bonnette was not alone in his interpretation of *LG* ¶25. He had supporters in the Philosophy Department, particularly fellow faculty members Joseph Dieska and Marianist father Richard Dombro. In his 1968 article "'New Theology' and the Old Faith,"[20] Dieska interpreted *LG* ¶25 in a way similar to Bonnette. Father Dombro, in the 1965 eight-page memo sent to Father Roesch, recommended "thinking with the Church" and "being FAITHFUL to the *thought of the Church* and of not deviating from it" (emphases added by Dombro).[21] Dombro also circulated an assembled packet of pertinent quotations from Vatican II documents and their commentaries regarding the magisterium, development of doctrine, and academic freedom. *Lumen Gentium* ¶25 was one of the texts included.[22]

Of the four accused faculty members, only Eulalio Baltazar responded directly to the accusation that in his "public utterances and writings" he

---

quotes from is the second of seven paragraphs in ¶25. It is the same paragraph quoted by Roesch at the beginning of the faculty meeting.

19. Obviously, there is another issue involved: the responsibilities of teachers in Catholic schools. This issue will be dealt with in a later chapter.

20. Joseph L. Dieska, "'New Theology' and the Old Faith," *Focus on the University of Dayton*, July 1968, 11, 13. Dieska also relies on papal primacy to support his position. Although Dieska's work was published after Bonnette's, the author believes—based on her communication with Bonnette—that Dieska was Bonnette's advisor on theological issues.

21. Richard J. Dombro, October 19, 1965, memo to Raymond A. Roesch, 5.

22. The packet of quotations has a handwritten title (appears to be Father Dombro's writing), "Quotes from 16 Documents re: Magisterium." Each quote has a page number and a notation of which document or commentary the quote came from and what it concerns (the magisterium, development of dogma, or academic freedom). The unidentified source of the quotes appears to be *The Documents of Vatican II*, ed. Walter M. Abbott, SJ (New York: Guild Press/Herder and Herder, 1966). My thanks to Dr. Dennis Doyle for his assistance in identifying this text. We do not know to whom this packet of quotations was distributed.

maintained a "position that is contrary to the Church's Magisterium."[23] As a former Jesuit seminarian, Baltazar was trained in both philosophy and theology. Baltazar pointed out that Bonnette had a "naïve understanding of theology... [that] fails to distinguish between formulation and content.... Any departure from this formulation is taken to mean a departure from Catholic truth.... Bonnette seems never to have heard of this long-accepted distinction, as was evidenced by his shock on hearing me say that there is such a thing as the evolution of dogma."[24] Baltazar recommended that Bonnette read articles on the changeability of church positions written by theologians Jean Danielou and Joseph Ratzinger, who later became Pope Benedict XVI.[25]

❦

Roesch's view of the faculty's responsibility to adhere to and respect church teaching changed over time and can be traced in three publications spanning 1964 through 1966: the 1964 remarks at the opening of the fall term, the 1965 remarks, also at the opening of the fall term, and then finally the 1966 *Annual President's Report*. All three publications were intended for the faculty, although the 1966 *Annual President's Report* was also written for the board of trustees, alumni, and friends of the university. It is worth examining each of these in succession, referring to them by the year in which they were published.

Father Roesch's remarks to the faculty at the term-opening faculty meeting in September 1964 were published later in the *Monday Morning Memo*, a newsletter for the UD faculty and staff. Roesch "reassures" the faculty that the Marianists "welcome [the faculty] in their role as associates... in carrying out the purposes of [the] Marianist institution." Roesch states that one of the reasons the Society of Mary was founded was for "the apostolic work of cooperating in the salvation of souls." To accomplish this goal, the Marianists engage in the work of education. Roesch goes on to say that the University of Dayton is "rightly characterized" as a

23. Eulalio R. Baltazar to Raymond A. Roesch, n.d., 1.

24. Baltazar to Roesch, n.d., 2–3.

25. The two articles recommended by Baltazar are Jean Danielou, "Pluralism within Christian Thought," *Theology Digest* 10 (Winter 1962): 67–70, and Joseph Ratzinger, "The Changeable and Unchangeable in Theology," *Theology Digest* 10 (Winter 1962): 71–76. See also Baltazar to Roesch, n.d., 3.

"Catholic institution of higher education" and that each year "we strive ...
to make that phrase take on deeper and fuller meaning."[26] Roesch added:

> "Catholic" refers, of course, to our deep conviction regarding our relation-
> ship to Almighty God and to the moral code that governs that relationship.
> All of you are aware that whether you be of our religious faith or not, you
> have accepted the principle that no doctrine contrary to the Catholic faith
> may be taught or advocated publicly while you are in our employ. But such
> a negative restriction is simply not sufficient to characterize us as a Catholic
> institution of higher learning. Bringing our students to know and love vir-
> tue requires positive action on our part.
>
> ... [Our students] need the example and active support of persons whom
> they sincerely respect.... As cooperators with the marianists [*sic*], you are in
> a powerful position to influence the lives of these young men and women.
> We hope and trust that you will take this responsibility seriously, and that
> you will do all that you can to foster in these young adults a love for Chris-
> tian virtue which will stand them in good stead for the rest of their lives.
> Under no conditions should you ever condone any action on the part of
> your students which is contrary to the ideals and objectives of the Christian
> education which the University proposes to profess.[27]

Thus, in 1964, Roesch emphasized the Catholic identity of the institution, with Catholicity referring to faith and especially moral behavior.
Roesch reminds faculty that "saving souls" is a Marianist goal and that
all faculty have a role to play in passing on the Christian tradition to
students.

Roesch also addressed the faculty at the beginning of academic year
1965–66. He reminded the faculty that the University of Dayton is a Catholic and Marianist university and told them that teachings in Paul VI's
1964 encyclical *Ecclesiam Suam* must be their "guideline" for keeping the
university Catholic and Marianist. Specifically, Roesch quoted paragraphs
47–49, which warn that "many of the faithful" think that the way to reform the church is for the church to adapt its "way of thinking and acting
to the customs and temper of the modern secular world." Those who are
fascinated with worldly life regard conformity to it as inescapable and a

26. Raymond A. Roesch, "A Catholic Institution of Higher Learning," *Monday Morning Memo*, September 14, 1964, 4.

27. Roesch, "Catholic Institution."

good thing to do. Paul VI pointed out that this "phenomenon of adaptation (to the secular) is noticeable" in philosophy and ethics and that doctrines such as naturalism and relativism undermine Christianity.[28]

Certainly, this speech is similar in tone to the 1964 lecture. It may have been written with the philosophy faculty in mind,[29] since by this time the controversy was underway in Philosophy Club meetings, student columns in the *Flyer News*, and Baltazar's proposed curriculum change. Recall that the 1965–66 academic year began with Dr. Richard R. Baker assuming the chairmanship of the department[30] and five new faculty—including Dennis Bonnette—joining the Philosophy Department. John Chrisman also returned to the faculty after a year of doctoral work in Toronto. Perhaps this speech was Roesch's way of trying to tamp down the controversy before the academic year began.

By the end of the academic year, Roesch's emphasis changed, as shown in his 1966 *Annual President's Report* distributed to the board of trustees, alumni, faculty, and friends of the university, where Roesch answers "no" to the question posed as the title of his report: "Is a Catholic University a Contradiction in Terms?" The majority of the report deals with academic freedom. What is pertinent is Roesch's view that "we[31] have accepted that [the Catholic university has] a duty to hand down a tradition of doctrine, morals and conduct to its students, but [that] is not its primary function." Rather, "the student must be given a commitment, but there comes a time when instruction must cease, and inquiry must begin."[32]

28. Paul VI, *Ecclesiam Suam*, accessed July 11, 2003, http://www.vatican.va/holy_father/paul_vi/encyclicals/documents/hf_pvi_enc_06081964_ecclesiam_en.html; Roesch, address to the faculty, August 30, 1965, Philosophy Controversy file in the office of the provost, University of Dayton. The author reviewed this file in 1997 and took notes on its contents, and in 2003 requested permission to review the file again. Permission was granted, but the file could not be located.

29. This particular speech was located by the author in the Philosophy Controversy file in the office of the provost, University of Dayton. The fact that this speech was filed in this particular file is an indication that the provost (or his secretary) thought this speech was connected to the controversy. One possible explanation is that Roesch wrote the speech with the Philosophy faculty in mind and that this was known to the provost, Father Charles Lees, who assumed his position in summer 1965.

30. Previously, Richard R. Baker served as interim chairman.

31. Presumably Roesch is referring to the Marianists at the University of Dayton.

32. Roesch, 1966 *Annual President's Report*, 5.

Nine months prior to this point, Roesch had stressed the importance of thinking with the church and not adapting to the secular world. Now he encouraged the faculty to embrace the same modern world he warned them against the previous fall. In the 1966 annual report, Roesch stated that the "Catholic college has a duty to maintain a critical independence"[33] from the church and that Catholics

> have lost much by paying scant heed to truths and insights propounded by those whose point of view differs or is even antithetical to our own. Non-Catholic positions in theology and philosophy, put forward by some of the finest scholars of our day, contain much truth.[34]

The content of the 1965 fall speech stressed unity with the church, while the 1966 annual report stressed a critical independence from the church.

What happened to change Roesch's vision of the University of Dayton as a Catholic university? There are several possibilities. In the 1966 annual report, Roesch refers to "some problems arising on the East Coast"[35]— namely, the controversy that erupted at St. John's University in New York in December 1965. The Vincentians, the order that founded St. John's, terminated thirty-one professors. In response, the faculty went on strike, students demonstrated, and the AAUP issued one of its strongest censures ever.

Second, a committee of the University of Dayton's faculty forum met throughout academic year 1965–66 to discuss service conditions at the university, such as faculty pay and governance, issues similar to those battled over in the St. John's case.[36] Any Catholic college administrator would want to keep the situation at his own school from escalating into a confrontation like St. John's. Third, several reports issued in spring 1966

33. Roesch, 1966 *Annual President's Report*.
34. Roesch, 1966 *Annual President's Report*, 7.
35. Roesch, 1966 *Annual President's Report*, 1.
36. During academic year 1964–65, approximately ten University of Dayton professors decided to meet weekly to "discuss matters pertinent to the welfare of the University." These informal gatherings represented a "response to the fulfillment of a spontaneous felt need on the part of a few professors concerned with excellence at the University of Dayton." The faculty forum took up the same issues in 1965–66, forming a committee called the Committee on Service Conditions Affecting the Life of the Mind. Most of the participants in the 1964–65 discussions were members of the formal committee; "Preface," faculty forum committee, University of Dayton, "Service Conditions Affecting the Life of the Mind," September 26, 1966, AUD.

were critical of Catholic institutions, especially the Danforth Commission report on church universities and the American Council on Education assessment of quality in graduate education. These national reports judged Catholic institutions of higher education as inferior, especially at the graduate level.

It is not surprising, then, that Roesch's 1966 annual report to faculty and alumni addressed the apparent contradiction of a university being Catholic.

In summary, those on opposite sides of the "Heresy" Affair differed sharply in their understanding of the proper response to church authority. Bonnette, Dieska, and Dombro believe that all church teachings must be accepted on personal and intellectual levels. Their interpretation of *Lumen Gentium* ¶25 leaves no room for dissent on church teachings related to faith or morals. They follow Alfredo Cardinal Ottaviani and the minority bishops at the Second Vatican Council. Baltazar, on the other hand, in the light of the majority at Vatican II, views church teachings as open to interpretation and development. Neither side is alone in its views within the church, the Marianists, and the faculty of the university. For this reason, the controversy is important and of interest beyond the University of Dayton.

Father Roesch's dilemma was to find a way to show that the university was both Catholic *and* a real university. He correctly described *Lumen Gentium* ¶25 as "the heart of the controversy," indicating that he understood the concerns of Bonnette and his supporters. However, Roesch had also come to see that being a Catholic university meant the University of Dayton must be academically legitimate.

1. Dennis Bonnette, AM, assistant professor of philosophy.

2. Thomas Casaletto, MA, instructor of philosophy.

3. Joseph Dieska, PhD, associate professor of philosophy.

5. Edward W. Harkenrider, PhD, professor of philosophy.

4. Fr. Richard J. Dombro, SM, assistant professor of philosophy.

7. *John M. Chrisman, MA, assistant professor of philosophy.*

6. *Eulalio R. Baltazar, PhD, assistant professor of philosophy.*

8. *Randolph F. Lumpp, MA, instructor of theological studies.*

9. *Lawrence Ulrich, MA, instructor of philosophy.*

 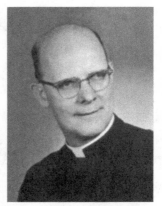

10. *Richard R. Baker, PhD, professor and chair of philosophy.*

11. *Fr. Matthew Kohmescher, SM, associate Professor and chair of theological studies.*

12. *Administrative Council. Seated: Bro. Joseph Mervar, Bro. Thomas Schick, Fr. Charles Collins, Fr. Paul Wagner, Fr. Charles Lees, Fr. Thomas A. Stanley, Fr. Nobert Burns; standing: Fr. George B. Barrett, Fr. Raymond Roesch, Bro. Elmber C. Lackner.*

13. Fr. James Darby, SM, provincial and chair of the Board of Trustees.

14. Fr. Thomas A. Stanley, SM, provost.

15. Fr. Raymond A. Roesch, SM, president.

16. Archbishop of Cincinnati,
Karl J. Alter (center) and
University President,
Fr. Raymond A. Roesch, SM
(right).

17. Philosophy
Club, 1966-67.
From left, John
M. Chrisman
(moderator),
Sandra Polaski, Jim
Wade, and Paul
Campbell.

SPEAKERS SPONSORED BY THE PRESIDENT'S AD HOC COMMITTEE ON ACADEMIC FREEDOM

19. William Doane Kelly, PhD.

18. Rosemary Lauer, PhD.

20. Leslie Dewart, PhD.

22. Fr. Gregory Baum, theologian and source for Fr. Roesch's lecture.

21. Fr. John L. McKenzie, SJ.

23. Fr. William J. Cole, SM, associate professor of theological studies; author of "Working Paper Presented to the Faculty for Critical Consideration; Purposes of the University of Dayton."

CHAPTER 5

TENSIONS BETWEEN THE MAGISTERIUM AND THOSE DOING THEOLOGICAL INQUIRY

[Doctrinal formulae] can, it is true, be made clearer and more obvious; and doing this is of great benefit. But it must always be done in such a way that they retain the meaning in which they have been used, so that with the advance of an understanding of the faith, the truth of faith will remain unchanged.

—Pope Paul VI, in *Mysterium Fidei*, September 3, 1965

If the "heart of the controversy" was the response Catholics owe to the official teachings of the church and if the University of Dayton was to be an academically legitimate Catholic university, Roesch, and indeed all presidents of Catholic universities in the sixties, needed to tackle the question: how can a theology or philosophy scholar be both academically credible and faithful to the church? More to the point, to what extent can scholars disagree with noninfallible teachings? First, we will look at the views of Bonnette and his supporters who made the charges, followed by the responses of those charged: Baltazar, Chrisman, Ulrich, and Lumpp. We will then return to Roesch's March 1967 address to the faculty to see how he approached this dilemma.

❦

Dennis Bonnette's October 28, 1966, letter to Roesch detailing the "deviations from Catholic doctrine which are present in our University" included charges that Baltazar, Chrisman, Ulrich, and Lumpp *"publicly,* either in talks given on this campus, or in their writings, revealed their explicit disagreement with Church teaching" in matters such as contraception, polygenism, situation ethics, abortion, and "the right of the Church to teach and guide Her faithful in matters of faith and morals."[1] As we have seen, in the view of Bonnette and his supporters, a faculty member at a Catholic university should not publicly disagree with any official church teachings.

Baltazar's response to the accusation letter shows that he views himself and other philosophers and theologians as

> advisors of the Pope, helping by their researches the formulation of an encyclical or the Church's position on a given question, and who, by the very nature of their work are already beyond an encyclical when this is formulated, ever seeking for more adequate formulation, ever probing the depth of Christian truth. It is in this context that scholars try to see whether contraception, situation ethics, polygenism are compatible with Christian experience or not. Such reflections and explorations are entirely in accordance with the mind of the Church.[2]

In response to Bonnette's objection that Baltazar defended birth control by contributing a chapter to *Contraception and Holiness* in October 1964, Baltazar stated that the church was reexamining her traditional position. He pointed out that "many cardinals, bishops, theologians,... a vast number of the Catholic laity... [and] fifty-three out of the sixty members of the papal commission favor[ed] some sort of change in the traditional doctrine." Baltazar indicated that Professor Bonnette "propose[d] as definitively solved what is precisely being re-examined."[3]

Chrisman believed that his views were "respectably within the bounds of current Catholic speculation." He insisted that he had "the right and (in loyalty to the church) the duty to utter and discuss them on our campus."

---

1. Dennis Bonnette to Raymond A. Roesch, October 28, 1966, 1.
2. Eulalio R. Baltazar to Raymond A. Roesch, n.d., 10.
3. Baltazar to Roesch, n.d., 4–5.

He gave three reasons: "(1) that the university is the appropriate place for the Church to listen to and learn from its own members because (2) the teachings of the Church are in constant need of relevant reformulation since (3) truth is a living, organic, growth of human consciousness."[4]

Lawrence Ulrich's October 11, 1966, Philosophy Club presentation on situation ethics led to him also being accused in Bonnette's letter to Archbishop Alter. In response to Bonnette's charges, Ulrich indicated that since Vatican II, "the Church is struggling to understand herself and her function in the world." He knew about Cardinal Ottaviani's letter and Pope Pius XII's two 1950s instructions condemning situation ethics, but "to his knowledge, none of these documents could be construed in any way as infallible teaching of the universal Church."[5]

As support for his views on the magisterium, Ulrich attached the remarks of Pope Paul VI to the faculty and students of Milan's Catholic University of the Sacred Heart on April 5, 1964. In the sermon, Paul VI discussed

> the problem of relations between the two magisteria, ecclesiastical and secular, that which is based on divine thought and that based on human, that deriving from faith and that from reason.... It is an age-old question that a Catholic university solves not by separating one kind of thought from another, the purely religious from the strictly rational, as if they were foreigners speaking different languages, but rather by uncovering and developing their respective areas of competence and their contributions to each other.[6]

Ulrich also quoted John Courtney Murray, SJ, in the introductory comments to the Declaration on Religious Freedom:

> [The document] raised with sharp emphasis the issue that lay continually below the surface of all the conciliar debates—the issue of the development of doctrine.... But the Council formally sanctioned the validity of the development itself; and this was a doctrinal event of high importance for theological thought in many other areas.[7]

4. John Chrisman to Raymond A. Roesch, n.d., 3.
5. Laurence P. Ulrich to Raymond A. Roesch, November 22, 1966, 1.
6. Paul VI, "The Task of Catholic Universities," *The Pope Speaks* 10, no. 1 (1965): 44–45; attached to Ulrich to Roesch, November 22, 1966, 5.
7. Ulrich to Roesch, November 22, 1966, 2; John Courtney Murray, SJ, "Comments on

In his response to Bonnette, Randolph F. Lumpp, the lone theologian among those charged, pointed out that "all theologians always and everywhere do not agree with every word uttered by the Magisterium nor should they." He gave the examples of Paul VI differing with Karl Rahner and Edward Schillebeeckx on polygenism and of theologians and bishops differing with the magisterium on contraception. Lumpp indicated that theologians recognize the "need to apply the same techniques of literary criticism to the Magisterium as we have already applied to scripture: the statements must be placed in the historical context in which they were composed and uttered." Although the ordinary magisterium should be approached with "reverence and respect," one might "well find oneself bound in conscience to disagree." Lumpp's sources for his response were the works of two well-known scholars, John Henry Newman's *Essay on the Development of Christian Doctrine* and Father John L. McKenzie's *Authority in the Church.*[8]

❦

In his March 1967 faculty address, Roesch tries to reconcile academic credibility with faithfulness to the church. He indicates that the primary issue for the university is "the exact and proper role of the Magisterium," which is "one of the most vexing and highly debated questions in the Church today."[9] Roesch continued, "Theologians are making a distinction between the 'infallible Magisterium' and the 'authentic Magisterium,'"[10] but have "difficulty in trying to identify the exact force of tenets in the latter area." To help "identify his position" on the role of the magisteri-

---

the Declaration on Religious Freedom," in *The Documents of Vatican II with Notes and Comments by Catholic, Protestant, and Orthodox Authorities*, ed. Walter M. Abbott, SJ (New York: Guild and America Press, 1966), 673. Also available at https://openlibrary.org/books/OL5989600M/The_Documents_of_Vatican_II.

8. Randolph F. Lumpp to Raymond A. Roesch, November 21, 1966, 2–3.

9. Raymond A. Roesch, carbon copy of a typed manuscript of the lecture, n.d., 4, Roesch papers, series 91–35, box 6, AUD. Future quotes from this manuscript appear parenthetically in this chapter.

10. Today we would refer to the "authentic magisterium" as the "ordinary and universal magisterium"; see John Boyle, "The Ordinary Magisterium: Towards a History of the Concept," *Heythrop Journal* 20 (1979): 380–98 and 21 (1980): 91–102; Richard R. Gaillardetz, *Witnesses to the Faith: Community, Infallibility and the Ordinary Magisterium of Bishops* (New York: Paulist, 1992), 18–35; Ladislas Orsy, SJ, "Magisterium: Assent and Dissent," *Theological Studies* 48 (1987): 473–97.

um, Roesch stated that he relied on unidentified theologians on campus and on three theologians who attended the Second Vatican Council—Father Eugene H. Maly, Father Bernard Häring, and Father Gregory Baum (3).

Maly, the least well-known of the three, was a scripture scholar at Mount St. Mary's Seminary of the West in Cincinnati and the personal theologian for Cincinnati's Archbishop Karl J. Alter. He was president of the Catholic Biblical Association of America, coeditor (with Mother Katherine Sullivan, RSCJ, and Passionist father Barnabas Ahern) of *The Bible Today*, as well as *peritus* at Vatican II. In the latter position, he worked on the American bishops' press panel, explaining the happenings at the Council.[11]

Maly was a friend of then-Marianist Gerard J. E. Sullivan,[12] a Latin teacher at Mount St. Mary's Seminary and an associate professor of languages at the University of Dayton. Upon hearing about the controversy, Maly suggested to Sullivan that Father Roesch "might profit from the advice of Father Bernard Häring, CSsR, considered to be the world's foremost moral theologian."[13] With Sullivan and Maly working out the details, Roesch and Häring met on Saturday, February 25, 1967, in a Cincinnati hotel where Häring stayed during one of his frequent visits to the United States.[14]

Häring, a German Redemptorist, was known for his 1954 book *The Law of Christ: Moral Theology for Priests and Laity*, a three-volume, groundbreaking text that focused on living like Christ rather than the traditional manualist approach of cataloging sins.[15] Father Häring served on the Preparatory Commission for the Second Vatican Council and as secretary

---

11. Each day after a session at the Second Vatican Council, U.S. news reporters met with the press panel, who answered questions and explained the happenings at the Council. Each member of the press panel was an expert in a specific area; "New Program Arranged for U.S. Newsmen," *Vatican II: 50 Years Ago Today*, accessed December 3, 2013, http://vaticaniiat50 .wordpress.com/2012/10/20/new-program-arranged-for-u-s-newsmen/.

12. Gerard J. E. Sullivan, email message to the author, May 17, 2002. Sullivan had master's and doctoral degrees. He left the Marianists in the 1970s.

13. Sullivan, email message to author, May 17, 2002.

14. Sullivan, email message to author, May 17, 2002.

15. Barbara Stewart, "Bernard Haring, 85, Is Dead; Challenged Catholic Morality," *New York Times*, July 11, 1998, section A, 9, accessed January 26, 2007, LexisNexis.

to the editorial committee that drafted *Gaudium et Spes*, the Pastoral Constitution on the Church in the Modern World.[16]

Roesch's written source on the role of the magisterium was Father Gregory Baum's January 1967 *Concilium* article "The Magisterium in a Changing Church,"[17] described by Roesch as "one of the finest and most authoritative treatments of the Magisterium" and one that was "widely accepted" as assured to him by both Häring and Maly (4).

Gregory Baum was born in 1923 in Berlin, Germany, to a Jewish mother and Protestant father. After making his way to Canada as a war refugee in 1940 and being interned in refugee camps under military control, he continued his education and ultimately earned bachelor's (mathematics and physics) and master's (mathematics) degrees. In 1946, he became a Catholic and shortly thereafter entered the Augustinian order (1947). He was ordained a priest in 1954 and completed the requirements for a Doctor of Theology degree from the University of Fribourg in 1956.[18] His work on ecumenism led to his serving as a Vatican II *peritus* for the Secretariat of Christian Unity, where he played a part in writing *Dei verbum*, the Dogmatic Constitution on Divine Revelation. After the Council ended, Baum taught theology at the University of Saint Michael's College in the University of Toronto.[19]

Paraphrasing Baum, Roesch told the faculty that "despite the difficulties" in knowing the role of the magisterium, the Catholic theologian and philosopher is "willing to engage in theological inquiries, even if some of his conclusions change or reinterpret the apparent meaning of past conciliar statements or papal encyclicals" (4–5). Roesch cited the Second Vatican Council as evidence that doctrinal positions develop over time. Since the Catholic theologian also wants to "remain in union with the

16. In his first year as pope, Paul VI chose Häring to give the annual retreat to him and the Roman Curia. Later, when Father Häring told Catholics to follow their consciences regarding *Humanae Vitae*, he was investigated by church officials; http://www.alfonsiana.edu/In%20Memoriam/EN%20-%20IM%20Haring2.htm.

17. Gregory Baum, OSA, "The Magisterium in a Changing Church," in *Man as Man and Believer, Concilium: Theology in the Age of Renewal*, vol. 21, ed. Edward Schillebeeckx, OP, and Boniface Willems, OP (New York: Paulist Press, 1967), 67–83.

18. "Comment on This Issue," *Christian Century*, April 6, 1966, 418.

19. For additional information on Baum, see his memoir, *The Oil Has Not Run Dry: The Story of My Theological Pathway* (Montreal: McGill-Queen's University Press, 2016).

Catholic Church," Roesch carefully points out that the theologian is tentatively expressing his opinions, contributing to dialogue, and refusing to "engage himself wholeheartedly in his own convictions" unless "accompanied by... the Church" (5).

To show that scholars may "respectfully suggest a different formulation of doctrine or practice," Roesch quotes from Paul VI's 1965 encyclical *Mysterium Fidei* ¶25:

> They (doctrinal formulae) can, it is true, be made clearer and more obvious; and doing this is of great benefit. But it must always be done in such a way that they retain the meaning in which they have been used, so that with the advance of an understanding of the faith, the truth of faith will remain unchanged.[20]

As Roesch continued his remarks to the faculty, he said that Häring "emphasized that doctrine must be constantly studied, otherwise the Church will be outmoded." But Häring also cautioned Roesch that "an individual must be an expert in the history of dogma in order to be able to interpret any of the past pronouncements of the Magisterium, because these pronouncements apply to certain problems at a certain time under certain historical-social-cultural conditions." Changes in conditions may result in questions about "whether or not the pronouncement applies with equal force in the new situation" (5–6). Häring continued that not everything can be changed. Church doctrine that is "solemnly defined can never change," as "declared explicitly in the First Vatican Council's Dogmatic Constitution on the Catholic Faith, ¶4: "The meaning that Holy Mother Church has once declared, is to be retained forever, and no pretext of deeper understanding ever justifies any deviation from that meaning" (6).

While the meaning of a doctrine may never change, "the repetition of an ancient creedal formula may not... communicate the same truth" in a new historical situation. Häring emphasized to Roesch that "the teaching of the Gospel must apply to man's problems as he experiences them today." The truth of Christ's message is universal. It "applies to man's life

---

20. *Mysterium Fidei*, September 3, 1965, http://w2.vatican.va/content/paul-vi/en/encyclicals/documents/hf_p-vi_enc_03091965_mysterium.html.

in any age, but not necessarily in the same formulation." This raises the question of who "acknowledge[s] the discovery of new knowledge and incorporate[s] it into [church] teaching" once that new knowledge is "proven to be true" (6). Roesch said that this is the task of the church's magisterium, a point with which Bonnette and his supporters agree. However, Roesch continues in words that echo those of the accused: "If the Magisterium is not responsive to human problems, it loses its role as a guide" (7).

To emphasize and support the view that new knowledge must be blended with "Christian morality and the teaching of Christian doctrine" in order to be "relevant to man's actual conditions of life," Roesch cites *Gaudium et Spes (GS)* ¶62[21] before continuing that "it cannot be taken for granted that the continuity of the infallible and general Magisterium necessarily implies the immutability of doctrinal formulae" (7).

Häring called to Roesch's attention ¶43 of *Gaudium et Spes*, where laymen have a role in suggesting solutions. *GS* recognizes that some of the faithful will disagree with others "rather frequently and legitimately so" and that proposed solutions may be "easily confused by many people with the Gospel message." Bonnette worried that students could not tell the difference between the teachings of some faculty and those of the gospel message. *GS* reminds "people to remember that no one is allowed… to appropriate the Church's authority for his opinion." Rather, they should "always try to enlighten one another through honest discussion, preserving mutual charity and caring for the common good" (7).

❦

In summary, Baltazar, Chrisman, Ulrich, and Lumpp, supported by Roesch, believed they had the right to "express their difficulties with the official non-infallible positions of the magisterium."[22] They felt that this is

21. *Gaudium et Spes* ¶62: "Let them blend new sciences and theories and the understanding of the most recent discoveries with Christian morality and the teaching of Christian doctrine, so that their religious culture and morality may keep pace with scientific knowledge and with the constantly progressing technology. Thus the knowledge of God is better manifested and the preaching of the Gospel becomes clearer to human intelligence and shows itself to be relevant to man's actual conditions of life"; translation used by Roesch, "Statement Relative to the Controversy," 3–4.

22. Gregory Baum, in *Search* (reprinted in *Commonweal*, November 25, 1966), typed and attached to John Chrisman to Raymond A. Roesch, n.d.

what they were "supposed to be doing," since "the role of Catholic philosophers and theologians" is to "develop and explore the depth of the truths of Christianity."[23] "How can the pope decide on a given question without the previous research of philosophers, theologians, etc., seeing the pros and cons of a question, testing ideas by talking about them, writing about them?"[24]

Dennis Bonnette and those who supported him could support much of what Father Roesch said. The problem for them was that the accused faculty, in their view, did not differentiate between their opinions and the teachings of the church.

In chapter 6, Roesch will explain to the faculty the basis for the apparent contradiction between the findings of the university and the archbishop's commission.

23. Eulalio R. Baltazar to Raymond A. Roesch, n.d., 11.
24. Baltazar to Roesch, n.d., 10.

THE BASIS OF THE UNIVERSITY'S REACTION TO THE ARCHBISHOP'S REPORT

Catholic theologians standing fast by the teaching of the Church and investigating the divine mysteries… must proceed with love for the truth, with charity, and with humility.

— Second Vatican Council, Decree on Ecumenism, ¶11

Having laid out the causes of the controversy, Father Roesch proceeded to explain the apparent contradiction that those "who made the charges amply demonstrated" that "some statements made by the four accused professors differed with certain specific pronouncements of the Church's Magisterium," and Roesch's conclusion that the four were innocent of those same charges. Three items shaped Roesch's view: a new attitude toward the truth; the canonist's report; and the perceived intervention of the archbishop. Roesch explained each of these to the faculty, and, at the end of each explanation, he stated the university's position reached as a result of studying that particular item.[1]

---

1. Raymond A. Roesch, carbon copy of a typed manuscript of the lecture, n.d., 14, AUD, Roesch papers, series 91–35, box 6. Future quotes from this manuscript appear parenthetically in this chapter.

Roesch could not ignore a new attitude in the church that was replacing "certitude and the Magisterium." Certitude is the neo-Scholastic understanding of certainty with which any particular truth can be known. Traditionally, "when it is a question whether any particular truth is contained within the deposit of revelation, the certainty of faith can be obtained only from the authority of the 'teaching Church.'"[2] What is different in the sixties is that a "new attitude toward ... the 'absoluteness' of sacred truth" has developed that is "characterized by an awareness of [a] certain relativity of all human knowledge." It does not matter whether the knowledge is of "human or divine origin." Since we are conscious of the "limitations of human knowledge," there is a "positive openness to truth based upon the appreciation that no man and no institution has [sic] a monopoly on any kind of truth." Truth is limited by the quality of the possessor; in the limitations of the transmitter; and in its applicability to the human situation (14a).

For Roesch, this new attitude is the result of a "new epistemology which is a healthy development over the smugness of scientism and over the triumphalism of metaphysicism" (14a). He credits Fathers Eugene Maly and Bernard Häring with "confirming and explaining [these principles] in detail" during his meeting with them on February 25, 1967, and declares that "we at the University of Dayton" find "logic in [these] principles which are widely held by many of the Church's leading theologians" (15).

Roesch continues explaining this attitude by directly quoting Father Gregory Baum, although in the lecture Roesch does not credit Baum.[3] Historical studies of doctrinal definitions are only beginning, and "we have no hermeneutical principles for the interpretation of the ecclesiastical Magisterium." Since we do not know what "the application of form criticism will do to the doctrinal statements of the past, we are sometimes unable to answer in a definitive manner the question, 'What is the Church teaching on this or that subject?' even when such a subject has

2. *1917 Catholic Encyclopedia*, s.v. "Certitude," 1917, accessed on February 15, 2007, http://www.newadvent.org/cathen/03539b.htm.
3. Baum, "Magisterium in a Changing Church," 67–83. Roesch gives Baum credit in his written statement.

been treated in ecclesiastical documents." Furthermore, the Second Vatican Council's understanding of divine revelation has made "the Catholic theologian more conscious of the transcendence of God's Word over any and every expression of it in the Church" (15).

Roesch begins discussing this new attitude toward truth with the words "we submit that," making it sound like he agrees with this position. However, at the end of this section, he says the university does not advocate any specific position, but "considers it its duty to guarantee true freedom of position for any scholar on its campus" (15). The faculty who hold positions such as those described by Baum, Maly, Häring, and others are free to pursue them.

THE CANONIST'S REPORT

"Weighing importantly" in the university's investigation was the report of the canonist. Roesch described the canonist as a "recognized authority in canon law, a member of a major religious order, a priest of the Archdiocese of Chicago, and a person familiar with academic and university problems, having rendered decisions in like cases previously" (16). The canonist was later identified as Jesuit priest James I. O'Connor from the Bellarmine School of Theology of Loyola University in North Aurora, Illinois.

O'Connor was recommended to Roesch by Jesuit priest Victor Nieporte, a Cincinnati native and executive vice president of Xavier University.[4] Father O'Connor held degrees from Xavier University, West Baden College,[5] the Catholic University of America, and the Pontifical Gregorian University in Rome. With T. Lincoln Bouscaren, SJ, O'Connor was editor of several volumes of *Canon Law Digest* and *Canon Law Digest for Religious*. O'Connor was also the sole author of *Canon Law Digest*, volume VII.[6]

4. Roesch, personal notes on visit with Archbishop Karl J. Alter on October 29, 1966, series 91–35, box 5, AUD.

5. The West Baden Springs Hotel near French Lick, Indiana, was sold to the Jesuits for one dollar in 1934. The Jesuits converted the hotel into a seminary, West Baden College, which operated from 1934 to June 1964; "West Baden Springs Hotel," accessed August 6, 2014, http://www.indianahistory.org/our-collections/collection-guides/west-baden-springs-hotel-cirkut-photographs.pdf/.

6. O'Connor's degrees are Xavier University, Litt.B., 1934, M.A., 1935; West Baden College,

Roesch provided O'Connor with Bonnette's two accusation letters and asked the canonist to deal with the ecclesiastical issues in Bonnette's letters. Bonnette twice cited Canon 1325, §2,[7] against John Chrisman. Since Canon 1325, §2, under the 1917 Code of Canon Law, defines a heretic—"one who having been baptized and retaining the name of Christian, pertinaciously denies or doubts any of the truths that one is under obligation of divine and Catholic faith to believe"[8]—Father O'Connor felt it was "necessary at the outset to determine whether or not the conditions for a charge of heresy were present" (16).

For Chrisman to be judged a heretic, Bonnette must prove that Chrisman "act[ed] with conscious and intentional resistance to the authority of God and the Church or, in fuller form, he ... den[ied] or call[ed] in doubt some article of faith which he knows has been proposed by the Church as a truth to be believe[d] as divinely revealed."[9] O'Connor found no basis for such a judgment. Roesch explained that the "accuser has since protested the characterization of his charges as formal accusations of heresy" (16).

On the charge that one of the professors "eloquently defended situation ethics in precisely that form which has been condemned by the Holy Father," the canonist focused on the words "condemned," "Holy Father," and "precisely" (17). O'Connor pointed out that situation ethics was "interdicted" by the Holy Office, not the Holy Father.[10] To prove that one of the accused defended situation ethics in a certain form would mean

---

Ph.L.,1938, S.T.L.,1944; Catholic University of America, J.C.B., 1946; Pontifical Gregorian University, Rome, J.C.L., 1948, J.C.D., 1950. O'Connor, with T. Lincoln Bouscaren, SJ, was editor of *Canon Law Digest*, vols. 4, 5, and 6, from 1958–69 and of *Canon Law Digest for Religious*, vol. 1 and supplements, 1964²–67; printed entry from *Contemporary Authors Database*, accessed on August 25, 2003.

7. Canon 1325, §2: Post receptum baptismum si quis, nomen retinens christianum, pertinaciter aliquam ex veritatibus fide divina et catholica credendis denegat aut de ea dubitat, haereticus; si a fide christiana totaliter recedit, apostata; si denique subesse renuit Summo Pontifici aut cum membris Ecclesiae ei subiectis communicare recusat, schismaticus est; 1917 Codex Iuris Canonicis, accessed August 10, 2014, http://www.jgray.org/codes/cic17lat.html.

8. G. A. Buckley, *New Catholic Encyclopedia*, vol. 6 (Palatine, Ill.: Jack Heraty and Associates, 1981), s.v. "Sin of Heresy."

9. James I. O'Connor, SJ, to Raymond A. Roesch, November 20, 1966, 2, Roesch papers, series 91–35, box 5, AUD.

10. To "interdict" is to forbid in a formal way.

that the accuser would have to prove what the Holy Office intended in its instruction and that the professor "singly and knowingly acted against the precise form of situation ethics interdicted by the Holy Office" (17a). When worded this way, it was obvious that Bonnette could not prove this charge.

The third matter taken up by the canonist was the charge that Chrisman had denied the existence of purgatory. Roesch told the faculty that in response to this charge, the accused faculty member wrote, "It is now impossible to remember my exact words (the remark...was in my present opinion too concise), but if they conveyed what I meant, I said that 'I'm not sure there is any such place as purgatory.' My objection to purgatory as a place of fire is that of Karl Rahner." The canonist commented "that it seems the accuser was letting himself be swept along by isolated words and phrases without apparently investigating their true meaning and interpretation. As it happens," he wrote, "it is the accuser who is mistaken about the Church's teaching on the fire of purgatory" (17a). O'Connor listed ten sources on purgatory that Bonnette should read.

Roesch continued to quote the canonist: "Since the accuser so strongly opposes the accused because they think that some of the Church's teaching should be formulated in a somewhat different way from its present formulation, how does he reconcile his attitude in this regard with Vatican Council II's statement as explicitly set forth in its Decree on Ecumenism ¶11?" (17). Roesch then read to the faculty the full three paragraphs of ¶11:

> The way and method in which the Catholic faith is expressed should never become an obstacle to dialogue with our brethren. It is, of course, essential that the doctrine should be clearly presented in its entirety. Nothing is so foreign to the spirit of ecumenism as a false irenicism, in which the purity of Catholic doctrine suffers loss and its genuine and certain meaning is clouded.
>
> At the same time, the Catholic faith must be explained more profoundly and precisely, in such a way and in such terms as our separated brethren can also really understand.
>
> Moreover, in ecumenical dialogue, Catholic theologians standing fast by the teaching of the Church and investigating the divine mysteries with

the separated brethren must proceed with love for the truth, with charity, and with humility. When comparing doctrines with one another, they should remember that in Catholic doctrine there exists a "hierarchy" of truths, since they vary in their relation to the fundamental Christian faith. Thus the way will be opened by which through fraternal rivalry all will be stirred to a deeper understanding and a clearer presentation of the unfathomable riches of Christ (17b).

Roesch's final quotes from the canonist's letter indicate that Bonnette and his supporters "seemed inclined to 'sin' on the side of orthodoxy." The canonist wonders how to defend some actions of the Second Vatican Council from the "accuser's apparent position that no aspect of Catholic doctrine or practice can ever be questioned in any way" (18).

PERCEIVED INTERVENTION OF THE ARCHBISHOP

With the doctrinal issues covered, Roesch returns to the intervention of the archbishop. As far as Roesch knows, "the archbishop has not communicated personally with any of the accused professors." Roesch thinks this is "significant" in that the archbishop could have done this "in virtue of his being their shepherd and their admission of obedience to him" (18).[11]

Considerably more important to the faculty was the relationship of the archbishop and the university. Roesch acknowledged that as a Catholic university, the University of Dayton has "accountability to the local Ordinary in matters which pertain to the preservation and teaching of Catholic doctrine, as such and opposed to the science of theology as an autonomous academic discipline." The archbishop has publicly declared his understanding and respect for the "role of the scholar in theological research." But the archbishop also "rightfully demonstrates a pastoral concern for the spiritual welfare of the members of his Archdiocese" (18).

Roesch claimed that the archdiocesan authorities "did not actually interfere in the University's affairs, though such an impression might well

11. The phrase "admission of obedience" is a curious one. It implies that at some time, the four accused admitted that they were obedient to the archbishop. However, three of the four (Chrisman, Lumpp, and Ulrich) do not recall making any such admission, even implicitly.

be inferred from the news release and articles which have appeared, and which were not refuted promptly by the University." Roesch justifies the university's silence by saying, "We were respecting confidences" (19).

The university's contention is that the archbishop's concern was primarily pastoral and that he was urged on by a "few local pastors" who were "disturbed by the effect of some of the teachings promulgated here, which were upsetting the personal lives of members of their parishes." Roesch notes that the university "singled out this same concern in [their] earliest releases concerning the controversy" (19–20).

Referring to the fact-finding commission report, Roesch thinks this pastoral effect is "what is intended by the phrase 'the difficulty extends further in the University community.'" He acknowledges the pastoral role of the Catholic university, but also says, "It is clear that Catholic institutions have been unable to define their pastoral specifications in the past without crippling academic freedom." The implication is that it is a new time for Catholic universities. They "must not relate [their] academic role to [their] pastoral function, that is, must show to all that freedom in the academic realm is in the best service of the community of the faithful" (20).

Roesch feels the university can "relate and harmonize the academic freedom of our faculty and students to the spiritual well-being of the University community." He points out that the Catholic university is not the Catholic Church; and its

> *raison d'etre* is not identical or coterminus with that of the Church. One deals with the sanctification of man through faith in Christ, and the other with the civilization of intelligence through a humanistic and scientific process. These processes can be related, but they must never be confused (20).

Roesch has every confidence that the ad hoc committee will draw up "guidelines" that will "clarify these roles" (20).

The archbishop's report indicated that "since the University's orientation is primarily toward undergraduate education, complex issues which require a multinimity of responses, rather than a unanimity of responses, should be submitted to an inter-subjective dialogue only within the confines of graduate faculty gatherings" (20–21). Some of the faculty wondered if the university was in accord with that statement. Roesch stated that "such a suggestion runs counter to [the university's] policy that any scholar speaking on any topic in the field of his competence is free to voice his opinion." However, Roesch adds that the scholar must voice his opinion "responsibly, which in this case, would certainly mean that he must judge the maturity and educational preparation of his audience and adjust his remarks accordingly" (21).

In this section of Roesch's lecture to the faculty, it is clear that Bonnette made a mistake when he included the word "heresy" in his letter to the archbishop. The canonical interpretation of "heresy" allowed the university to say that the four faculty were cleared of the charge of *heresy*, a charge Bonnette claims he did not intend. Use of the word "heresy" led to this incident being called the "heresy" affair in a university publication with the use of quotes indicating that it was not really about *heresy*.

CHAPTER 7

THE UNIVERSITY'S INVESTIGATION AND ACADEMIC FREEDOM

In order that they may fulfill their function let it be recognized that all the faithful, whether clerics or laity, possess a lawful freedom of inquiry, freedom of thought and of expressing their mind with humility and fortitude in those matters on which they enjoy competence.

—*Gaudium et Spes,* ¶62

Father Roesch needed to defend the archbishop's role of preserving and teaching Catholic doctrine in his archdiocese, but even more to defend the validity of the university's investigation, the results of which were released in Roesch's December 3, 1966, letter to the faculty and staff. As Roesch continued his lecture to the faculty, he described the investigation in three parts, all pertaining to those charged: the evidence against them, the examination of the evidence that included their credentials, and their intentions. His explanation included the crisis in the role of authority that was part of the climate of the sixties. Roesch also examined the behaviors of both sides in the conflict and attempted to reconcile the results of the university's investigation with that of the archbishop's fact-finding commission. He concludes this section of his lecture by addressing future behaviors of the faculty.

❦

In his lecture, Roesch stated that, at the outset, the university knew "it could not judge the dogmatic implications of statements taken out of context and interpreted by members of an audience."[1] Therefore, the four accused were asked to submit copies of their prepared speeches if available and to write a "thorough explanation of their position in light of the charges made." The collected documentation totaled forty-five pages. Roesch did not mention who reviewed the documents, but he indicated his satisfaction "with the evidence supporting the competence of these faculty members" (22).

As to the credentials of those charged, the university knew their academic qualifications when it hired the faculty because the university received "favorable credentials [*sic*] from those who knew them" (22–23). Each time the university renewed their teaching contracts, it evaluated them "in the light of the evidence reported by their colleagues, their chairmen, and their students." Furthermore, those who examined the forty-five pages of evidence prepared by the accused "were of the opinion that there were no doctrines expressed contrary to the universal Magisterium." The key phrase in the latter sentence is the word "doctrines," since Roesch previously recognized that some statements of the accused "differed with certain specific and recognized pronouncements of the Church's magisterium" (23).

In its inquiry, the university also looked at the "intentions" of the accused. Roesch expressed satisfaction that the accused are "practicing Catholics, who love the Church, who want to advance the Gospel, and who seek the truth honestly, fearlessly, and openly." These faculty are "trying to face the problems of the day." In proposing "new solutions," they realize that "many of their hypotheses could be questioned, but as scholars, they want to express these hypotheses" that they "try to support... with solid reasons." They "claim that truth might be found anywhere, even in areas previously considered 'off-limits'" (23). Roesch believed they were

1. Raymond A. Roesch, carbon copy of a typed manuscript of the lecture, n.d., 21, AUD, Roesch papers, series 91–35, box 6. Future quotes from this manuscript appear parenthetically in this chapter.

seeking answers in accord with the Gospel, that they wanted to add their efforts to that of the Church of which they are a part, and they were seeking that deeper and fuller meaning of the truth and revelation which demonstrates that the message of Christ is relevant to the lives of His followers in every age (24).

For these reasons, the university "declared them innocent of the charges as made in the two letters of accusation" (24).

Roesch noted that the sixties were a time of crisis in the role of authority and, on behalf of the university, "accepted a part in the debate discussing the role of authority." After acknowledging that "legitimate authority does and must exist," Roesch said its role is not to "silence those who are thinking, and reasoning, and studying" (24). He followed that with a quote from an unnamed source, who said that "silencing and suspension are not instruments of debate." Roesch indicated that the university agreed with the French hierarchy when the bishops said that

condemnations will not make intellectual problems go away; that the job of teaching authority is not primarily to denounce errors, but to teach the truth; and that some traditional formulations of doctrine are insufficient, demand further research, and must be studied in relation to the true problems of the time (24–25).

By this time, it had to be clear to the audience that Father Roesch was upholding the views of those charged. He publicly supported the "right that the dissenting faculty members had, to voice their fears." He also said that he respected their "conscientious disagreement" with the university's conclusions as a result of its investigation. From there, it was all downhill from the perspective of Bonnette and his supporters. Roesch objected "most strenuously" to the methods that the "dissenting faculty members" used. He would rather have seen them come forward in the "academic arena with scholarly presentations in those same areas of modern day problems, and suggest solutions which may have been superior to those presented by the four professors, whose honesty, integrity and competency, they questioned" (25).

As if his criticism were not enough, he added that Father Bernard Häring was also "appalled" at their methods. Father Häring said that the "first step in any accusation is to establish the competency of those who are accusing." In other words, the accusers should have "established that they are knowledgeable in the history of dogma; that they know how to interpret precisely the Magisterium which they contend is being flaunted, and that they must substantiate their charges" (26).

So far, Roesch has supported the accused and objected to the methodology of the accusers while questioning the latter's competency to interpret the statements of the accused. Since the position of the accusers has already been supported publicly by the archbishop's fact-finding commission, Roesch needed to clarify where the university stood in relation to the theological and philosophical positions of the accused. He tells the gathered faculty that his defense of the accused "must in no wise be construed as either an endorsement or a condemnation of the academic positions set forth by these men" (26). Qualified theologians and philosophers should analyze their positions. Roesch says that

> their declarations were not being taught subversively as though representing those of the Church; they gave no evidence that they were denying the authority of the Church to teach infallibly; [and] they did not intentionally ridicule the traditional and widely accepted Magisterium of the Church (26–27).

Rather, they were trying to point out that many traditional positions are inadequate for the problems of the present day. Roesch agreed with the accused that "stating and arguing for a position contrary to the ordinary Magisterium is not advocating a commitment to it against one's religious convictions. Faith may rightly supersede reason" (27).

Although Roesch supported the four charged, he also stated that it is

> our considered and expressed judgment that much of our present difficulty stems as much from the *way* and *manner* in which certain statements were made, as with their questioned content. We have privately called the attention of some of these men to the inappropriateness of the way in which they spoke, especially insofar as it seemingly showed a flippant attitude and irreverent handling of the Magisterium; insofar as it was uttered in a way which shocked the audience, which was in no way prepared for the effect which they produced; and insofar as they may have neglected to announce

the distinction between a generally accepted ecclesiastical position and their own proposed solution (27).

Roesch "believe[s] that to varying degrees these four professors were pedagogically at fault." Referring back to his December 3, 1966, letter at the end of the university's investigation, Roesch says that "we are well aware of the confusion that may have arisen in the minds of some of the hearers" (28). In the same letter, he quoted Archbishop Alter, who called the university's attention to the

> care that must be taken to avoid disturbance of mind and a species of scandal, or at least wonderment, on the part of the ordinary student or hearer, because of the way and/or the occasion in which one or other Catholic tenet, dogma, or practice may be subjected to academic examination and discussion (28).

It must have been a bit confusing to the faculty as they listened to Roesch support those charged while trying to also support the archbishop. The faculty knew the archbishop's commission wanted the University of Dayton to set guidelines to ensure its faculty acknowledged and preserved the magisterium of the church, had due reverence for it, and accepted its true function (29). That being the case, "to what extent [were] the four accused professors... going to have to alter their teachings?" Roesch responded that they are "free to teach as they see fit" as long as they "confine their utterances" to their area of competence; as long as they "acknowledge, respect and pay due reverence" to the magisterium; and "as long as their competence is continually attested to by their colleagues, chairmen, students and dean" (29).

Roesch "hopes and trusts" that every member of the University of Dayton staff, including the accused and accusers, better understands how "academic controversies can best be resolved, and that they want to continue their professional careers on the University of Dayton campus" (29–30).

The primary way Father Roesch expected to resolve future academic controversies was through the recommendations of the ad hoc committee. He expected the committee's report to be submitted directly to him and that it would be published as an official university document. He told the faculty that "the heart of the task put before the Ad Hoc Committee is to demonstrate that paragraph 25 of the Constitution on the Church, as well as all the other recommendations of Vatican II, are fully applicable on a Catholic campus" (30).

Roesch knew that the wording in the university's faculty contract could be problematic in this regard, so part of the committee's task was to draw up a "satisfactory and logical explanation" of the wording pertaining to the university's "function with relation to the deposit of faith and Christian morality." The president expected that once the committee's "guidelines" were accepted formally by the faculty and administrators, they would become university policy. After that, any action "deliberately contrary" to the guidelines would be a contract violation. For this reason, Roesch wanted the faculty to formulate the guidelines. On the other hand, he also wanted "some solidly Catholic authorities" to be among the experts invited to assist in the committee's process (31).

The faculty had also been thinking about how to handle future academic controversies. One of the ten questions posed to Roesch indicated their approach: "Since the problems of academic freedom are continuous, might it not be possible for the ongoing committee of a faculty senate to adjudicate them?" This was a loaded question in that no faculty senate existed at the University of Dayton. In fact, the Marianist administration and board of trustees repeatedly refused permission to form a senate and empower it to act on behalf of the faculty. In his response to this question, Roesch again rejected the idea of a faculty senate but said that he expected the ad hoc committee to recommend an academic freedom committee as part of the university's faculty forum, which consisted of faculty and administrators. He added that if such a recommendation was not made, he would suggest one himself because he was "strongly of the opinion that the reaction of one's peers is the surest safeguard against any abuse of academic freedom. A man who is too proud to submit his conclusions to the scrutiny of his colleagues is not a true scholar" (32).

To show that these guidelines were expected to be in line with church teachings, Roesch added that the guidelines must make possible the "full implementation" of the recommendation of ¶62 in Vatican II's document *Gaudium et Spes*:

> In order that they may fulfill their function let it be recognized that all the faithful, whether clerics or laity, possess a lawful freedom of inquiry, freedom of thought and of expressing their mind with humility and fortitude in those matters on which they enjoy competence (32).

Another concern of the faculty was finding itself "informed initially thru public news media" even on "matters highly relevant to the University's teaching community." They asked Father Roesch, "What provisions are being made to directly impart communications to the faculty?" In response, Roesch indicated that in the case of this controversy, each release was distributed on campus before it went to the media, although the "lead time was not always very great." He shifted some of the burden back on the faculty when he said that one of his reasons for a short lead time was that "violations of confidential material to the news agencies is [*sic*] not unknown on this campus." Roesch indicated that "deadlines are important and ... if we would release our communication too far in advance it seems inevitable that someone will violate the deadline" (32–33).

Unwilling to take sole responsibility for communicating to the faculty through the media, Roesch asked that faculty "accord us the same courtesy of prior information" when they "have something of importance to bring to the attention of their colleagues and the administration." Some of the "deleterious effects" of releases with incomplete information could have been avoided if "some faculty members and students" consulted with those "holding responsible positions in the University" (33).

Roesch pointed out that faculty have "correlative responsibilities" in regard to academic freedom. They have an obligation to distinguish between their "personal convictions and generally accepted and proven conclusions" and to present relevant data fairly to their students in order to "discourage sensationalism" (33).

He went on to say that it was his conviction that "intellectual freedom does not rule out commitment, but that it makes it possible and personal."

Freedom does not require neutrality, neither on the part of the institution, nor that of the individual. It does not even require neutrality toward the task of inquiry and learning, nor toward a value system. And yet, I would recall to your attention that it is possible to distinguish between the pursuit of a point of view and a formal commitment to it (33–34).

Surely, Bonnette and his defenders did not feel supported in this section of Roesch's lecture. In spite of the fact that they wrote scholarly papers early in the controversy and tried to work with various members of the administration for a way to resolve the controversy, Roesch rejected their methodology.

As was the case from the beginning of the controversy, it is clear from this portion of Roesch's lecture that the university administration supports those accused. One wonders if Baltazar, Chrisman, Ulrich, and Lumpp heard Roesch say that the university is in this difficulty because of their actions; that the accused did not make clear their own speculation versus the church's teachings. Regarding the magisterium, on the one hand, the accused "did not intentionally ridicule" it; on the other, they "seemingly showed a flippant attitude and an irreverent handling of the Magisterium." Perhaps the key word for Roesch is "intentionally." Maybe he could not believe the accused would intentionally ridicule the magisterium.

Roesch ended his lecture by describing the future climate at the University of Dayton. He reiterated a sentiment voiced by Father James Darby, the chairman of the university's board of trustees, in one of his interviews where Darby "declared that those who are not tough enough intellectually and spiritually to study under a true concept of academic freedom, be they faculty or students, will unfortunately be disturbed... at the University of Dayton." Why? Because "intense academic debate is not for the ill-informed or timorous." If only one academic position is acknowledged by the faculty, "indoctrination would surely follow and, without a challenge, [the university's] scholars could soon become demagogues" (34–35).

Roesch stated that both sides are welcome at the University of Dayton. The "conservative and traditionalist" has a place. He should teach his position with all the conviction he can muster. Some will welcome his position and "find in it comfort and security." But he must also "accept the challenge to engage in academic debate,... to both argue and listen." The liberal is also welcome. "He, too, must be ready to discuss, and prove, and revise, and meet every challenge hurled at him" (35).

Roesch called on the faculty to "relegate our concern for personal rights to a secondary position and by abandoning a defensive posture, strike out through positive action to build a healthy academic atmosphere and to measure up to our responsibilities as a faculty on a university campus" (35–36).

He concluded by acknowledging that the university community learned much during the controversy. Roesch reminded the faculty that in his December 3, 1966, letter, he predicted that the results of this experience would have long-reaching effects on the University of Dayton. He hoped that "we would be proud of how we brought [the resolution] about." Roesch emphasized that a campus should be a lively place and to "have a campus that cares about theology and philosophy is an honor and a distinction" (36).

Roesch thanked the "faculty who do not profess the Catholic faith" for their "respect of the sincerity that has been evidenced." He trusts that "they are aware that there will be no interference with their academic freedom" (36). Quoting Darby, Roesch said:

> The University of Dayton, while experiencing the tensions of the modern day, in no wise shrinks from her responsibility to her student body and the University community as a whole to reflect openly and objectively the living thought of our times. In such a commitment, we accept unquestionably the risk demanded by a sincere pursuit of the truth (36–37).

Roesch concluded by wishing that each faculty member "use this presentation for study, for encouragement and... for inspiration" (37).

❦

The faculty reacted to Roesch's remarks with a thunderous standing ovation. They believed Roesch was distancing the university from ecclesiastical control and moving toward academic legitimacy within the wider academic community. Many faculty wrote to Father Roesch after his address. James McGraw, the director of the university's Technical Institute, described the standing ovation as a "heartfelt expression of confidence, pride and approval."[2] Professor of theological studies and Marianist father William Cole said that he was "proud to have [Roesch] as President at this time."[3] John Steinbruegger, director of the university's Special Sessions office, wrote that the lecture was "absolutely unprecedented evidence of our having achieved a level of maturity and stature that many never believed possible for the University of Dayton." It made him "extremely proud" to be a part of the university.[4]

Others, such as associate professor of biology Joseph J. Cooney, wanted to give Roesch's statement "the widest possible circulation to dispel the extremely poor national image which has resulted from this affair.... our image is poor in the world of academe."[5] Indeed, Rocco Donatelli, the chair of the faculty forum, indicated to Roesch that the forum "voted to use funds to publish in suitable national media—all or part of the President's statement."[6]

Some of the faculty members directly involved in the controversy reached out to Roesch. Eulalio Baltazar wrote, "[You] came through with flying colors. I am confident that from henceforth, the University will continue to grow vigorously."[7] Gonzalo Cartagenova contributed thoughtful suggestions for Roesch's published statement. He believed Roesch based "his entire pronouncement on a theory [form criticism applied to the magisterium] that is not truly representative of the general theological thought." He thought the same conclusion could be reached by "a positive understanding of freedom and its applications to academic freedom."

2. James McGraw to Raymond A. Roesch, February (*sic*) 1, 1967, Roesch papers, series 91–35, box 6, AUD.

3. William J. Cole to Raymond A. Roesch, March 3, 1967, Roesch papers, series 91–35, box 6, AUD.

4. John Steinbruegger to Raymond A. Roesch, March 1, 1967, Roesch papers, series 91–35, box 6, AUD.

5. Joseph J. Cooney to Raymond A. Roesch, March 8, 1967, Roesch papers, series 91–35, box 6, AUD.

6. Rocco Donatelli, letter from the faculty forum to Raymond A. Roesch, March 20, 1967, Roesch papers, series 91–35, box 6, AUD.

7. Eulalio R. Baltazar to Raymond A. Roesch, March 2, 1967, Roesch papers, series 91–35, box 6, AUD.

True freedom implies an intelligent goal accepted willingly by the individual as good for him. True academic freedom demands consequently an intelligent goal accepted by both faculty and students willingly as good for them. Of the essence of this freedom is a sense of responsibility that restrains the individual from doing that which will jeopardize the attainment of his goal.[8]

Cartagenova also suggested that Roesch not use Gregory Baum as an authority. Instead, he recommended quoting Jesuit priests from Woodstock, John L. McKenzie and Joseph A. Fitzmyer. Cartagenova was not the only one who questioned the wisdom of using Baum in the lecture. Marianist father Edwin M. Leimkuhler said "the conservatives gloated over Baum"[9] being included, while Marianist William Cole felt, even before Roesch's talk, that Baum could be misleading. He wondered whether Maly and Häring specifically approved of that section of Roesch's lecture.[10]

After Roesch rewrote his statement for publication, he sent a copy to Dennis Bonnette and Joseph Dieska. He asked them to meet with him and the provost. Roesch hoped they "were now in a position to join forces, move forward, and solve this problem which is common to all Catholic universities."[11] Bonnette responded the next day, declining to meet with Roesch. Bonnette found Roesch's statement to be "theologically unsound" and "personally offensive to those of us who followed our conscience." Bonnette thought it ironic that Roesch would seek his counsel when the salary in his new faculty contract was frozen, a "punitive" action for the second consecutive year. To Bonnette, this action "looks like a deliberate humiliation to a professor who defended the faith." He concluded:

8. Gonzalo Cartagenova to Raymond A. Roesch, March 3, 1967, Roesch papers, series 91–35, box 6, AUD.

9. Edwin M. Leimkuhler to Raymond A. Roesch, March 15, 1967, Roesch papers, series 91–35, box 6, AUD.

10. William J. Cole to Raymond A. Roesch, March 3, 1967, Roesch papers, series 91–35, box 6, AUD.

11. Raymond A. Roesch to Dennis Bonnette, April 7, 1967, Roesch papers, series 91–35, box 6, AUD.

Too many human souls may be at issue in this current "academic" controversy for me to allow my decision or analyses to be made on primarily personal grounds. In the long run, it shall not be you, or I, or the University of Dayton itself, which shall decide the principles in contention here, but rather such properly theological questions shall be decided by Rome and no one else.[12]

Bonnette knew he had written to the Vatican and, apparently, expected them to intervene at some time in the future.

12. Dennis Bonnette to Raymond A. Roesch, April 8, 1967, Roesch papers, series 91–35, box 6, AUD.

CHAPTER 8

RESOLUTION OF THE CONTROVERSY

The Ad Hoc Committee for the Study of Academic
Freedom at the University of Dayton

*The University of Dayton ... is a church-related institution of higher learning ... that] seeks, in
an environment of academic freedom, to foster principles and values consonant with Catholicism and with the living traditions of the Society of Mary.*

—University of Dayton Statement of Purposes, May 14, 1969

When Father Roesch declared Eulalio Baltazar, John Chrisman, Lawrence Ulrich, and Randolph Lumpp innocent in early December 1966, he
believed they were pedagogically imprudent rather than guilty of openly
advocating teachings contrary to the magisterium. Roesch thought that
much of the controversy was "due to an improper understanding of the
proper role of a Catholic university and Catholic scholars."[1] In an effort to
clarify these roles, Roesch established an ad hoc committee to

> proceed immediately to conduct an open discussion directed toward estab-
> lishing clear directives for the pursuit of truth in academic debate on the
> University of Dayton campus. [The committee] will be free to consult with
> and to invite recognized authorities to help identify the issues, especially

1. Raymond A. Roesch to members of the UD faculty and staff, December 3, 1966, 2.

the question of how a scholar can resolve the tensions that sometimes exist between the two magisteria [divine and human].[2]

Roesch believed this question was one facing every Catholic institution of higher learning. He hoped that "charity, prudence and wisdom characterize our search for the correct understanding of [the university's] role in the world of education."[3]

Roesch intended the committee members to be full-time faculty members nominated by the faculty forum and the five professors involved in the controversy: Dennis Bonnette and the four charged.[4] To represent the faculty-at-large, the faculty forum nominated Richard R. Baker, professor and chairman of the Department of Philosophy; Ellis A. Joseph, chairman of the faculty forum and associate professor and chairman of the Department of Teacher Education; and Joseph J. Kepes, associate professor and chairman of the Department of Physics.[5] Dennis Bonnette refused to cooperate because he could "find no Catholic who follows the magisterium of the Church *and* who is willing to sit on [the] *ad hoc* committee for the purpose of 'liberalizing' [the university's] notion of academic freedom."[6] Dieska also refused to participate when asked by Fathers Roesch and Lees.[7]

2. Roesch to UD faculty and staff, December 3, 1966.

3. Roesch to UD faculty and staff, December 3, 1966, 2–3.

4. Roesch to UD faculty and staff, December 3, 1966, 2.

5. Aggie Taormina, "Faculty Forum Censures Eight Philosophy Professors," *Flyer News*, December 16, 1966, 1. Although the *Flyer News* reported who the faculty forum nominated, there is no record in the minutes of the vote to indicate this action. There is a record that the faculty forum approved the following criteria for membership on the committee: (1) members must be "interested," (2) "no administrators above the position of chairman," (3) members must be "teaching faculty with six or more equivalent hours," and (4) members must be "holders of the doctorate"; faculty forum, minutes of first special, executive meeting 1966–67, December 9, 1966, 2. Although these criteria were moved, seconded, and voted on, the minutes for the February 3, 1967, meeting say that the criteria for serving were not set by the forum. The information that the criteria were not set by the forum was in response to a letter from Dean Leonard Mann, who thought that eliminating anyone above the position of chairperson discriminated against administrators and denied their essential rights as faculty members. The minutes do not say who set the criteria. Dean Mann's letter was sent to the "chairman of the Forum Committee on Revision of the Forum Constitution and Faculty Participation in University Government"; faculty forum, minutes of the fifth regular meeting, February 3, 1967, 1.

6. Raymond A. Roesch, "Chronology," personal notes, Roesch papers, series 91–35, box 5, AUD.

7. Joseph Dieska to Leonard A. Mann, May 30, 1968, 5. Dieska's letter to Mann states

William Doane Kelly, instructor in the Department of Theological Studies and in his first year at the University of Dayton, recalls being nominated by Baltazar, Chrisman, Ulrich, and Lumpp.[8] Kelly held a bachelor of arts degree from St. Peter's College, a master of arts from St. John's University in New York City, and a Ph.D. (1964) from the University of Ottawa in Canada.[9] Prior to his appointment at the University of Dayton, Kelly was an assistant professor of theology at St. Edmund's Seminary in Burlington, Vermont. Father Matthew F. Kohmescher, associate professor and chair of the Department of Theological Studies, also represented the accused.[10]

The AAUP nominated Joakim Isaacs,[11] instructor in the Department of History, along with other faculty members. Isaacs was an instructor in history with an A.B. degree from Fairleigh Dickinson University (1958) and an M.S. from the University of Wisconsin (1962). He came to the University of Dayton in 1964. Father George Barrett, vice president of the university, made the choice to seat Isaacs on the committee.[12] A one-time office mate of Dennis Bonnette, Isaacs believed he was able to represent Bonnette's side on the committee even though he was an orthodox Jew. Isaacs was "sympathetic" or at least "not antagonistic" to Bonnette's view.[13]

---

that he refused to participate because he worried "to what extent will it be possible to conduct Catholic colleges toward their goals and objectives if [non-Catholics] will be pulled into the administration and policy-making organs of the university and college." The ad hoc committee members listed in the *Flyer News* article were all Catholic. [At the time, Isaacs was not listed as a member.] Perhaps Dieska was involved in conversations about putting non-Catholics on the committee and refused to participate when it became apparent that a non-Catholic was going to be added.

8. William D. Kelly, email to the author, February 25, 2002; also in Taormina, "Faculty Forum Censures Eight Philosophy Professors," 1.

9. The topic of Kelly's doctoral dissertation was "A Determination of the Value of the Concepts of the Covenant and the People of God Derived from Representative Contemporary Jewish, Protestant and Catholic Theologians as a Basis of Ecumenical Dialogue and Agreement." Later in his career, Kelly became a Westar Institute fellow involved in the Jesus Seminar.

10. Taormina, "Faculty Forum Censures Eight Philosophy Professors," 1.

11. Isaacs spent most of his career teaching at Marymount College in Tarrytown, New York. He currently lives in Israel.

12. Raymond A. Roesch to Alfred Bannan, January 10, 1967. In 1966–67, Bannan was an assistant professor in the History Department at the University of Dayton and the first president of Dayton's AAUP chapter.

13. Joakim A. Isaacs, telephone interview with the author, April 2, 2002.

The committee was rounded out with the inclusion of Marianist father William J. Cole, associate professor in the Department of Theological Studies. His degrees include a B.S. from the University of Dayton (1947) and S.T.B. (1952), S.T.L. (1954), and S.T.D. (1955) degrees from the University of Fribourg. His sympathies lay on the conservative side.

In individual appointment letters, Roesch told committee members that they were to clarify "the role of a Catholic university and the meaning of responsible academic freedom for a scholar on a Catholic campus." Roesch said the committee must be mindful of the admonition of the archbishop that "care must be taken to avoid disturbance of mind and a species of scandal, or at least, wonderment on the part of the ordinary hearer, because of the way and/or the occasion in which one or other Catholic tenet, dogma, or practice may be subjected to academic examination and discussion." Roesch asked that all interested faculty be included in the committee's work because "the outcome...will to a great extent define academic freedom on this campus."[14]

On January 13, 1967, Roesch announced the membership of the committee and named Ellis Joseph as chair. The committee immediately got to work using a number of approaches. First, they researched the topic of academic freedom, including asking every chair at the university to discuss the topic of "academic freedom and the University of Dayton" within one's department and to submit a report to the committee. Second, students and faculty were given the opportunity to appear before the committee in small sessions. A number of them did so, including Lawrence Ulrich, one of the faculty members involved in the controversy.[15] Finally, the committee arranged for speakers from within and outside the campus, using whenever possible speakers who were already coming to campus during the 1967 spring semester. What follows is a review of the speakers in the order they spoke on campus: Dr. Rosemary Lauer, Dr. William Doane Kelly, Jesuit father Neil G. McCluskey, Dr. Leslie Dewart, and Jesuit father John L. McKenzie.

14. Raymond A. Roesch to individual committee members, January 3, 1967, various ad hoc committees, 1966–69, v. 2, box 30, folder 2, AUD.

15. Minutes for the ad hoc committee for the study of academic freedom at the University of Dayton, March 6, 1967, 1, various ad hoc committees, 1966–69, v. 2, box 30, folder 2, AUD.

The ad hoc committee kicked off its campus discussions on January 25, 1967, with a three-member panel discussing "Why a Catholic University?" Panelists were Dennis Bonnette, Ellis Joseph, and Rosemary Lauer,[16] who had been previously scheduled to speak on campus. A 1950 University of Dayton philosophy undergraduate with a master's and doctoral degrees from St. Louis University, Lauer was one of the thirty-one professors fired by St. John's University, New York City, in early 1966. Dr. Richard Baker, chair of Philosophy, moderated the discussion.[17]

Lauer criticized Catholic universities for being "inferior" because "priority in Catholic colleges is not given to the requirements of scholarship." She believed that Catholic colleges emphasized "maintenance of theological orthodoxy, submission to ecclesiastical authority, and conservation of the rights of religious orders." She suggested that Catholic universities be separated from the teaching function of the church to liberate institutions from ecclesiastical authority (the solution of Sister Jacqueline Grennan, president of Webster College in St. Louis, who left the Sisters of Loretto and secularized the college), and to "eliminate religious orders, at least as they exist today, as owners and operators of colleges and universities."[18] As Lauer put it after she was fired by St. John's, "the Catholic Church should get out of higher education because churches and universities don't mix."[19]

Bonnette responded that universities were created in a Catholic culture and in a pluralistic society such as our own, "'contending philosophical and religious viewpoints' are healthy." He maintained that

16. Lauer was born in Delphos, Ohio. She taught at Rosary College in Illinois from 1952 to 1958 and Manhattanville College in New York in 1958 and 1959 prior to going to St. John's University in 1959. Her doctoral dissertation was on Voltaire. Later in her career, Lauer became a spokeswoman for women's equality within the church.

17. "Dr. Lauer Views University as Community of Criticism," *Flyer News*, January 20, 1967, 1.

18. "College-Church Separation Issue Debated by Old Foes," *Catholic Telegraph*, February 3, 1967.

19. Philip Gleason, *Contending with Modernity: Catholic Higher Education in the Twentieth Century* (New York: Oxford University Press, 1995), 310.

academic freedom consists in a freedom not only to hold what you would choose to hold or teach what you would choose to teach, but it also consists in the free choice of collectivities of faculty and students to establish themselves with a special purpose in mind, and they ought to be free to establish a university designed for the communication of that tradition in all the richness and wealth which it may entail."[20]

Joseph defended the traditional rationale supporting the existence of Catholic institutions of higher learning, arguing that the basis for a Catholic university's existence is sound, because "we do not wish to affirm a human nature as closed in upon itself or absolutely self-sufficient" when we pursue the study of man.[21]

DR. WILLIAM DOANE KELLY

The February 2, 1967, presentation of Theological Studies faculty member William Doane Kelly is remembered more for the reaction to it than for its thesis. The Intellectual Frontiers series, sponsor of his lecture entitled, "The Catholic University, a Band of Secular Prophets," described the topic as answering this question: "Is a declericalized, secularized Catholic university desirable and possible? If so, what process will bring about necessary changes? What will be the relationship of the Church? Will the university be unique?"[22]

Kelly began with views first expressed in his January 1966 *Commonweal* article "What Is a Catholic College?"[23] He emphasized declericalization of Catholic colleges, by which he meant that the lay faculty "should have more say in the operation and decision-making procedures of the university."[24] Keep in mind that at this time in the history of the University of Dayton, there were no members of the laity in the upper administration of the university. All university-level administrators and two of

20. "College-Church Separation."
21. "College-Church Separation."
22. "Intellectual Frontiers 1967," brochure, series 7JD, box 26, folder 5, AUD.
23. William Doane Kelly, "What Is a Catholic College?" *Commonweal*, January 28, 1966, 494–97.
24. William Doane Kelly, "The Catholic University: A Band of Secular Prophets," Intellectual Frontiers presentation, February 2, 1967, 1–2. A copy of the presentation was given to the author by Kelly.

the four academic deans were Marianists. Kelly also recommended the "juridical and legal separation" of the university from the "local and universal Church." Kelly believed that the result of such moves would be "creativity" and "genuine academic freedom and respect."[25]

Early in his lecture, Kelly addressed the topic of heresy by distinguishing between language in "theological statements and propositions" and faith that is "the response of the whole man to the other.... To accuse someone of heresy is to get at the deeper recesses of faith in the human person which is behind the formulation of language." Kelly continued that "heresy trials are inhibiting to responsible thinkers. Dialogue and discussion are not." He went on to say that "heresy... is poor theology" best met by "improving the thought and climate where theologizing occurs." Given the context and timing of Kelly's lecture, presumably, he was referring to the controversy at the University of Dayton, although no one was accused of heresy, and the archbishop's investigation was not a "heresy trial."[26] Kelly's solution was for the Theological Studies Department to "handle poor theology in the same way that any other department in the university concerns itself with weak members. What do you do with a weak... engineer? The problem is the same."[27]

Kelly next spoke on secularization, a sixties concept that was in vogue after the 1965 publication of Harvey Cox's *The Secular City: Secularization and Urbanization in Theological Perspective*. Indeed, Cox participated in a University of Dayton joint-sponsored lecture at a Dayton church a few months earlier. Presumably, some of Kelly's audience attended Cox's lecture.[28] Kelly used wording that he later incorporated into the ad hoc committee report: "Secularization means to come of age, to come into the time and forms of the city of man today. It means a new freedom for all men in which men perfect the world, in a non-religious way." Using

25. Kelly, "Catholic University," 3.

26. Bonnette does not recall attending this lecture; Dennis Bonnette, email to the author, September 12, 2003.

27. Kelly, "Catholic University," 4.

28. UD press release, October 19, 1966, 1. The lecture, part of UD's Religion in Life series, was cosponsored by Wright State University, Antioch College, and United Theological Seminary and took place at Westminster Presbyterian Church on November 3, 1966; press releases, series 7J (A2), AUD.

wording that was not incorporated into the ad hoc report, Kelly continued that secularization meant "the Church turns her full attention to this world in all her modernity." Kelly objected to a "preoccupation with metaphysics and the ecclesiastical world... with some ideal world and not this one."[29]

Kelly supported his case with scripture and doctrine. He used the Old Testament and the Epistles of Paul to emphasize that "men must assume responsibility for this world," which Kelly defined as "secularity."[30] He recommended thinking of the incarnation as "the revelation of the fulness [sic] of what it means to be truly human" rather than "stressing the divine entering this world and therefore giving us at some point a divine world." The incarnation was "not a message" but "the dynamic process of evolution" so that the "Christian battlefield" was "ultimately in the secular life." For the church to form

> its own culture and atmosphere... is to put the emphasis in the wrong place. Randolph Lumpp, John Chrisman, Lawrence Ullrich [sic], Eulalio Balthazar [sic] are to me putting the emphasis in the secular and concrete problems of life. Situation ethics, contraception, and abortion are very important practical problems and ones that must be undertaken by university professors who have a firm desire to take responsibility for the total process of life and history, and not to give this responsibility to others. This is the message of Jesus: take responsibility for life and this world before the other.[31]

Some of the audience heard that the church's teachings on the incarnation were incorrect, that the church emphasized the wrong things, and that the accused were correct because they were taking responsibility for the here and now.

Kelly continued:

> Religion is failing because it often attempts to provide too much security and too little of the mystery of what is really before us. Religion has been good for mental health, important for correct behavior and valuable for nationalistic purposes. Man is proving that he does not need God as a prob-

29. Kelly, "Catholic University," 4.
30. Kelly, "Catholic University," 5–6.
31. Kelly, "Catholic University," 7–8.

lem solver. This is why the process of secularization has been so valuable for religion, it is throwing man back on the basic awareness of the mystery of the other, and giving man the opportunity to assume responsibility.[32]

Kelly then presented his vision for the University of Dayton. He hoped that it could be "secularized," but that would require "Jews, Protestants, Catholics, Buddhists, Hindus, and other men filled with the mystery of being and hope for the future" to join us in the "task of creating a secular humanism."[33] The "major concern" of theology in such a university is to be

the light of prophecy, and its shepherd and mentor. It must have one eye on the Bible, the other eye on the traditional development of religious thought and life, and a highly sensitized ESP on the secular developments of the new age and its ways of life. This will lead us, we hope, to a new, non-religious and non-Church form of humanistic prophecy.[34]

Kelly wanted the "layman's vision, his witness, his prophecy" to be incorporated into the secular, and he did not want such prophecy "preoccupied with ecclesiastical structure.... The ecclesiastical structure in this vision will only taste the power that comes from secular service and ministry. A fruit which some have already found quite succulent."[35]

Kelly catalogued prophecy in both the Old and New Testaments and spoke of all being given the gift of prophecy at the sacrament of confirmation.[36]

The shape for the future [depends] upon the undertakings initiated in the Church by individuals who are charged or endowed by their office or by a talent that God has awakened. The Catholic university has that charge, office, and talent. [He] hope[s] it will be charismatically awakened by a quickening of the prophetic Spirit.[37]

Kelly emphasized the importance of the Spirit as a guide "as we move to secular forms." He also said, "We must have a theologically correct idea of

32. Kelly, "Catholic University," 10.
33. Kelly, "Catholic University," 11.
34. Kelly, "Catholic University," 12.
35. Kelly, "Catholic University," 13.
36. Kelly, "Catholic University," 16.
37. Kelly, "Catholic University," 17.

the Church as the secular people of the other and really be led by these implications."[38]

From this point on, Kelly began saying things that must have shocked many in the audience. He asked if the religious realize "how it appears to others" when "they stand in the center of a religious tradition, wearing clothes of other ages, and yet claim that they live in this age?" He wondered if

> the vows of poverty, chastity, and obedience, and stability as in the Marianists, [should] be the representative value [sic] of secular Christianity?... [He] put forth new vows [of]... materialism, sexuality, and freedom, and for an addition from the secular city, mobility and worldly communication.[39]

Kelly believed the "Marianists may have greater possibilities for developing secularity than presently realized" because Father William Joseph Chaminade, the French founder of the Marianists, was "a forerunner" of Christian secularity. Kelly offered the new vows to the Marianists and asked, "Will you implement these today as did Father Chaminade in his?"[40]

Kelly announced "tidings of great joy. The secular kingdom of the other is at hand." He proposed speaking out "your convictions and values," whether they be about "birth control and situation ethics, or a recommendation that the archbishop, the Pope, or the local pastor resign." He proposed electing the local bishop and developing a new method for choosing pastors. He spoke of his conviction that

> Pope Paul is not theologically and personally qualified to be the Pope, that the archbishop should resign because of old age, and that [his] own pastor in Dayton should move out of [the] parish because he does not understand the local secular needs.... It would be better at this time to pick a non-clerical person for the position of bishop, probably a married person would be more suitable.

At this point, the Marianist provost, Father Charles Lees, walked out. Later Lees said that he walked out

---

38. Kelly, "Catholic University."
39. Kelly, "Catholic University," 18.
40. Kelly, "Catholic University."

as a form of protest against what, in my estimation, was an unscholarly and un-Christian disparagement of the Vicar of Christ on earth, of the successor to the Apostles in this Archdiocese, and of the pastor of souls in one of the parishes in the Dayton community. One can be a scholar without failing against Christian charity, and one can be a Christian without failing against scholarship. Speaking not as Provost but as a member of the University community, I am of the opinion that Dr. Kelly's lecture lacked both scholarship and Christian charity.[41]

Kelly's other suggestions included the seminary being in a university, the laity taking courses in the seminary, and "complete freedom to experiment" with liturgical forms. Kelly called for the "layman [being able to] put the Eucharist in his own hands and mouth,"[42] a practice that was not instituted in the United States until 1978. One can only imagine how the audience reacted when he continued, "Will you priests here at the university please start demanding liturgical innovations. [*sic*] You do not have families, so I cannot see why you worry about losing your jobs. Since you have this freedom of celibacy, why not let us see some more risk?"[43]

Kelly concluded his lecture by paraphrasing 1 Samuel 10:5–7:[44]

And there, as you come to the secular city, you will meet a group of humanists coming from the inner city, the laboratories, the skyscrapers, the theaters, the bureaucracy, the universities. They are coming with poems, paintings, novels, IBM cards, guitars, and much scientific apparatus; many are dressed in white jackets. Then the Spirit of the secular man, the director and direction of process, will grant you a perception, and you shall prophesy with them, and you shall be turned into a secular humanist. And as

41. Carol Giver, "Dr. Kelly Delivers Secularism Lecture," *Flyer News*, February 10, 1967, 7.

42. Although Communion under both species was discussed at the Second Vatican Council, the practice was not authorized for Sundays and holy days in the United States until 1978, more than a decade later; Mark E. Wendig, "Reception of the Eucharist under Two Species," *Pastoral Liturgy*, accessed on February 25, 2017, http://www.pastoralliturgy.org/resources/0705ReceptionEucharistTwoSpecies.php.

43. Kelly, "Catholic University," 20.

44. The New Standard Revised Version of 1 Samuel 10:5–7 is, "After that you shall come to Gilbeath-elohim, at the place where the Philistine garrison is; there, as you come to the town, you will meet a band of prophets coming down from the shrine with harp, tambourine, flute, and lyre playing in front of them; they will be in a prophetic frenzy. Then the spirit of the Lord will possess you, and you will be in a prophetic frenzy along with them and be turned into a different person. Now when these signs meet you, do whatever you see fit to do, for God is with you."

Samuel said to Saul, I say to you, "When these signs come to you, do as the occasion demands; for the Other is with you."[45]

Not surprisingly, an "emotionally charged" question-and-answer period followed the lecture.[46]

Campus reaction to Kelly's lecture, as reported in *Flyer News*, was generally negative. Kelly's department chair, Father Kohmescher, said that Kelly's examples "might have been better explained and therefore grasped in the proper light." Dr. Richard Baker, chairman of Philosophy, said, "If to be brash, arrogant and insulting is to be prophetic, then, I suppose, Dr. Kelly did speak in a prophetic voice." Two persons—Lawrence Ulrich from Philosophy and Missionaries of Africa priest S. Byron Mutch from the Department of Theological Studies—said that misinterpretation occurs if the listeners focus on the sensationalism rather than Kelly's ideas.[47]

Coverage of Kelly's lecture and an interview with him appeared in the next afternoon's *Dayton Daily News*. In general, the article focused on the sensationalist statements made in the lecture, although mention was made that Kelly was on the ad hoc committee "to study issues involved in the recent doctrinal dispute." In response to a question about whether it was risky to speak out, since the archbishop's commission was still investigating, Kelly replied, "I didn't feel it was too risky to speak out because I wasn't concerned with [the commission] or what they would think." From the standpoint of the local pastors, however, Kelly's appointment to the ad hoc committee must have been alarming. It is not surprising that Father Roesch sent a handwritten letter of apology to the archbishop. In it, Roesch indicated his impression that Kelly was "both arrogant and lacked charity in his statements." Roesch was embarrassed that a faculty member "not only cast a pall of suspicion over the privilege of academic freedom on our campus" but that he also made "disparaging remarks" about the archbishop.[48]

45. Kelly, "Catholic University," 22–23.

46. Department of Theological Studies, minutes of the meetings of February 8 and 9, 1967, 2, "Academic Freedom" file, Department of Religious Studies, University of Dayton.

47. Giver, "Dr. Kelly Delivers Secularism Lecture," 1 and 7.

48. Raymond A. Roesch, handwritten letter to Archbishop Karl J. Alter, February 3, 1967,

A few days after Kelly's lecture, his department met for a departmental meeting, and Kelly's lecture was an agenda item. Kohmescher introduced the topic by noting that the "discussion should be limited to the content of the talk." The main concern for some was Kelly's statement on the pope. "Fr. Cole suggested that the department go on record for or against the statement that the Pope was 'unqualified' to hold the office of the papacy." This led to a discussion of departmental responsibility for statements by individual members and a seconded motion that the department go on record as "supporting the right of any member... to speak out regardless of whether... all agree or not." Father Cole proposed an amendment to the motion that was seconded "with the understanding that [the member] is responsible for his use of academic freedom and can be judged by his peers."[49]

In the discussion that followed, Kohmescher stated his opposition to both the motion and the amendment because "the right of freedom is not in jeopardy in the department." No vote was recorded for the original motion, but the amendment did not pass (9 FOR, 9 AGAINST, and 1 abstention).

Cole then tried another approach, asking Kelly to "read his statement for the sake of those who were not at the talk." Another member of the department objected because he did not want to hear the statement out of context. At this point, someone motioned that discussion be closed on the topic, and the motion was seconded. The recorded minutes show Cole making a final statement of his position: a faculty member has "a right to say what he wants, but it is not an infringement on his academic freedom for his peers to judge the statement." The vote to close the discussion was 15 YEA to 4 NO.[50]

This departmental discussion is important because it is very similar to departmental discussions that took place in the Philosophy Department leading up to the controversy. One faculty member (Cole) challenged an-

series: Belmont Ave. general files, University of Dayton, Controversy "Academic Freedom, etc.," 1966–67, 1.6 Abp Alter, AAC.

49. Department of Theological Studies, minutes of the meetings of February 8 and 9, 1967, 2, "Academic Freedom" file, Department of Religious Studies, University of Dayton.

50. Theological Studies minutes, February 8 and 9, 1967.

other (Kelly) about an issue, and the discussion went nowhere. A vote was taken that ended in a draw until they voted to adjourn. Throughout the discussion, Father Cole tried various ways to challenge Kelly's assertion about the pope, and was thwarted at every attempt. Cole correctly indicated that with academic freedom comes responsibility and judgment by one's peers. Those present at this meeting seemed to want academic freedom, but were less willing to accept their responsibility for challenging their peer. Finally, during the discussion, Kelly commented that his original statement was taken out of context. This is the same response of the accused in the philosophy controversy. Kelly remained at Dayton for one more year before leaving to teach at the University of Windsor in Canada, where his contract was not renewed after one year. In response, there was a sit-in by students, and, ultimately, an academic freedom case taken up by the Canadian Association of University Teachers. It was found that Kelly's academic freedom was violated because the chair of Theology said he disagreed with Kelly's ideas.[51]

FATHER NEIL G. MCCLUSKEY, SJ

Jesuit father Neil G. McCluskey, former vice president of Gonzaga University and visiting professor at the University of Notre Dame, was scheduled to speak at the University of Dayton as part of the School of Education Lecture Series. McCluskey was born in Seattle and educated at Gonzaga University (bachelor's and master's, 1944 and 1945), Alma College—now Jesuit School of Theology at Berkeley—(S.T.L. degree in 1952), and Columbia University (Ph.D., 1958).

McCluskey's scheduled topic fit right into the campus conversation: Catholic colleges and universities in the post–Vatican II era. He drew on the Second Vatican Council's Decree on the Apostolate of the Laity to show that the temporal order, including the academic world, enjoys God-given autonomy and that the layman has an obligation and the competence to deal with the temporal world. McCluskey enumerated a list of problems in Catholic higher education—"the dominance of reli-

---

51. William Doane Kelly, email message to the author, February 24, 2002.

gious orders, reliance on old-world tradition, amateurish administration, short-sighted financial policies, confusion between pastoral and academic areas, insularity from the main stream of contemporary thought, and lack of definition of purpose"—all of which he believed "flow from the non-recognition of the character of the work of higher education."[52]

McCluskey placed most of the blame on religious orders that were not moving Catholic institutions fast enough: "The government and ownership of a collegiate institution are things that simply have to flow from the character of higher education," not from the "monastic, or conventual, or ecclesiastical" community.[53] In the United States, Catholic institutions are chartered through the state. They therefore are "stewards of public trust" with an obligation to civil authority. In other words, Catholic higher education serves the church, but it also serves a wider public.[54] McCluskey did not want to "empty Catholic institutions of their reason for existence." Rather, he wanted the laity to join in and "recognize the basic commitment of schools of the [religious] order of bringing Christ to men." Staff may need to be educated about the religious order's commitment but, "if we have not produced lay men and women leaders in the community who are as much dedicated as we to what we are trying to do in education, then we have failed anyway and we ought to go out of business."[55]

Regarding academic freedom, philosophers and theologians must have the same academic freedom as do scholars in other disciplines. He argued that "there is no more academic justification for the entry of a local bishop... into the university discipline of theology than there is for the local governor or mayor to intrude into the field of political sci-

52. Neil G. McCluskey, SJ, transcript from tape recording of talk at the University of Dayton, 1, AGMAR, University of Dayton Philosophy Controversy 1966, cat. DAY 6, doc. R15. At Notre Dame, McCluskey worked with Father Theodore Hesburgh on projects related to the International Federation of Catholic Universities and was the principal author of the Land-O'Lakes document. He was one of the leading advocates for sharing control of educational institutions with the laity. McCluskey, laicized in the mid-1970s, died on May 27, 2008; Neil J. McCluskey, SJ, telephone conversation with the author, February 24, 1999. For a more in-depth look at McCluskey's concepts from his University of Dayton address, see chapter 7, "Catholic Higher Education: Its Prospects," in Neil J. McCluskey, SJ, *Catholic Education Faces Its Future* (Garden City, N.Y.: Doubleday, 1968): 215–55.

53. McCluskey, transcript of talk at the University of Dayton, 3.

54. McCluskey, transcript of talk at the University of Dayton, 8–9.

55. McCluskey, transcript of talk at the University of Dayton, 10.

ence."[56] The official magisterium has "only an indirect influence" in that "the church speaks authoritatively to consciences of her members in the academic community just as she does to the consciences of her members holding elective office in political society." Is there a risk to the church's influence being indirect? It is "no greater than that taken by God himself when he created thinking beings."[57]

The ideas expressed by Father McCluskey at Dayton, shocking to many, appeared a few months later in the "Statement on the Nature of a Contemporary Catholic University," a publication of the International Federation of Catholic Universities under the leadership of its president, Father Theodore M. Hesburgh, CSC, then president of the University of Notre Dame. McCluskey was given credit as the principal author of the statement—known as the Land O'Lakes Statement, because the final version was drafted at a lodge in Land O'Lakes, Wisconsin—signed on July 23, 1967, by twenty-six academic and ecclesiastical leaders. Viewed as a "declaration of independence" from all authority outside of the higher education community, it continues to be a contentious document.[58] On the fiftieth anniversary of the document's signing, articles such as "The Land O'Lakes Statement Has Caused Devastation for 50 Years," "The Document that Changed Catholic Education Forever," and "Showing its Age? The Land O'Lakes Statement Could Use an Update" appeared.[59]

DR. LESLIE DEWART

Dr. Leslie Dewart, professor of philosophy at St. Michael's College, University of Toronto, came to the University of Dayton in March 1967

---

56. McCluskey, transcript of talk at the University of Dayton, 11.

57. McCluskey, transcript of talk at the University of Dayton, 12.

58. The Land O'Lakes Statement is available at http://archives.nd.edu/episodes/visitors/lol/idea.htm.

59. Patrick Reilly, "The Land O'Lakes Statement Has Caused Devastation for 50 Years," *Cardinal Newman Society*, July 20, 2017, accessed October 17, 2017, https://cardinalnewmansociety.org/land-o-lakes-statement-caused-devastation-50-years/; John J. Jenkins, CSC, "The Document That Changed Catholic Education Forever," July 11, 2017, accessed October 17, 2017, https://www.americamagazine.org/faith/2017/07/11/document-changed-catholic-education-forever; Massimo Faggioli, "Showing Its Age? The Land O'Lakes Statement Could Use an Update," *Commonweal*, October 31, 2017, accessed November 16, 2017, https://www.commonwealmagazine.org/showing-its-age.

at the request of his doctoral students John Chrisman and Lawrence Ulrich. At the time, Dewart was receiving a lot of attention—both good and
bad—for his book *The Future of Belief: Theism in a World Come of Age*.[60]

Dewart gave two presentations at Dayton. The first—a lecture entitled, "What is happening in the Church?"—was part of the Intellectual
Frontiers series and was attended by more than one thousand.[61] Dewart
began by recognizing that recently the word "confusion" keeps turning
up in Catholic discussions, conversations, and articles—confusion with
the many unexpected changes that have been "introduced into the prac-
tices, doctrines and attitudes of the Church." Catholics had not anticipated such changes because "most Catholics assumed that they would
be impossible," and yet, they occurred. Catholics were now questioning
what the changes mean for an "unchangeable dogmatic truth." They have
lost their "psychological security" because of the presumed stability of the
object of faith.[62]

Dewart cited two developments as to why Catholics assume their
faith cannot change. The first event was a conscious decision on the part
of the church in the late eighteenth/early nineteenth centuries to preserve
itself and its cultural form as the world changed socially, politically, eco-
nomically, scientifically, and culturally. This isolated and centralized the
church and, in Dewart's words, prevented "the fermentation of Catholic
thought by contemporary intellectual experience."[63]

During this time, it came to be accepted that there was a "unique,
rigid and eternal Catholic opinion on almost any subject, the orthodoxy
of which could usually be measured by its compatibility with papal pronouncements."[64] Here Dewart seemed to be describing Dieska, Dombro,
and Bonnette. He continued by giving the example of Scholasticism as
the "unique, chosen philosophical instrument of the Catholic faith." He

60. Leslie Dewart, *The Future of Belief: Theism in a World Come of Age* (New York: Herder
and Herder, 1966).

61. For more information on Dewart and his role in the sixties, see William L. Portier,
"The Genealogy of 'Heresy': Leslie Dewart as Icon of the Catholic 1960s," *American Catholic
Studies* 113 (Spring–Summer 2002): 65–77.

62. Leslie Dewart, "What Is Happening in the Church?," talk given at the University of
Dayton, n.d., 1. A copy of the talk was given to the author by John Chrisman.

63. Dewart, "What Is Happening," 2–3.

64. Dewart, "What Is Happening," 3.

ridiculed this choice, calling it a "well-meaning but abysmal delusion."[65] Change was needed within the church, and Pope John XXIII's call for the Second Vatican Council was "nothing less than convert[ing] a potentially disruptive explosion into a call for constructive creativity." Dewart described the changes brought about by the Council revolutionary.[66]

Dewart then pondered why the church did not adapt when the world changed in 1789 and beyond. The reason, he believed, lies in the cultural origins of Christianity. To be catholic or universal, the church adopted a "Hellenic cultural form in place of its original Hebrew form." Dewart argued that this was useful for the church at that time, but now it is time for the church to "transcend its original Hellenic cultural form," a process he called dehellenization, which he believed would bring Christian belief in line with contemporary human experience.[67] Dewart blamed the church for not moving past its Hellenic culture on ideas within that culture: "immutability, stability, and impassivity."[68]

Dewart concluded by answering his question, "What is happening in the Church today?" by saying, "We are undergoing a process of rapid dehellinization, generally unprepared for, reluctantly undertaken, and forced upon the Church by history itself only after the disparity between faith and experience has reached a critical point." The church must "develop itself thru the creation of new cultural forms."[69] Therefore, "reconceptualization of the Catholic faith in novel forms is legitimate."[70] And "unwarranted stability" may be "unfaithful to the Catholic tradition and to the Christian spirit." In terms of the situation at the University of Dayton, he [Dewart] seemed to be implying that Chrisman and Ulrich's novel approaches were legitimate and Bonnette, Dieska, and Dombro may have been unfaithful to the Catholic tradition.

Dewart's second presentation was on March 17, 1966, at an open hearing of the ad hoc committee. Information about the event is from a news article in the Archdiocese of Cincinnati's newspaper, the *Catholic Tele-*

65. Dewart, "What Is Happening," 4.
66. Dewart, "What Is Happening," 5.
67. Dewart, "What Is Happening," 12.
68. Dewart, "What Is Happening," 13.
69. Dewart, "What Is Happening," 14.
70. Dewart, "What Is Happening," 15.

graph. According to Dewart, "a deeper understanding of the notion of teaching would remove tensions now existing between officials of the church and Catholic universities." No teacher, including the magisterium, can just "pass on" the truth. It is the "function of the intellect to inquire, to develop itself, not to take over ready made or otherwise even revealed truth." Dewart criticized the bishops for their "simplified" view of teaching, which he summarized as, "God has given the Church and specifically the hierarchy a truth which they have to look after and pass on, and their job is to see that this heritage is not dissipated or devalued."[71] Dewart's view was that

> the deposit of faith... has been entrusted to the Church; that is to say, has been entrusted to a social historical process, because that is what the Church is.... It has not been entrusted to the magisterium. The magisterium is a function for the sake of, for the welfare of, that deposit of faith given to the Church as a whole. The function of the magisterium is one of serving the Church in relation to the deposit of faith.[72]

Dewart recognized that the sixties were a "critical period" in the church's history. He believed the church was "liquidating the first 2,000 years of Christianity." Presumably, Dewart was referring to the process of dehellenization, which he advocated in his book and in his previous lecture. He believed that "in no time in our history, not even in the First Century, have we been challenged as deeply nor have we responded so sincerely, that is, from the bottom of our heart [*sic*], as we are at the present time."[73]

FATHER JOHN L. MCKENZIE, SJ

The ad hoc committee minutes for March 6, 1967, indicate that Jesuit John Courtney Murray, Paulist Eugene Burke, and Jesuit John L. McKenzie of the Theology Department at the University of Notre Dame were

71. "Philosopher Examines Idea of Magisterium," *Catholic Telegraph Register*, March 24, 1967, B4.
72. "Philosopher Examines."
73. "Philosopher Examines."

invited to appear before the committee in open hearings.[74] McKenzie accepted the invitation and addressed the university community on April 17, 1967. His topic was "The Magisterium and the University."

McKenzie began by defining "magisterium" as "the office of school-master." He did not think the church was "instituted to be anyone's schoolmaster," but "magisterium" was designated "a theological principle" when it was declared by those "assembled at the First Vatican Council that the Church is empowered to teach, and in that Council the object of its teachings was described as 'faith and morals.'" McKenzie looked for the "roots of this commission to teach matters of faith and morals" in the New Testament. There he found that the "exclusive mission of the Church" is to "proclaim the gospel," which to him meant to teach what the church has learned from her founder and about him.[75] When the church says, "Something is of her faith," the church is a "witness to what the Church believes." He defines morals as "how Christians should live." At this point, however, McKenzie adds that these objects of the church's teaching have undefined limits and that, at times, the "men who bear the teaching authority of the Church" have "failed to meet their mandate" or "exceeded their mandate." Galileo is an example of the latter.[76]

Turning to the university, McKenzie says it is

supposed to deal with learning; it's supposed to preserve it, increase it, and transmit it.... Over the centuries... there has arisen a certain body of method, technique and principles which have become identified with the university.[77]

McKenzie reminds his audience that

the first modern universities were founded under ecclesiastical auspices and remained under them for several hundred years.... One of the earliest encounters of the University of Paris with the Archbishop of Paris was the

74. Minutes for the Ad Hoc Committee for the Study of Academic Freedom at the University of Dayton, March 6, 1967, 1, various Ad Hoc Committees, 1966–69; v. 2, box 30, folder 2, AUD.

75. John L. McKenzie, SJ, "The Magisterium and the University," April 17, 1967, 1, series "The Philosophy Controversy," AUD.

76. McKenzie, "Magisterium and the University," 2–3.

77. McKenzie, "Magisterium and the University," 4.

diocesan synod in which the Archbishop of Paris condemned as heretical, rash, vagarious and offensive to pious ears the writings of Thomas Aquinas.... Thomas Aquinas (at that time quite recently dead) encountered an Archbishop who obviously could not recognize good theology when he saw it.[78]

According to McKenzie, it follows that the university is a "possible limit" to the teaching authority of the church.

If you look at the history of the relationship between the magisterium and the university and the principles behind it, McKenzie claims that you get into a "discussion of what the magisterium has done, and what the magisterium has done it can do." This falls apart when you come to Galileo, and "then you're left without any principles." If it does not work for Galileo, McKenzie sees no reason to argue what the magisterium has done it can do in other instances.[79]

If one were to risk formulating a principle, McKenzie argues that "perhaps among the objects of infallibility *is not the determination of the object of teaching.*" He does not wish to destroy infallibility, but what the church teaches is "not the object of academic study or academic instruction." The church is proclaiming the gospel "to the simple [and] to the learned and it is the same gospel that is proclaimed to both." McKenzie believes the problem in the Western church is that we have an educated class. When the gospel is proclaimed, its reception differs. The faith of the simple is not the same as the faith of the learned.[80]

This leads McKenzie to state "that [the magisterium] is not competent to settle questions of learning except by the methods of learning and when it does settle them by methods of learning it is no longer acting as the Church." The church can speak to a "particular historical situation," but we should be aware that there may need to be "'adjustments' in the moral teaching of the Church over the centuries." McKenzie then gives examples such as slavery, usury, the morality of war, and possibly, contraception that was being considered at that time.[81]

78. McKenzie, "Magisterium and the University."
79. McKenzie, "Magisterium and the University," 5.
80. McKenzie, "Magisterium and the University," 5–6.
81. McKenzie, "Magisterium and the University," 6–7.

McKenzie notes that, rightfully, academics do not want nonacademics interfering in academic proceedings. "But is the teaching authority a nonacademic body?" McKenzie thinks not. The teaching authority meets the definition of an academic body, and, if the magisterium wants to discuss "academic questions," then it should "discuss them in academic terms or we cannot discuss it with them." This leads to a discussion of the need for academic freedom for scholars. Without academic freedom, McKenzie believes Catholic universities will cease to exist:[82]

> In [McKenzie's] own life of scholarship the magisterium has created... not even minor problems. [He] has lived with it—[he] won't say happily, but at least peacefully. The problems arise not from what we call the magisterium, as the official teaching body of the church, but rather from its somewhat overzealous unofficial protectors, who, it seems have not realized that as only the Church can declare what she believes, so only the Church can declare what is heresy. No other body is empowered to define this. It is not a word which can or ought to be used in any academic discussion, because no academic man has any more business saying something is heresy than he has saying that something is of faith.... But if he measures something which goes on in the present time against the standards of the past, the proper word, if one is to be used in discussion, is not that something is heretical, but that something is wrong.... That word is offensive enough.[83]

McKenzie suggests that there ought to be some sort of "public ritual of repentance" in the church for those who "charge their fellow Christians with heresy and can't make it stick." He equates a theologian's orthodoxy with a woman's virtue: "Once it's doubted, it's gone." He thinks the "university community here could furnish a model for the Catholic community at large by the use of that temperate language which we like to think is characteristic of the highest scholarship."[84]

Since the university and the magisterium must meet in the world of learning, he continues, it must be the magisterium that makes a reparation, "if only since they, practically, have been unsympathetic to free discussion and which has tried its hand in areas where its incompetence

---

82. McKenzie, "Magisterium and the University," 7–8.
83. McKenzie, "Magisterium and the University," 9.
84. McKenzie, "Magisterium and the University."

was proved, but not discouraged." One does not need to look back to Galileo. Pius IX's *Syllabus of Errors* in the nineteenth century has all been disproved. And yet when "we meet the magisterium... we just listen.... When it engages in matters in which it has no competence... then somebody must say something, unless we are to have Galileo cases by the dozens rolling out of the Vatican Press." McKenzie knows that someone will bring up the "safety of doctrine," but you cannot "build a fence around it" without "paralyzing its force."[85]

McKenzie ends his lecture by talking about the fragility of the Catholic university. He is afraid the church might make a statement on the university and the magisterium and that it "could entirely wreck the Catholic university," which needs "constant nurturing and protection." He suggests that

> no one in the academic community should say to himself that because I teach a secular discipline this is not my concern. If he really believes in what we usually call the academic community it is very much his concern. The whole body bleeds, not just the organ that is cut. And [McKenzie] think[s] that in the strife, scholars have proved themselves beyond a doubt to be authentic, dedicated Christians, and authentic, dedicated scholars. The Catholic university will have all the strength it needs in order to preserve itself in doing what we somewhat perhaps immodestly believe only a university can do.[86]

In general, McKenzie's message to the ad hoc committee is that the university should distinguish itself from the magisterium. The issue in the University of Dayton controversy, however, was not the magisterium unjustly calling an academic a heretic. It was an academic saying other academics were teaching contrary to the magisterium. The faculty members involved were not civil. They did not use "temperate language" toward each other. They were not an example for the church.

85. McKenzie, "Magisterium and the University," 10.
86. McKenzie, "Magisterium and the University," 11.

Before finalizing its report, the ad hoc committee invited Society of Mary members Father Thomas Stanley and Brother Gerard J. E. Sullivan to discuss the Marianist tradition of education and the University of Dayton. From the committee minutes, we know that Stanley stressed that

a. no artificial distinction between the sacred and the secular be made;

b. the University of Dayton needs to devote much attention to continued study of its purposes; and

c. a part of any distinctive ethos at the University of Dayton would focus upon a sense of mystery—heuristic as well as theological.[87]

Father William Cole's personal notes on Father Stanley's remarks indicate the need for a definition of Catholic university. Stanley suggested that the committee look to particular Marianists who have written about Catholic education for its special characteristics. He was disappointed at the lack of treatment of the faith as a characteristic of the university, which he described as an illumination, something people carried with them in whatever they do.[88]

Brother Gerard Sullivan read a position paper on "Special Characteristics of the University of Dayton as a Marianist Catholic University." Before he addressed his topic, Sullivan reviewed some of the early history of Father Chaminade and the Marianists, stressing that Father Chaminade's "whole interest lay in using every possible means to bring every possible person, first of all, a better life, particularly from the moral point of view, which sometimes required rescuing them from their unhealthy selves."[89] Sullivan suggested using Chaminade's approach as a "new manner of viewing the goals of the Marianists... at the University of Dayton."[90]

87. Minutes, May 25, 1967, 1, various ad hoc committees, 1966–69, v. 2, box 30, folder 2, AUD.

88. William J. Cole, notes on Father Thomas Stanley's remarks, May 25, 1967, 2, series "The Philosophy Controversy," AUD.

89. Gerard J. E. Sullivan, "Special Characteristics of the University of Dayton as a Marianist Catholic University," May 25, 1967, series "The Philosophy Controversy," AUD.

90. Sullivan, "Special Characteristics," 3.

By the time the ad hoc committee concluded its report in July 1967, its tasks had changed somewhat, given developments during the first six months of 1967. In the preface, the committee summarized the tasks "in the developmental order in which they were made public":

1. To study the guidelines of academic freedom on our campus.
2. To provide guidelines to eliminate future difficulties.
3. To give the university a *better chance* to be free from fault in the future.
4. To formulate a satisfactory and logical explanation of the intent of the university contract pertaining to the preservation of the deposit of faith and Christian morality on campus.
5. To demonstrate that paragraph 25 of the Constitution on the Church, as well as all the other recommendations of Vatican II, are fully applicable on a university campus.
6. To establish criteria that define the true posture of the theologian and the philosopher on campus.
7. To treat the question of how appropriate respect is to be paid the proper role of the church's magisterium.[91]

Task number 1 was the initial mandate for the committee. Number 2 was from the archbishop's fact-finding commission. Numbers 3 and 6 were from Father Darby in his press release after the issuance of the fact-finding commission's report and in his letter to the editor of *Ave Maria*, respectively. Numbers 4, 5, and 7 were from Father Roesch's faculty address.

Recognizing the enormity of their tasks, the committee structured the report in five sections:

1. Treating the developmental serial performance in Catholic higher education;
2. Considering the university learning strategies and the magisterium;

91. President's ad hoc committee for the study of academic freedom at the University of Dayton, "Academic Freedom at the University of Dayton," July 1967, 3.

3. Concerning a new *gemeinschaft* for the University of Dayton,

4. Freedom of discussion by faculty and students; and

5. Freedom of mode of expression by faculty and students.

The first three sections respond to the controversy in the Philosophy Department. The committee found E. G. Williamson's national empirical study, "The Role of the President in the Desirable Enactment of Academic Freedom for Students," "helpful in identifying the last two sections."[92]

Section 1 defines "serial performance" as "an extended sequence of performances which have some relation to one another in an overall pattern."[93] This section looks at a developing (rather than regressing) sequence of events related to Catholic higher education. The committee initially looked at American Protestant institutions of higher education to see if the "prevailing ethos" was similar to American Catholic institutions. Since the foundations differed, the report turned to the specific development of Catholic higher learning. The committee looked at the Greco-Roman period when Christians used existing schools without accepting all the purposes of the schools.[94] Then they considered developments in the Middle Ages, the Reformation, and the Council of Trent before turning to the founding of Catholic colleges in the United States. The focus on the United States is on the educational psychology in church documents from U.S. plenary councils in the 1800s to Pius XI's *Christian Education of Youth*, to the Jesuits at Boston College, and to Cardinal Mercier in Belgium from the mid-twentieth century to the Second Vatican Council. The report shows the church developing over time with the emphasis after Vatican II on "dialogue, understanding others, and most of all, the recognition 'that man's response to God in faith must be free.'"[95] The committee concludes this section by stating that "Vatican

92. Ad hoc committee report, July 1967, 4. E. G. Williamson's study appeared in *Educational Record* 46 (1967): 351–75.

93. Abraham Kaufman, "Teaching as an Intentional Serial Performance," *Studies in Philosophy and Education* 4, no. 4 (December 1966): 364, quoted in Ad Hoc Committee Report, July 1967, 5.

94. For this portion of the report, the committee "drew heavily" on Bernard J. Kohlbrenner, "The Catholic Heritage," in *Heritage of American Education*, ed. Richard E. Gross (Boston: Allyn and Bacon, 1962), 103–32.

95. Walter M. Abbott, SJ, ed., *The Documents of Vatican II* (New York: Guild Press/Herder and Herder, 1966), 639, quoted in Ad Hoc Committee Report, July 1967, 13.

II seems to be willing to risk the expression of knowledge by mode of inclination rather than exclusively by mode of discursive reason; it seems to be willing to recognize that expressed heuristic strategies are germane to theology and philosophy as well as the other realms of meaning, even though such expressions may be more 'risky.'"[96]

Section 2 focuses on learning strategies related to the university and the magisterium. It is a mixture of educational theory applied to an understanding of the magisterium as the teaching authority of the church and to the university, which is focused on learning rather than teaching. Ultimately, the committee concludes that the scholar and non-scholar interact with the magisterium in different ways.[97] Section 2 also deals with the necessity of the philosopher and theologian to be aware of and able to assume the postures of other disciplines—namely,

individual liberty, idiosyncrasy in the mode and method of investigation, a kind of humility which yields a mistrust of one's brain to reach grand conclusions, a self-correcting attempt to defeat one's own conclusions, a willingness to tolerate a success which may come after a series of intelligent failures, a willingness to admit sometimes the only certainty is uncertainty, and lastly to realize that intellectual work is not so much to be interpreted as the calisthenics of discovery but as an art of investigation.[98]

These postures allow "men ... [to] hold authority not according to any system of rules, but because of learning, competence and success in a given academic sphere." These "personal achievements ... give one the right to make pronouncements."[99]

Section 3, on a new *gemeinschaft* for the University of Dayton, attracted the most attention.[100] After recognizing the "dedication and service" of the Society of Mary, the committee called on the current faculty, staff, and administrators to "understand the tradition they have received, develop it in the present, and give it a new direction for the future." The committee

96. Ad Hoc Committee Report, July 1967, 14.
97. Ad Hoc Committee Report, July 1967, 18.
98. Ad Hoc Committee Report, July 1967, 19–20.
99. Ad Hoc Committee Report, July 1967, 20.
100. The meaning of *gemeinschaft* is "a spontaneously arising organic social relationship characterized by strong reciprocal bonds of sentiment and kinship within a common tradition"; *Merriam-Webster Dictionary*, https://www.merriam-webster.com/dictionary/gemeinschaft.

saw the purpose of a Marianist university as "fulfilling Mary's role, that is, to create an environment of scholarship, a university, so that... [the] Word may pass into present-day American and international culture."[101]

How does a Catholic university function in the sixties to serve this purpose? The committee states, "The Catholic university should not be ... an arm of indoctrination of the universal Church or of the local Church." Rather, it continued that a Catholic university should "investigate, probe, and search for truth and the interpretation of reality and the mystery of life and existence" that leads to the "ultimate purpose—to discover the mystery of what is really before man, to keep man open to this mystery, to the future, and to an encounter with the other."[102]

The Catholic university is "not limited to being the transmitter for the official teachings of the Church (although this could occur in some disciplines)." The Catholic university's "chief interest" is "perfecting the world in a *non-religious* way." This meant that the university is "to be secularized ... to come of age, to come into the time and forms of the city of man today."[103]

The committee goes on to talk about the *gemeinschaft*—that is, "the dimension of *mutual participation*," of the church, religious communities, and "sub-institutions of the Church" such as Catholic hospitals and universities.[104] While "a debt of gratitude" is owed to those who created the institutions, "tremendous changes have begun" since the Second Vatican Council, and the Catholic university must be a university. The university *"as an institution"* cannot "pass judgment on any individual's loyalty or fidelity to the larger church community." *Lumen Gentium* ¶25—the paragraph Father Roesch described as the "heart of the controversy"— "applies to an individual's freely chosen, personal relationship to the Church."[105] The relationship of Catholic universities to the official magisterium is therefore "indirect, that is, the teaching Church speaks to the consciences of Catholic members of an academic community... [rather

---

101. Ad Hoc Committee Report, July 1967, 24.
102. Ad Hoc Committee Report, July 1967, 25.
103. Ad Hoc Committee Report, July 1967.
104. Ad Hoc Committee Report, July 1967, 26.
105. Ad Hoc Committee Report, July 1967, 27.

than to the university], its schools or fields of learning, including theology."[106] A Catholic university "jealously maintains its independence of all outside authority, but unlike [its secular counterparts], respects the apostolic concern of the local Bishop, including his authority to teach the faithful and his right to speak to situations anywhere which might be the occasion of moral and spiritual harm."[107]

On an academic level, a professor is judged according to the standards of his academic peers. A professor's "relationship to his chosen religious affiliation" is "determined by himself and his Church," and the university cannot "control the stance, attitude or determination which a religious group takes toward an individual in a university."[108]

Until the sixties, the *gemeinschaft* of the Catholic university was determined primarily by the sponsoring religious order. This becomes problematic when the "structures of the larger Church community as represented in the religious community tended to become... superimposed on the university structure."[109] The committee maintained that "the *gemeinschaft* of the university should be created by scholars and should not be determined by the structure of the Church or the structures of the religious community associated with the university or its way of life." "The University's future direction should be determined by the faculty... the heart and mind and soul of the university."

> If the University of Dayton were to [turn immediately to its own faculty to determine and shape its future in a spirit of scholarly, Catholic, Christian democracy,] ... it could very well become a type of Catholic university of the future and lead other American Catholic and non-Catholic private universities to new patterns and perspectives.[110]

If the University of Dayton immediately created and implemented "proper University structures" that reflect the above *gemeinschaft*, "an environment will be created in which controversies, difficulties, and problems will contribute to the growth of the University in full accord with the

106. Ad Hoc Committee Report, July 1967.
107. Ad Hoc Committee Report, July 1967, 28.
108. Ad Hoc Committee Report, July 1967.
109. Ad Hoc Committee Report, July 1967.
110. Ad Hoc Committee Report, July 1967, 29. The emphasis is that of the committee.

spirit of Vatican II—the Church moving forward as the People of God."[111]

Sections 4 and 5 deal with practical issues related to freedom of discussion and freedom of mode of expression. Sources for these sections include the AAUP and the Association of American Colleges. Section 4 states that faculty have "complete freedom" to express their views, and the "university's sole concern should be for the academic performance of the faculty member... not on his particular personal point of view or interpretation of the material presented." The criteria in judging student discussion should be that "such meetings be conducted in an orderly and responsible manner." Probably the most important practical recommendation of the committee is the formation of a standing faculty committee "to make a thorough investigation of any alleged abuse by faculty and students of the right of freedom of speech."[112]

Section 5 lays out seven "basic principles" for all members of the academic community, particularly scholars, to follow in their pursuit of truth: (1) be accurate; (2) exercise proper restraint; (3) show respect for the opinions of others; (4) make it clear in which capacity you are acting (as a professional scholar, a private citizen, and so forth); (5) consider your audience; (6) be a servant of the community, not its tool; and (7) form "within the academic community a committee to hear and judge cases involving members of the instructional staff accused of having exceeded the tenets of academic freedom."[113]

The ad hoc committee report was completed in July 1967. When the report was released to the faculty in September 1967, the *Dayton Daily News* focused on the secularization sentence and ran a story with the headline, "Faculty Group Wants a Secular UD." Father Roesch "declined comment," but Brother Elmer Lackner, vice president for public relations, stated that "the report... is strictly for the faculty and their perusal and recommendations for any deletions or additions. This certainly is not the report in final form."[114]

111. Ad Hoc Committee Report, July 1967, 30.
112. Ad Hoc Committee Report, July 1967, 32.
113. Ad Hoc Committee Report, July 1967, 34–36.
114. Bill Clark, "Faculty Group Wants a Secular UD," *Dayton Daily* News, October 10, 1967, 1 and 4.

Roesch's October 2, 1967, letter to ad hoc committee members sheds more light on what actually happened. Apparently, the committee could not "unanimously agree" on a text. Roesch acknowledges the possibility of a minority report that would "perhaps be more to the point of establishing clear directives for the pursuit of truth in academic debate" on the campus. Roesch felt that "much of [the committee's] work, reflection and thought [was] missed in [the] report." The committee therefore was invited to an administrative council meeting on October 5, 1967, to discuss how to proceed. Roesch indicated that "uppermost in our intention is that the term 'Marianist Catholic University' both collectively and individually will apply in their fullest connotation to U.D."[115] At the same time as Roesch was inviting the committee to his administrative council meeting, he sent copies of the invitation letter to all vice presidents and asked them to inform their own councils of the upcoming action on the part of the administrative council. Roesch wanted to make it clear that the ad hoc committee report was not "accepted and endorsed" by the administration.

The administrative council decided to ask the faculty to "evaluate the report" and submit "remarks and suggestions" to the ad hoc committee. Each academic department was also asked to "discuss the document and report the results of the discussion to the Provost."[116] Every department and more than sixty individuals responded. In summary, "Only a few departments and individuals accept[ed] the report more or less *in toto*.... A strong segment of faculty... support[ed] an entirely different view of academic responsibility and freedom on a Catholic campus."[117]

In December 1967, Marianist father John Nichols, a first-semester assistant professor in philosophy, was asked to "carry on the work of the President's *ad hoc* committee" as editor of the report.[118] Within six weeks, the Marianist superior general reassigned Nichols to the seminary in Fribourg, Switzerland. No amount of pleading on the part of Fathers Darby

115. Raymond A. Roesch to individuals on the Ad Hoc Committee for Setting Guidelines for Scholarship [*sic*—there is no indication why the correct name of the committee was not used], October 2, 1967, various ad hoc committees, 1966–69, v. 2, box 30, folder 2, AUD.

116. Charles J. Lees to members of the faculty, October 10, 1967, 1.

117. Raymond A. Roesch to members of the faculty, December 6, 1967, 1.

118. "News from the University of Dayton," press release, December 18, 1967, press releases, series 7J (A2), AUD,.

and Roesch and Brother Leonard Mann, the dean of the College of Arts and Sciences, could stop the reassignment from happening, so Marianist father William Cole, professor of theological studies and member of the ad hoc committee, was "asked to begin again on this study independently" of Nichols's work.

By mid-March 1968, Cole's report was presented to the faculty as a "working draft of a University statement on objectives and purposes."[119] Cole divided the report into sections on the meaning of a university, Catholic, Marianist, and Dayton. In the Catholic section—twenty-nine pages of the fifty-three-page document—Cole dealt with the relationship between the university and the church, including the "true autonomy of the university" and the "compatibility of autonomy and a real institutional commitment to the Church."[120] Cole looked at the role of theology and philosophy in a Catholic university while indicating that "freedom in the teaching of philosophy and theology cannot be divorced from a respectful relationship to the Magisterium."[121] He also explored the "fear that Catholic universities will not long remain Catholic" if the institution and the sponsoring body are separated. Cole suggested that "the University of Dayton, like many Church institutions, must prove the feasibility of reconciling freedom, responsibility, and institutional purpose as these are involved in the religious character of the college."[122]

Cole's report, along with other documents, including a John Nichols essay on "The Strategic Contribution of the University of Dayton to American Higher Education," became the source materials for a fall 1968 faculty seminar studying the purposes and objectives of the University of Dayton.[123]

The university's board of trustees approved a one-page statement of

119. Raymond A. Roesch to members of the faculty, March 15, 1968, 1.

120. William J. Cole, "Working Paper Presented to the Faculty for Critical Consideration; Purposes of the University of Dayton, A Catholic Marianist University in Dayton, Ohio," 18, AUD.

121. Cole, "Working Paper," 29.

122. Cole, "Working Paper," 47.

123. "Source Material Proposed for Faculty Seminar on Study of Purpose and Objectives of the University of Dayton, 'A Marianist Catholic University,'" Fall 1968. Copy of the booklet given to the author by Michael Barnes. It is also available in the AUD.

purposes on May 14, 1969. The statement affirmed that the University of Dayton is a "church-related institution of higher learning" that "seeks, in an environment of academic freedom, to foster principles and values consonant with Catholicism and with the living traditions of the Society of Mary." It "deliberately chooses the Christian worldview as its distinctive orientation in carrying out what it regards as four essential tasks: teaching, research, serving as a critic of society, and rendering public service."[124]

After the approval of the "Statement of Purposes," the board of trustees approved "Regulations on Academic Freedom and Tenure" on June 30, 1969. The "Plan for the Seventies" led to amendments to the university's articles of incorporation, bylaws of the corporation, constitutions of the University of Dayton, and bylaws of the board of trustees. A "Statement of Student Rights, Responsibilities and Freedoms" was approved by the board on October 15, 1971, while the corresponding "Statement of Rights and Responsibilities for Members of the University of Dayton Community" was created and approved by the board on May 25, 1972. One might expect the latter statement to address the relationship of faculty to the magisterium, but it did not mention the magisterium. The statement does call on members of the UD community to respect the rights of others and "deal with their fellows in justice and civility," something that did not happen during the controversy. A statement addendum, approved by the executive committee of the board of trustees prior to distribution of the documents to community members in September 1972, clarifies the university's relationship with the church as:

the right as a civil corporation to administrative autonomy in the profession of its Church relatedness. Ecclesiastical authority has the right to make known that it questions or rejects conclusions reached by members of the University Community; but in doing so makes use of its own jurisdiction and due process; and does not attempt to enjoin the academic due process of the University.[125]

124. University of Dayton, "Statement of Purposes," in *Documents Pertaining to Academic Freedom and Tenure at the University of Dayton*, Fall 1969, 1. Copy of the booklet given to the author by Michael Barnes. It is also available in the AUD.

125. "Addendum," Statement of Rights and Responsibilities for Members of the University of Dayton Community, May 25,1972, 11. Copy of the booklet given to the author by Michael Barnes. It is also available in the AUD.

As the seventies unfolded, the University of Dayton returned to the topic of purposes with the formation of a board of trustees committee on objectives and purposes. The committee, under the leadership of Marianist fathers William J. Ferree (chair from 1970 to 1976) and William R. Behringer (chair from 1976 to 1977), included board members, faculty, administrators, and students. After producing a first draft, the committee solicited "comments and criticism" from the entire university community.[126] The resulting document, "The Purposes and Nature of the University of Dayton," was approved by the board of trustees on October 20, 1977. This document remains the university's official statement of its purposes and nature.

The statement has two sections:

1. An explication and analysis of the university's purposes as set forth in the articles of incorporation; and
2. A correlation of this and two more recent official statements, arranged in the order of precedence established by the constitution of the university.[127]

Section 1 is "limited to matters of definition and history," while Section 2 is a more extended "commentary and re-interpretation for [the seventies]" of the first.[128]

For the purposes of this book, section 2 is the most relevant. The section begins by recognizing that "the University, like all other human institutions, is passing [through profound changes] at this moment in history." This change is the "passage of civilization from 'Subsistence' to 'Development,' which many theologians like to characterize as 'Mankind coming of age.'" From there, the section discusses, paragraph by paragraph, the Nature section of the university's constitution.[129]

---

126. James L. Heft, memo to the goals and purposes committee, May 30, 1977, 1, objectives and purposes committee, series 2BC, AUD.

127. "The Purposes and Nature of the University of Dayton," accessed November 4, 2017, 5–6, https://udayton.edu/rector/_resources/files/PurposeNature.pdf.

128. Raymond A. Roesch, cover letter to the university community, n.d., "The Purposes and Nature," 2.

129. The Constitution of the University of Dayton was renamed "Code of Regulations of the Corporation" and the language of the five Nature items updated in 2014 and again in 2017. The items are still essentially the same as approved in 1977.

Two items in the Nature section pertain to this book: the University of Dayton's commitment as a private institution and its commitment as a Catholic university. The statement describes the university as a "private institution in a pluralistic society" that has "chosen as its option the Christian world-view as a distinctive orientation and insists only that human problems be first approached from that philosophical position." The statement explains that this approach does not refer to "particular positions... but rather to a general attitude and orientation.... Those engaged professionally by the University are to be informed of this orientation and are expected to have the personal integrity to respect it in their teaching, research and other professional pursuits."[130] Key to the goal of working out its commitment to the Christian worldview is dialogue with all traditions. Those from other traditions are asked to "respect the right of the University to express *institutionally* its own fundamental orientation." The statement summarizes this section as "sufficient personal integrity to respect institutional integrity."[131]

In describing the university's commitment as a Catholic university, the statement says the university "accepts the validity of revealed as well as reasoned truth and is committed to genuine and responsible academic freedom, supported by proper respect for the Church's Magisterium." The university "operates under a civil charter and assumes the stance of a Catholic University by free and voluntary option, without executive control of the Church [or] financial dependence on it." Although autonomous from the church, the university "recognizes the Magisterium of the Catholic Church as the authentic definer and interpreter of what is and is not Catholic." The university expects that "scholarly criticism" by a theologian's colleagues will

> render unnecessary any direct involvement of ecclesiastical authority. However, in times of great controversy, the institution's commitment may be challenged just as one's personal stance may be called in question. Just as in the ordinary course of events, these times of crisis are to be characterized by a "proper respect for the Church's Magisterium."[132]

130. "Purposes and Nature," 17.
131. "Purposes and Nature," 18.
132. "Purposes and Nature," 19.

The university recognizes the right of the church to follow its own due process and "make public its judgment that a given professor in the University, who professes to represent the Catholic tradition on a certain issue, does not, in fact, do so." This is not to be considered a "condemnation of either the individual or the University."[133]

In such a situation, the individual and the university need to come to an understanding of how "institutional integrity and academic freedom can best be maintained."[134] It may be the case that the "individual could usefully or conveniently perform a quite different function such as that of the representation of a different tradition." The statement goes on to clarify:

> The concern to identify the specific function of a professor with relationship to the University's commitment should not be understood as an opposition to a legitimate pluralism within a tradition. For example, theologians in their work are free to question, to develop their own hypotheses, to search for more adequate interpretations and formulations, to publish and defend their views on a scholarly level and to study theological sources, including pronouncements of the Magisterium; although in their teaching they must take prudent account of the maturity and previous preparation of their students. The encouragement of scholarly contributions to the development of Church teaching is, in fact, one of the functions of a Catholic University within the Church.[135]

When the statement was written, the University of Dayton stated that it was unique among other Catholic universities because of the way "the different roles and procedural norms of the University and of the Magisterium have been set forth." The university was "conscious of breaking new ground." Indeed, a review of similar documents of twenty Catholic colleges and universities[136] in existence in the sixties reveals that no other

133. "Purposes and Nature," 20.

134. "Purposes and Nature,"

135. "Purposes and Nature," 21. The university's statement includes Thesis 12 of the International Theological Commission's "Theses on the Relationship between the Ecclesiastical Magisterium and Theology," approved on June 6, 1976. Thesis 12 deals with the due process procedure of the magisterium. In a footnote, the statement also discusses the definition of heresy and the importance of dialogue between a theologian and the magisterium.

136. The institutions surveyed, in alphabetical order, are: Boston College, the Catholic University of America, College of St. Benedict, College of St. Thomas, Creighton University,

Catholic institution addressed the issue of the relationship of the institution to the magisterium or the church in its governance documents. For the University of Dayton to have the issue in its current documents (as of this writing) is a nod to the importance of the "Heresy" Affair in the university's history.

The administration of the University of Dayton and the Archbishop of Cincinnati counted on the ad hoc committee to bring an end to the controversy and prevent future controversies from occurring. The committee's work was a step in the right direction, but it took an additional ten years of work to craft a document that has withstood the test of time. Along the way, the University of Dayton developed faculty policies such as the "Academic Freedom and Tenure" document and created faculty governance groups such as the academic senate and various academic freedom and tenure committees. These policies and groups—steps that the University of Dayton took to achieve academic legitimacy—are a safeguard against the development of future controversies similar to the "Heresy" Affair.

DePaul University, Georgetown University, Loyola Marymount University, Marquette University, St. John's University (Minnesota), St. John's University (New York), St. Louis University, St. Michael's College, Santa Clara University, University of Detroit Mercy, University of Notre Dame, University of San Francisco, University of Scranton, Villanova University, and Xavier University (Ohio).

CHAPTER 9

THE CHURCH BEHIND THE SCENES

Authority exercised with humility and obedience accepted with delight are the very lines along which our spirits live.

—C. S. Lewis, "Membership," in *The Weight of Glory and Other Addresses*

When one is on the outside of a controversy, it sometimes looks like the powers that be are unaware of what is going on and, therefore, are not doing anything about the situation. However, most administrators try to work behind the scenes before going public. The church, in particular, tries to work behind the scenes. Such was the case with the "Heresy" Affair. This chapter will examine the actions of the all-Marianist University of Dayton board of trustees, the all-Marianist president's administrative council, the local archbishop, Karl J. Alter, the apostolic delegate in Washington, D.C., the Congregation for the Doctrine of the Faith at the Vatican, the Marianist superior general, Father Paul-Joseph Hoffer, and the Marianist provincial, James M. Darby. All were involved in the situation at the University of Dayton.

C. S. Lewis, "Membership," in *The Weight of Glory and Other Addresses* (San Francisco: HarperSanFrancisco, 2001). My thanks to Mark Masthay for bringing this quote to my attention.

There is evidence that the all-Marianist board of trustees was aware of the issues involved in the controversy. On December 4, 1963, the topic of honorary degrees was discussed. It was noted that a *nihil obstat* was required for honorary degrees to be given to "ecclesiastics"; namely, the archbishop needed to approve any priests being given honorary degrees. This led to a discussion of the role of diocesan authority over the university. The board wondered if the proper line of authority was through the president or the chairman of the board. They speculated that "in time there should be some clarification."[1] This issue came up again in 1967 when the provincial, Father Darby, asked the archbishop to give him the report of the archbishop's fact-finding commission as provincial, not as chairman of the board. Darby wanted the report to be given to the Marianists, not to the University of Dayton. Why? Because by doing what Darby requested, the archbishop would not appear to be exercising ecclesiastical authority over the university.

The board of trustees was concerned about what to do about the Philosophy Department. At their March 15, 1965, meeting they discussed the deteriorating situation in the department. Their understanding was that philosophy at Georgetown University was "invaluable." They discussed possibilities to improve the situation at the University of Dayton: rewrite the courses listed in the catalog; bring in a visiting professor from Georgetown for a semester; provide better training for well-qualified faculty members; hire someone to be head of the department; and finally, "Hope for the better is based on John Nichols, SM, at Louvain to come to UD."[2]

Father Roesch's all-Marianist administrative council was also concerned about the growing controversy. In spring 1966, they interpreted the unrest in the Philosophy Department to be a "clash between old and

1. Board of trustees, minutes, December 4, 1963, board of trustees minutes, January 19, 1963–Nov 4, 1970, series 2BA (1), box 2, folder 5, AUD.

2. Board of trustees, minutes, March 15, 1965, board of trustee's minutes, January 19, 1963–Nov 4, 1970, series 2BA (1), box 2, folder 5, AUD.

new ideas." They were aware of Father Francis Langhirt's letter to the archbishop that went "so far as to accuse certain department members of heresy." After discussing the issue, the records of the meeting state that the council believes that "academic freedom and search for truth must be allowed and does not feel that the Administration should place specific regulations or limitation on the members of the Philosophy Department."

The conversation continued at the June 2, 1966, administrative council meeting when someone reported that some faculty members at St. John's University contributed to the cause of the dismissed individuals, seemingly implying that some UD faculty members could make the case against other UD faculty members.

The June 16, 1966, meeting minutes indicate a difference of opinion between the board of trustees and the administrative council. The council had received a memo from the board of trustees pointing out that the University of Dayton is an apostolic mission. The board believed the university had a "quasi-contract with Catholic parents to strengthen the faith of their children."[3] The board had compared Dayton's official statements on academic freedom to the American Association of University Professors (AAUP) statement published in autumn 1965. They concluded that the AAUP statement did not apply to members of the Society of Mary because under their vow of obedience, they are obliged, "within the realm of truth, to direct their teaching toward the fulfillment of an apostolic mission as determined by others." The same applied to lay faculty "based on shared willingness to cooperate with the purposes of the Marianists."[4] After discussion, the administrative council indicated there are "limitations within the framework of the University's goals." The question was how to express those limitations, both general and specific, given that, in teaching, there is a difference between imparting truth and pursuing truth.

3. Board of trustees, memo 65–33, June 16, 1966, 3, administrative council minutes, 1965–1966, series 87-3, box 3, AUD.
4. Board of trustees, memo 65–33, 4.

On the same day that Dennis Bonnette wrote his accusatory letter to Archbishop Karl J. Alter, he sent a second letter to the archbishop and included his document "Some Principles Relating to Theology and Philosophy at the University of Dayton." He informed the archbishop that, three weeks previously, on September 26, 1966, he had sent the document to every member of the Philosophy and Theological Studies departments, to the academic council members, to the members of the general education committee, to the provost, to the president, and to the provincial. No one responded, either verbally or in writing. Bonnette could not believe this was the case because, in the document's final paragraph, he pointed out that, given the way philosophy was being taught at the University of Dayton, "we ought to be logically consistent and cease to refer to the University of Dayton as a 'Catholic' university." Bonnette thought if his statement was correct, something should be done about it; if it was wrong, he should be reprimanded or fired for "making such a wild allegation." Instead, nothing happened—to him a "sign of that theological 'indifferentism' against which Cardinal Ottaviani has warned."[5]

Roesch's personal chronology about the controversy indicates that he prepared a response to Bonnette's principles in a letter addressed to Bonnette with copies to the provost, dean, and chair of Philosophy. He never sent the response, however, because the provost, Father Lees, wanted to speak personally with Bonnette. Roesch indicates that he destroyed his response. Evidently, Lee's conversation did not happen in a timely fashion.[6]

Bonnette's next letter to the archbishop, again with a copy to the apostolic delegate, is dated December 1, 1966, the day Father Roesch told Bonnette and the accused that he intended to clear the accused of the charges. Bonnette wrote to the archbishop, protesting the lack of an investigation on the part of the university and the dismissal of the charges

5. Dennis Bonnette to Karl J. Alter, October 15, 1966, 1, "Controversy 'Academic Freedom': Bonnette, Dennis (Correspondence), 1966–67," Belmont Ave. general files, 1.6 Abp. Alter, AAC.

6. Raymond A. Roesch, "Chronology of the Bonnette Case," n.d., Roesch papers, series 91–35, box 5, AUD.

on "specious technicalities." Bonnette included Roesch's draft press release. In his final paragraph, Bonnette said,

> If the Roman Catholic Church is now too weak to enforce an effective investigation, even in this nationally observed case, then I assure you, Your Excellency, that no sincere Catholic will ever again risk his professional reputation in defense of the Faith.[7]

There is no record of a response on the part of the archbishop.

Bonnette supporter Joseph Dieska also wrote to Archbishop Alter about Roesch's upcoming December press release. He warned the archbishop that "I and several other professors in the Department of Philosophy will publicly protest, and they will demand an ecclesiastical investigation not only of the professors involved but also of the Catholic priests who are members of the Administrative Council of the University of Dayton." Presumably, the "Declaration of Conscience" was the public protest on the part of Dieska.

Six of the Philosophy faculty, including Dennis Bonnette, wrote to the archbishop on January 17, 1967, after the AAUP alleged that the archbishop's investigation "abridges the academic freedom of the University of Dayton Faculty." They wanted to know "whether the Church intends to act in such a manner that those of us who have sought to defend Her will be able to remain with dignity and function without harassment as Catholic professors in a truly Catholic institution." It was about time for them to sign their contracts for next year. They were trying to decide whether to stay at Dayton or seek employment elsewhere. They saw what happened at Webster College (complete secularization of the institution) and wondered if that would happen at the University of Dayton. They thought that it would "harm the University of Dayton's orthodoxy to lose those professors, especially in philosophy, who alone have shown vigor in defending the Faith."[8] The archbishop answered Bonnette, saying that he forwarded the letter to the fact-finding commission.

7. Roesch, "Chronology of the Bonnette Case," 1.

8. Paul Seman et al. to Karl J. Alter, January 17, 1967, 1. Other signers include Dennis Bonnette, Allen Rinderly, Hugo Barbic, Thomas Casaletto, and Joseph Dieska; "Controversy 'Academic Freedom': Bonnette, Dennis (Correspondence), 1966–67," Belmont Ave. general files, 1.6 Abp. Alter, AAC.

Bonnette replied in a handwritten letter on January 25. He understood why Archbishop Alter could not clearly answer their question as to whether they should seek other positions and hoped a clear decision would be forthcoming soon. He enclosed with his letter a newspaper article that showed the passage of the AAUP motion that the archbishop's fact-finding commission interfered with the university's academic freedom. For Bonnette

> The picture is quite complete now: Certain teachers *did* teach contrary to the Magisterium. The Administration either ignored or hid the facts. The faculty forum condemned those who defended the Faith. And now, the only other faculty representative body, the AAUP, has virtually condemned Your Excellency as well.[9]

Nearly a month later, Bonnette sent a three-page typed letter to the archbishop. He had listened to a tape of Father Darby's press conference about the release of the fact-finding commission's report. Bonnette was outraged at Darby's "deliberate misreading" of the report, but Darby's "most appalling statement" was in response to a question from a reporter who asked about John Chrisman, asking if he denied papal infallibility during a campus lecture. Darby did not reply to the reporter's question, but engaged in "doubletalk." Bonnette believed Darby did not "defend true doctrine when called upon to do so in order to avoid public scandal." Bonnette thought Chrisman and Darby were both guilty of heresy.[10]

Bonnette was also concerned about his teaching position. Darby made it clear that "those who feel strongly opposed to his line of thinking about academic freedom in a Catholic university might feel much more comfortable in other circumstances." When reporters asked whether Bonnette's contract would be renewed, Darby said the university does not "intend to renew [his] contract 'on other grounds.'" Bonnette knew that the fact-finding commission "urged the retention by the University of all those who signed the 'Declaration of Conscience,'" so Darby seemingly

9. Dennis Bonnette to Karl J. Alter, January 25, 1967, 1, "Controversy 'Academic Freedom': Bonnette, Dennis (Correspondence), 1966–67."

10. Dennis Bonnette to Karl J. Alter, February 19, 1967, 1–2, "Controversy 'Academic Freedom': Bonnette, Dennis (Correspondence), 1966–67."

was ignoring the commission. In the event that the archbishop wanted to listen to the tape, Bonnette gave a copy of the tape to George Barmann, the local editor of the *Catholic Telegraph*. Copies of the letter went to the apostolic delegate and to auxiliary bishop Edward McCarthy.[11]

Two weeks later, Bonnette sent Bishop McCarthy an excerpt from a fourteen-page document entitled, "Conscience and Contraception," by Basilian father Stanley E. Kutz, that was being distributed on campus to all faculty. Bonnette reported that the student council helped distribute the document, as did the university post office, but he did not know who paid the "rather large bill" for printing. The document implies that the magisterium is a *consensus fidelium*, an agreement (consensus) of the faithful. For Bonnette, this is "theological errancy... being promulgated by the UD administration."[12]

Bonnette's next letter to Bishop McCarthy was written on April 16, 1967. He enclosed a letter he wrote to Father Roesch declining to meet with Roesch to discuss the latter's lecture to the faculty. Bonnette thought the lecture was theologically unsound and indicated "no change in UD's thinking." Bonnette also told the bishop that he had resigned his position at Dayton. He asked for an "unhurried discussion" with McCarthy, along with Joseph Dieska, and the archbishop if available, before he leaves Dayton.[13]

Bishop McCarthy set up the meeting as requested by Bonnette, who was accompanied by Thomas Casaletto. Archbishop Alter was able to attend. Dennis Bonnette remembers the archbishop's dismay that the university's press release about the fact-finding commission report contradicted the archbishop's press release.[14]

Bonnette wrote a follow-up letter to Bishop McCarthy on May 12. From it we learn that the archbishop told Bonnette that he had "no jurisdictional powers over the University." Bonnette later realized that Alter must have meant he had "no positive and direct powers." He surely knew

11. Bonnette to Alter, February 19, 1967, 2–3.

12. Bonnette to Alter, February 19, 1967, 3.

13. Dennis Bonnette to Karl J. Alter, April 16, 1967, 1, "Controversy 'Academic Freedom': Bonnette, Dennis (Correspondence), 1966–67."

14. Dennis Bonnette, interview with the author, April 10, 1997.

he had "canonical negative powers to forbid a person to teach, to excommunicate, and to order out of the diocese."[15]

Bonnette got the impression that the archbishop wanted to "await the more thorough and comprehensive action of the Sacred Congregation for Seminaries and Universities." He, however, urged immediate action even if "by the criteria of ordinary circumstances, [such action] would be termed 'imprudent.'" Bonnette and Casaletto sympathized "with the difficulty attendant upon giving even 'symbolic' indication of His Grace's displeasure with the University of Dayton." They suggested that perhaps the *Catholic Telegraph*, with the archbishop's permission, could "take the wraps off" in an editorial.[16]

The letters to Bishop McCarthy continued into the summer. On June 2, Bonnette told the bishop that Randolph Lumpp was a "frequent visitor at the Holy Family rectory" where he met with Father Fay to discuss the "new-theology" in the absence of the pastor.[17] Bonnette heard from reliable sources that "Father Fay is joining his good friend, Mr. Lawrence Ulrich, on a trip to Toronto where Ulrich plans to marry." Bonnette continued that "one cannot help but wonder whether the influence of UD's 'new-theology' is a concern well beyond the limits of the academic community."[18] Bonnette also enclosed a marked-up article, "Situation Ethics: A Revolt Against Legalism," by John Chrisman, that was published in *Here and Now: A Christian Journal of Opinion*, a Dayton-based "independent enterprise of ecumenically oriented laymen and clergy."[19] Bonnette's markings indicate problems he sees with the article: abortion, contraception, moral relativism, pragmatism, and so on. In conclusion, Bonnette suggests that McCarthy read the book *Trojan Horse in the City of God*, by Dietrich von Hildebrand, "as a suitable 'translation' of Maritain's

15. Dennis Bonnette to Edward McCarthy, May 12, 1967, 1, "Controversy 'Academic Freedom': Bonnette, Dennis (Correspondence), 1966–67."

16. Bonnette to McCarthy, May 12, 1967, 2–3.

17. Randolph Lumpp has no recollection of Father Fay or of being in Holy Family rectory; Randolph Lumpp, email message to the author, October 5, 2017.

18. Dennis Bonnette to Edward McCarthy, June 2, 1967, 1, "Controversy 'Academic Freedom': Bonnette, Dennis (Correspondence), 1966–67."

19. John Chrisman, "Situation Ethics: A Revolt Against Legalism," *Here and Now: A Christian Journal of Opinion* (May 1967). A copy of this article was given to the author by Chrisman.

Les Paysan de la Garonne" because "their analysis of our precarious position is nearly univocal!"[20]

Bonnette also gave the marked-up article to the provost, Father Lees, and to Father Darby, who asked Father Lees to get a response from Chrisman and relay it to Bonnette. According to Lees, Chrisman

> regrets that [Bonnette] preferred to attack what [Bonnette] deem[s] a lack of orthodoxy rather than to address [himself] publicly to the very real problems involved. Mr. Chrisman declares that [Bonnette] realize[s] that the issues he discussed in his article are live issues, being discussed openly in the Christian community. If his article is illogical or un-Christian, Mr. Chrisman thinks a valid criticism would show how or why and that *Here and Now* would presumably welcome such a criticism, and he is certain that he would.[21]

Two weeks later, Bonnette sent Lees an eight-page, single-spaced detailed analysis of Chrisman's article. He asked Lees to forward the analysis to Darby and Chrisman, since Lees seemed to be acting as intermediary.

Bonnette's analysis begins by listing the many ways Chrisman deviates from church teachings: situation ethics, moral relativism, rejection of an objectively right order, pragmatism, rejection of objective norms outside of and independent of man, and "rejection of any morality based upon conformity of one's actions to the will of God."[22] Bonnette then provides a philosophical analysis of Chrisman's situation ethics that he believes is based upon an "irrational metaphysics and faulty epistemology." Chrisman appears to deny truth and applies psychological or physiological criteria to moral problems.

Bonnette devotes the last four pages of his response to the theological errors in Chrisman's treatment of the doctrine of creation. Here, Bon-

20. Dennis Bonnette to McCarthy, June 2, 1967, 1–2. Hildebrand's *The Trojan Horse in the City of God: The Catholic Crisis Explained* (Chicago.: Franciscan Herald Press, 1967) defends traditional Catholicism and points out the harm to the church that is happening because of the 1960s liberalization. Jacque Maritain's book *The Peasant of the Garonne: An Old Man Questions Himself about the Present Time* (New York: Holt, Rinehart and Winston, 1968) criticizes the new philosophy, which he believes is harming the church's spirituality and doctrine.

21. Charles J. Lees to Dennis Bonnette, July 17, 1967, 1, "Controversy 'Academic Freedom': Bonnette, Dennis (Correspondence), 1966–67."

22. Dennis Bonnette to Charles J. Lees, July 31, 1967, 1–3, "Controversy 'Academic Freedom': Bonnette, Dennis (Correspondence), 1966–67."

nette believes Chrisman "stumbles" into heresy when he says that "the world progressively brings itself into being." Bonnette indicates that while he has "always been prepared to explain or debate any of these points either privately or publicly, [his] concern, as is well known long ago transcended the realm of the purely academic." The reason he sent the article to Father Darby is that he has spiritual responsibilities.[23]

Bonnette sent his entire communication with Lees to Archbishop Alter on July 20, 1967. Bonnette said he did the analysis to point out to Father Darby that Darby was wrong when he indicated that "nothing was amiss" at the University of Dayton. Bonnette thought that the Marianist leaders should "prevent and condemn such teaching." He said there were "devout and loyal Catholics" among the Marianists and they oppose these teachings, but that their work is "rendered ineffective because of the suspicion aroused by the core of leaders and would-be leaders which is convinced that secularization is the wave of the future."[24] Bonnette sent a similar communication to Bishop McCarthy on July 31, 1967, so that "a permanent record of this correspondence be entered into ecclesiastical files *outside* the University. There may come a time when it will be relevant to show that the Marianist leaders were informed of these points."[25]

Bonnette sent one more letter to Bishop McCarthy in August. By this time, he had moved to New York to teach at Niagara University. Enclosed was a letter from Father Lees to Bonnette thanking him for speaking to him about Chrisman's situation ethics article. Lees tells Bonnette: "Amen to everything you have affirmed.... I am bewildered how a Christian can affirm what Mr. Chrisman teaches." Bonnette in turn wonders to Bishop McCarthy "where was Father Lees when the Administrative Council, of which he is a member, decided that nothing contrary to faith or morals was being taught?"[26]

Bonnette was not the only person writing to the archbishop and bish-

---

23. Bonnette to Lees, July 31, 1967, 4–7.

24. Dennis Bonnette to Karl J. Alter, July 20, 1967, 1, "Controversy 'Academic Freedom': Bonnette, Dennis (Correspondence), 1966–67."

25. Dennis Bonnette to Edward McCarthy, July 31, 1967, 1, "Controversy 'Academic Freedom': Bonnette, Dennis (Correspondence), 1966–67."

26. Dennis Bonnette to Edward McCarthy, August 24, 1967, 1, "Controversy 'Academic Freedom': Bonnette, Dennis (Correspondence), 1966–67."

op about the controversy. In an undated handwritten note labeled January 1967, Monsignor Tensing, the chair of the archbishop's fact-finding commission, wrote Alter about a unanimous "recommendation" from the commission. The recommendation was unstated, but the letter made the case that Father Stanley was "a source of much of the difficulty" at the University of Dayton. Tensing indicates that the Dayton-area parish priests were the first to give the commission this information, but many facts learned since then support their contention:

- The accused were hired while Stanley was provost.
- Stanley helped the accused.
- Stanley was the academic leader when "trouble first began to develop."
- Stanley was a leader in the recent faculty forum censure.

"Father Lees indicates that within the Administration officers looked to Stanley for philosophical and theological knowledge." There was "no one else to whom they could go for that kind of help."[27]

The archbishop's fact-finding commission did not know how to handle the facts they uncovered; they decided to pass them along to the archbishop. They suggested that perhaps his grace could bring up Stanley's involvement when he spoke with Father Darby.[28] There is no evidence that anything came of this suggestion. Stanley was not removed from his position at the University of Dayton, nor was he removed as a priest in the archdiocese. When he left Dayton in 1967, he took an elected position within the Marianist administration in Rome.

Bonnette's supporters in the Philosophy Department also contacted the archbishop. Father Dombro and Joseph Dieska sent a copy of the November 1966 *American Ecclesiastical Review* column about academic freedom in a Catholic college. They underlined the end of the column:

If a college does not measure up to this standard [that truth is taught by the Catholic Church], it should close its doors. And, it may be added, in

27. Robert M. Tensing to Karl J. Alter, January 1967, "Controversy 'Academic Freedom, etc.,' 1966–67," Belmont Ave. general files, 1.6 Abp. Alter, ACC.
28. Tensing to Alter, January 1967, 2.

these days when so many false notions are widespread, those who administer any Catholic school or college or university have a strict obligation in conscience to see that the teaching of the institution is fully in conformity with the teaching of the Catholic Church.[29]

Also in November 1966, while the university was conducting its own investigation, Dr. Dieska sent the archbishop a four-page letter that he had sent to Dr. Xavier Monasterio, his colleague in the Philosophy Department. Dieska's letter was a response to Monasterio's twelve-page paper, recently discussed in the department, on Monasterio's views on faith and philosophy in the university. Monasterio, a devout Catholic, held that it was not possible to do philosophy properly without having freedom to proceed rationally. He argued that philosophy had to be an autonomous discipline, just as mathematics and chemistry were autonomous disciplines.[30] Dieska found Monasterio's position "absolutely untenable" and quoted sources from the Second Vatican Council, other philosophers, Karl Rahner, and the Code of Canon Law to support his position that Catholic philosophy cannot be separated from religious faith.[31]

Dieska also sent the archbishop a four-page undated paper, "The Impact of Teilhard de Chardin upon Contemporary Philosophy and Theology." The paper appears to be based on Dieska's Spring 1966 *University of Dayton Review* article "Teilhard De Chardin or Thomas Aquinas?," which was also published in the March 1967 issue of *Social Justice Review*. Dieska points out the flaws in Teilhard's philosophical and theological thinking, his deviations from church dogmas, and his negative influence on the Catholic faith. In particular, Dieska holds Teilhard "responsible for a group of Catholic writers who refuse to submit their personal views on philosophical and theological questions to the teaching magisterium." The situation at the University of Dayton in his opinion falls into the latter category.[32]

29. Richard J. Dombro and Joseph L. Dieska, copy of column sent to Archbishop Karl J. Alter, "Controversy 'Academic Freedom, etc.,' 1966–67."

30. Xavier O. Monasterio, mimeographed paper, "Faith and Philosophy in the University," n.d. Copy of the paper given to the author by Monasterio.

31. Joseph L. Dieska to Xavier O. Monasterio, November 24, 1966, "Controversy 'Academic Freedom, etc.,' 1966–67."

32. Joseph L. Dieska, "The Impact of Teilhard de Chardin upon Contemporary Philosophy and Theology," n.d., 4, "Controversy 'Academic Freedom, etc.,' 1966–67."

Bonnette supporters Paul Seman and Thomas Casaletto reported to the archbishop on Father Roesch's March address to the faculty. Seman did so through a telephone call with Monsignor Sherman, who typed a report and sent it by mail to the archbishop. The key points for Seman were that Father Roesch quoted Gregory Baum saying that the universal magisterium must be interpreted with form criticism, that the men charged were not guilty because the magisterium is in doubt, and that the archbishop "tacitly admitted he had no jurisdiction over the University."[33] Casaletto sent a handwritten a two-page letter to Monsignor Sherman that was forwarded to the archbishop. He itemized thirteen points from the lecture, all reported accurately. Both Seman and Casaletto reported on the standing ovation that Roesch received, describing it as "thunderous" and "tremendous."[34]

Father Arnold F. Witzman, the founding pastor of the Church of the Ascension in suburban Kettering, Ohio, wrote to Father Roesch, with a copy to the archbishop, shortly after Roesch exonerated the accused in December. Witzman expressed his disappointment in Roesch's settlement of the dispute. He had talked to numerous people about the controversy and indicated that, due to the pastoral issues, it is "not a matter that concerns the University alone."

> The very fundamental issue is whether the University and its faculty are presenting the teaching of the church in such a way that our Catholic people can rely and trust it. One can quickly gather from students that very often the teaching of the Church is ignored, sometimes ridiculed, and at other times put in such a bad light that it is rejected by thinking people.[35]

Five Dayton pastors (Father James L. Krusling from St. Helen Church; Monsignor James E. Sherman from Our Lady of Immaculate Conception Church; Father Ernest Lucas, CPPS from St. Adalbert Polish Church; Father Titas Narbutas from Holy Cross Lithuanian Church; and Father

33. James E. Sherman, report of telephone conversation with Paul Seman, March 1, 1967, "Controversy 'Academic Freedom, etc.,' 1966–67."

34. Thomas Casaletto to James E. Sherman, March 1, 1967, "Controversy 'Academic Freedom, etc.,' 1966–67."

35. Arnold F. Witzman to Raymond A. Roesch, December 12, 1966, "Controversy 'Academic Freedom, etc.,' 1966–67."

Robert J. Lux, CPPS, from St. Joseph Church) wrote to Father Darby on February 23, 1967, and sent a copy to the archbishop. They began by stating that they knew the decision of the commission—that certain members of the University of Dayton faculty taught errors contrary to the magisterium—and that "the difficulty extends further into the University Community." They had hoped Father Darby would do all he could to rectify this situation and were saddened when he did not do so in his press release.[36]

The priests thought that the University of Dayton, under Darby's leadership, "should publicly, with humility, accept this decision, and with due submission to the rightful authority of the Church, implement it at once. Immediate assurance should be given to the anxious Catholic everywhere that this will be done. The good of souls requires it."[37]

The pastors agreed with the idea of the ad hoc committee but disagreed with the appointment of William Doane Kelly, who has "recently shown [by his lecture] his inability to qualify as a useful member" of the commission. They also thought that membership qualifications should state that the members be Catholic and well trained in Catholic philosophy and theology. They suggested that some members of the committee be chosen from outside the university community.[38]

The pastors asked Darby to consider the objectives of the university as stated in the faculty handbook and the official bulletin, that "the University is committed to 'the upholding of the true deposit of Faith and Christian morality.'" They considered this statement to be a "truly contractual agreement with each student and/or his parents, should the student be a minor."[39]

They pointed out that Pope Paul VI had designated "A Year of Faith" to "combat the errors of faith in our times" and suggested that the University of Dayton "launch a program of renewal in the Faith." The program should include "lectures, seminars, retreats, credit-hour courses, all

---

36. James L. Krusling et al. to James M. Darby, February 23, 1967, 1, "Controversy 'Academic Freedom, etc.,' 1966–67."

37. Krusling et al. to Darby, February 23, 1967.

38. Krusling et al. to Darby, February 23, 1967.

39. Krusling et al. to Darby, February 23, 1967, 2.

dealing with this most vital topic of our times.... Only the most qualified instructors or teachers should be called upon."[40]

It was evident the pastors knew what was happening on campus because at the end of their letter, they asked Darby to refute John Chrisman's statement, reported in the *Flyer News*, that "the Pope's infallible pronouncements are true only in the situation in which they are taught, and not necessarily so in every future situation."[41]

Darby did not reply to the pastors but wrote to the archbishop, complaining that the priests had not come to him first before going to the archbishop. There were inaccuracies in the letter—namely, the report of Chrisman's comment—but "no one, it seems, need check out anything directly with a person *before* he preaches from the altar or writes so surely on this subject."[42] There is no evidence that the archbishop responded.

Monsignor Sherman wrote frequently to Bishop Edward McCarthy throughout the controversy. In mid-December, he recommended that the archbishop not approve the university's ad hoc committee because Father Stanley was named a member of the committee. "It was when Fr. Stanley was Provost that all these accused teachers were imported, and he will do all he can to continue their work."[43] Sherman enclosed seven proposed guidelines that he felt the archbishop should "impose" on the university. The guidelines are worth exploring because they show how far Monsignor Sherman was willing to go to control the situation at the University of Dayton.

1. Philosophy and theology shall be taught according to the teachings of St. Thomas. Further amplification of the principles of Thomas are encouraged as long as there is no violation of the Ordinary Magisterium of the Church.
2. Every teacher of philosophy or theology "shall be cognizant of the Ordinary Magisterium of the Church."

40. Krusling et al. to Darby, February 23, 1967.
41. Krusling et al. to Darby, February 23, 1967.
42. James M. Darby to Karl J. Alter, February 28, 1967, "Controversy 'Academic Freedom, etc.,' 1966–67."
43. James E. Sherman to Edward A. McCarthy, December 14, 1967, "Controversy 'Academic Freedom, etc.,' 1966–67."

3. Any student may contest the teaching of a professor, or any attendant at a lecture may contest the teaching of a lecturer, where there is question of a violation of the Ordinary Magisterium. The professor in question must then defend his stand and prove conclusively that the Magisterium was not violated. The burden of proof shall be on the professor or lecturer. If the professor/lecturer does not make a correction within five days, "a public announcement of a correction shall be made by the University president."

4. A faculty member who has been charged on three occasions and found guilty by the Provost shall "automatically be relieved of his office."

5. When false systems of philosophy or theology are explained in classes or lectures, the lecturer or professor must also "uncover the errors of such false systems." Failing this, it will be presumed that the professor/lecturer is "guilty of espousing such errors."

6. When for ecumenical reasons, or for the sake of the better understanding of the views of another religion, or false philosophical system, a lecturer versed in such shall be invited to speak at the University, there shall be no charge made against him since the student will know beforehand that the views do not conform to the Church's views.

7. Catholic philosophy or theology shall be taught only by those possessed of degrees in philosophy or theology respectively, issued by a Catholic university. Professors of social sciences must have taken at least one year of training in Catholic philosophy and theology in a Catholic university, in order that they may know the basic elements of the Catholic viewpoint on moral questions related to social sciences.[44]

Clearly, orthodoxy is important to Monsignor Sherman. His requirements for teaching philosophy and theology are more restrictive than they were for most Catholic universities prior to the sixties. He also does not grant faculty protection of their positions and academic freedom. He appears to view the university as a seminary that the archbishop can control.

On January 10, Monsignor Sherman wrote to Bishop McCarthy to report that "it is pretty well known here that Father Thomas Stanley, for-

44. James E. Sherman, "Proposed Guidelines for Teaching at U.D.," "Controversy 'Academic Freedom, etc.,' 1966–67."

merly Provost, master-minded the whole problem that now exists at UD." Sherman had information that Bishop James E. McManus, the former bishop of Ponce, Puerto Rico, "ordered [Stanley] out of his diocese... when he, after many conflicts, countermanded orders which the bishop had given." Sherman suggested that McCarthy write to McManus to get "information and guidance" and provided McManus's current address in New York City. Sherman continued, "We priests feel that the only way to clean up the University is to remove him from the diocese completely." A postscript was added at the bottom of the letter: "Clippings enclosed. The false doctrines continue to be taught."[45] There is no evidence that McCarthy wrote McManus to inquire about Father Stanley's service in Puerto Rico, and, as mentioned previously, Stanley was not removed from the Archdiocese of Cincinnati. There is also no evidence in his Society of Mary personnel file to support Sherman's accusation that Stanley was removed from the diocese of Ponce in Puerto Rico.

Around the same time, James Miller, a University of Dayton alum from Dayton, then a graduate student in philosophy at the University of Ottawa in Canada, wrote to Archbishop Alter with observations about Father Stanley, Eulalio Baltazar, and Edward Harkenrider. Miller had read the media coverage and wanted Alter to know that Harkenrider was a fair and just professor who encouraged investigations of all modern philosophical positions. "His methodology is that of a true scholar not that of sarcasm and ridicule which Dr. Baltazar so adequately displays." He continued, "If Harkenrider leaves UD over these events it will be a disgrace to the faculty."[46] Miller also indicated that he had already written to Monsignor Tensing, the chair of the archbishop's fact-finding commission, about Baltazar. The timing of Miller's letter and his mention of Tensing indicates that he talked to one or more of the involved professors or administrators, since Miller knew about the commission before it was reported by the Dayton newspapers.[47]

45. James E. Sherman to Edward A. McCarthy, January 10, 1967, "Controversy 'Academic Freedom, etc.,' 1966–67."
46. James Miller to Karl J. Alter, January 1, 1967, 2, "Controversy 'Academic Freedom, etc.,' 1966–67."
47. Miller to Alter, January 1, 1967, 3.

We have seen that Marianist fathers John Elbert, Richard Dombro, and Francis Langhirt were on the side of the conservatives in the Philosophy Department. Marianist brother Edmund R. Schmid, a manager in the university's food service department, wrote Archbishop Alter in February 1967. He expressed his "sincere sorrow for all of the indignities and outrages committed against [the archbishop] this past year at the University of Dayton." Schmid assured the archbishop that the sentiments expressed by the various professors are "not shared by me, nor by my fellow Brothers." They hold their "heads in shame, and beg of your Grace forgiveness." Schmid prayed daily for the archbishop, hoping that the Blessed Mother "will guide and protect [the archbishop] during these trying times."[48]

In general, Archbishop Karl J. Alter's actions showed restraint. He investigated the situation in response to appeals from the Thomists and the local pastors. The findings of the investigation supported the university's solution—that is, the creation of the ad hoc committee—and purposely indicated that no faculty dismissals were recommended. From the perspective of the university, it could not have gone much better once the appeals were made to the archbishop.

On the other hand, it could have gone much worse for the university. In a letter to Father Paul-Joseph Hoffer, the Marianist superior general in Rome, Father Darby indicated that the archbishop

> threatened [the university] with the appointment by His Grace of *outside* authorities for theology and philosophy—to be put in charge of the departments on campus, at least as arbitrators representing the voice of the Church. This recommendation...was dropped because [Fathers Darby and Roesch] assured the Archbishop we could strengthen the departments *ourselves*. [The archbishop] let us keep our autonomy unencumbered.[49]

Presumably, the archbishop could not have made these faculty appointments without the cooperation of Father Roesch and the provost, Father Lees, who was responsible for faculty hiring and the appointment of

48. Edmund R. Schmid to Karl J. Alter, February 7, 1967, "Controversy 'Academic Freedom, etc.,' 1966–67."

49. James M. Darby to Paul-Joseph Hoffer, January 16, 1968, 2, AGMAR, cat. 4B10, doc. 6.2.

chairpersons. Given Father Roesch's lecture to the faculty, it is hard to imagine that Roesch would have cooperated. Allowing such an action on the part of the archbishop went against the way Roesch intended to take the university. Such an action, if known by the faculty and the wider academic community, would have been severely criticized by the rest of American Catholic higher education.

THE APOSTOLIC DELEGATE

The controversy exploded when Dennis Bonnette sent a carbon copy of his letter to Archbishop Karl J. Alter to Egidio Vagnozzi, the apostolic delegate, in Washington, D.C. While this is public knowledge, what has not been made public is the extent to which the apostolic delegate was involved in the controversy.

The carbon copy was not Dennis Bonnette's first communication with the apostolic delegate. As shown in chapter 3, Bonnette wrote Vagnozzi on September 12, 1966, asking the delegate to forward a letter to Cardinal Pizzardo, prefect of the Sacred Congregation of Seminaries and Universities, requesting guidelines for the academic council in dealing with the controversy in the Philosophy Department. There is no record of a response from Pizzardo.

Vagnozzi responded to the carbon copy of the accusal letter to the archbishop. He acknowledged the letter and the copy of the "specific charges concerning deviation from Catholic doctrine at the University of Dayton." He indicated that he will be "interested to learn the outcome of this latest action you have undertaken." Obviously, Vagnozzi was aware of other actions taken by Bonnette and his supporters.

On January 17, 1967, Dennis Bonnette sent a letter and photocopies to Vagnozzi—probably the January 17 *Dayton Daily News* article in which Eulalio Baltazar questioned the competency of the members of the archbishop's fact-finding commission. Vagnozzi replied almost immediately, thanking Bonnette for informing him of "recent developments" at the University of Dayton. Vagnozzi said he continued to "take serious interest in these events and [he looks] forward to having a copy of the findings of the board whose investigations concluded on January 17th."[50] Obviously, Vagnozzi was up to date on the happenings at Dayton.

On January 25, Bonnette sent a letter to Vagnozzi about the actions of the American Association of University Professors chapter at the University. Vagnozzi's quick response indicated that he could not make a "complete evaluation" of the situation until he received the final report from Archbishop Alter. He told Bonnette, "You may be sure of my hopeful prayers that the University will be able to maintain an atmosphere of freedom consonant with the teaching of the Church."[51]

Two days later, Bonnette sent a letter to Pope Paul VI about the situation. No copy of the letter exists. The Vatican secretariat of state asked the apostolic delegate to acknowledge the letter. Vagnozzi said that "the entire matter is under study by the Holy See. Therefore, you may be sure that the recent situation at the University of Dayton will be given a very careful review."[52]

Bonnette sent additional materials, presumably the *Dayton Daily News* story about William Doane Kelly's controversial campus lecture, to the apostolic delegate on February 3, 1967. On March 7, Bonnette sent Vagnozzi the circular by Basilian father Stanley E. Kutz that was being distributed on campus concerning the magisterium as a *consensus fidelium*, the faith of the faithful. The delegate encouraged Bonnette, saying, "The information you continue to provide is most helpful."[53]

Dennis Bonnette's next letter to Vagnozzi was very personal. He sought advice as to whether he should sign the teaching contract for the next academic year offered by the University of Dayton. Vagnozzi replied in a letter marked "Personal and Confidential" and counseled Bonnette to overcome his reluctance and remain at Dayton, confident that the situation will come under control. He prayed that "future action will bring peace to the University and to you personally."[54]

50. Egidio Vagnozzi to Dennis Bonnette, January 20, 1967, 1.
51. Vagnozzi to Bonnette, January 28, 1967, 1.
52. Vagnozzi to Bonnette, February 25, 1967, 1.
53. Vagnozzi to Bonnette, March 11, 1967, 1.
54. Vagnozzi to Bonnette, March 18, 1967, 1. Permission has been given by Apostolic Nuncio Archbishop Christophe Pierre to publish the contents of the letter; email from Dennis Bonnette to the author, September 2, 2017.

The correspondence to the apostolic delegate continued on March 23, when Bonnette told Vagnozzi about Bishop Fulton Sheen's invitation to Eulalio Baltazar to teach in his seminary. Vagnozzi appreciated Bonnette letting him know what was going on, but, of course, he could not "interfere with a decision that may have been made by His Excellency, Bishop Sheen."[55]

Bonnette's next letter to Vagnozzi informed him that he was leaving the University of Dayton. Vagnozzi "had sincerely hoped that it would be possible for [Bonnette] to remain at the University and by [his] teaching to give a fruitful dimension to its educative process."[56]

The final letter Bonnette sent to Vagnozzi reported on his and Tom Casaletto's meeting with Archbishop Alter and Bishop McCarthy. Vagnozzi replied that he could not "take any action except as directed by the Holy See."[57]

From his new position at Niagara University, Bonnette wrote two final letters to the apostolic delegate in the fall of 1967. By this time, Vagnozzi had returned to Rome, and the new apostolic delegate was Luigi Raimondi. The responses from the delegate were acknowledgments of receipt of the letters, sent by secretaries. Seemingly, the new delegate did not want to have the same relationship with Bonnette as did Vagnozzi.

Bonnette was not the only person at the University of Dayton communicating with the apostolic delegate. Father James M. Darby knew the apostolic delegate from Darby's service as president of the Conference of Major Superiors of Men (CMSM) from 1962 to 1967. Darby wrote to Vagnozzi on February 27 after the archbishop's fact-finding commission report was released. He told Vagnozzi:

> The Provosts have been in touch throughout with the various principals and were satisfied that, although they could not resolve the matter and placate both sides, they were assured that there was no compromise with our position as a Catholic university.[58]

55. Vagnozzi to Bonnette, March 28, 1967, 1.
56. Vagnozzi to Bonnette, April 21, 1967, 1.
57. Vagnozzi to Bonnette, May 25, 1967, 1.
58. James M. Darby to Egidio Vagnozzi, February 27, 1967, ASM(CIN), "Statements," University of Dayton Theology [*sic*] Controversy, 1967.

Darby corresponded with the apostolic delegate again in March and May in response to Vagnozzi's request for documents. In March, Vagnozzi asked for three copies of the transcription of Father Neil McCluskey's address on campus, and, in May, he requested three copies of Father Roesch's statement to the faculty.

In a January 1968 letter to the Marianist superior general, Father Paul-Joseph Hoffer, Darby indicates that he had "frequent meetings" with the apostolic delegate and that neither Father Roesch nor Archbishop Alter knew of the meetings. Darby believed the apostolic delegate was on the side of the university.[59] Hoffer, in a confidential letter to Darby, indicated his understanding of the situation: Darby told him the delegate "was on [Darby's] side, that means on the side of the accused."[60]

In the controversy at the University of Dayton, both sides—Dennis Bonnette and Father Darby—communicated with the delegate, trying to convince him that their side was correct. Egidio Vagnozzi, diplomat that he was, let both of them think he was on their side.

THE VATICAN

Previously, we saw that Dennis Bonnette wrote to the pope and the Sacred Congregation for Seminaries and Universities and expected that Rome would ultimately make a ruling on the Dayton controversy. In mid-February 1967, Father James Darby received a handwritten letter from Marianist father Pierre Humbertclaude, secretary for the Vatican Secretariat for Non-Christians.[61] Humbertclaude wrote that the "former Holy Office" asked about the controversy at the University of Dayton. They asked for the "facts necessary to give an opinion of the responsi-

---

59. James M. Darby to Paul J. Hoffer, January 16, 1968, 1.
60. Paul J. Hoffer to James M. Darby, January 10, 1968, AGMAR, cat. 4B10, doc. 5.
61. During World War II, Father Pierre Humbertclaude, served in Japan under the apostolic delegate to Japan, Archbishop Paolo Marella. Marella and Humbertclaude got the names and home addresses from POWs and wrote letters to their relatives in the U.S., Great Britain, Australia, New Zealand, and the Netherlands. By the end of the war, the apostolic delegate's files on the POWs contained 200,000 entries. Humbertclaude is the author of *Little Cultural Guide for the Use of the Missionary* (Tokyo: 1948); *Current Biography Yearbook 1964*, (U.S.A.: H. W. Wilson, 1964), printed copy of text accessed September 6, 2003.

bility or not of the accused, on the [motives][62] of the accusation, on the findings of the campus forum, of the archbishop's committee and of the investigation on the part of the Society of Mary as such."[63] Humbertclaude included a copy of a typed note in Italian on plain paper with the designation "Rome, February 6, 1967." The translated note reads:

> The Congregation of the Doctrine of the Faith has become involved in the case of Professor Bonnette, an instructor at Dayton University.
>
> The case was submitted to a preliminary investigation last November, the results of which were not satisfactory but that, in the main, revealed real inadequacies in the teaching of some instructors of the university (as per the accusations of Bonnette).
>
> A second investigation is underway. While this is going on, the Cong. Part. of Saturday 4 February 1967 has decided that the major superiors of the Marianists (Society of Mary), to which the aforementioned university belongs, be heard. It was also decided that His Eminence Marella[64] would enter into contact with Father Humbertclaude, requesting him to agree to provide all the information useful and necessary to elucidate the case.[65]

Humbertclaude concludes his letter by pointing out that "it was a gesture of friendship from the Holy Office to inquire thru Cardinal Marella and myself." In other words, the Holy Office—whose name was changed in 1965 to the Congregation for the Doctrine of the Faith (CDF)—was dis-

---

62. Humbertclaude's handwriting at this point is difficult to decipher. The word appears to be "mobiles."

63. Pierre Humbertclaude to James M. Darby, February 9, 1967, ASM(CIN), "Statements," University of Dayton Theology [sic] Controversy, 1967.

64. Paolo Cardinal Marella was the Cardinal Praeses of the Secretariat for Non-Christians. Marella was born in 1895 in Rome and died in October 1984. Pope John Paul II preached the homily at his funeral. Marella's appointments prior to the Secretariat included apostolic delegate to Japan, nuncio to France, and archpriest of St. Peter's Basilica. Marella presented the anti-Communist schema/draft to the Central Preparatory Commission for the Second Vatican Council. On the eve of the third session of the Council, he was one of twenty cardinals who signed a document attacking collegiality. His appointment to the Secretariat as its first president was not controversial, since he dealt with Shintoism and Buddhism while he was in Japan. He was already a curial conservative and therefore acceptable to the other members of the curia. Later, his lack of knowledge about the Muslim faith became problematic, as did the Secretariat's inactivity. In 1973, he was replaced in the Secretariat; Peter Hebblethwaite, *Paul VI: The First Modern Pope* (New York: Paulist Press, 1993), 276.

65. Humbertclaude, enclosure in envelope with letter to Darby; translation from Italian to English by Brother John of Taizé. A previous translation was provided to the author by Andria Chiodo.

creetly inquiring into the controversy. Rather than make a formal request to the Marianists, the CDF approached them through Father Humbert-claude and the cardinal for whom he worked.

Darby's response took nearly five single-spaced pages plus attachments. In general, Darby's letter was a chronology of the controversy. The attachments were Bonnette's October 15, 1966, accusation letter to the archbishop, Roesch's letter to the canonist, the canonist's response to Roesch, Eulalio Baltazar's position paper, Roesch's November 29, 1966, letter to Darby discussing the build-up of the controversy over several years and the involvement of the provosts,[66] and Darby's statement to the press after the fact-finding commission report was released.[67] There is no indication that Darby sent the archbishop's fact-finding commission's report.

Early in the letter, Darby states that the "accused denied the validity of the charges." He describes the four charged as "not heretical, not teaching and advocating anti-Catholic doctrine." Later, Darby indicates why no witnesses were called: "All charges in themselves were admitted by the accused.... [there was] no heresy, no deliberate intent to mislead."[68] In other words, the accused admit to saying what they were accused of saying, but they did not intend to mislead others. Therefore, in the eyes of the administration, they are not guilty of teaching and advocating "anti-Catholic" doctrine. However, the accused now see the "possibility of pedagogical indiscretions." Darby states that, according to Roesch, "stronger insistence was needed at the University to guarantee greater reverence for the Magisterium and a clearer presentation of its place and function." The solution to the latter problem is the formation of the ad hoc committee.[69]

After describing the whitewash accusation, the "Declaration of Conscience," and the faculty forum censure, Darby reported on Bonnette's use of the press and on Harkenrider's resignation from the faculty. Darby believes Harkenrider's resignation makes Bonnette "look very good." Darby recognizes that Harkenrider and Bonnette are

---

66. The author has been unable to locate this letter.
67. James M. Darby to Pierre Humbertclaude, February 1967, ASM(CIN), "Statements," University of Dayton Theology Controversy, 1967. No copy of Roesch's November 29, 1966, letter has been located in the University of Dayton Archives or the Society of Mary Archives.
68. Darby to Humbertclaude, February 1967.
69. Darby to Humbertclaude, February 1967.

devoted teachers but [they] are not comfortable amidst the tensions every-where present today and especially on the university campus. They definite-ly have a role to play but tend to frustrate their effectiveness by wanting everything letter-perfect, at once and all the time. The give-and-take of com-plex and real-life situations is too great a strain on them.[70]

Darby explains the formal entry of the archbishop into the investi-gation as "the Law demanded [the archbishop] respond to the appeal" of the faculty in their "Declaration of Conscience" and of the "various representatives from the Catholic community of Dayton," those unnamed representatives being the local Dayton pastors.

Darby states that the commission report "focuses on the relation-ship... between the four accused professors and the Magisterium of the Church." He made four points, three summarized in a more positive light than the wording used by the archbishop's commission as shown:

Darby	*Archbishop's Commission*
Magisterium is "offended but not in matters *de fide* (of faith)."	Teachings occurred which were "opposed to the teaching of the Magisterium" but "may not have been contrary to defined doctrines."
"Magisterium is mentioned without due respect."	"Lack of respect for the Magisterium."
"Magisterium is not always defined clearly enough."	Tendency to reduce the "Magisterium of the teaching Church to a mere consensus of individuals each teaching primarily in the light of his own insights."
"Pastoral effects of professor's presentations were not good enough."	This controversy is "more than a dispute between individuals"; "the difficulty extends further into the University community."

70. James M. Darby, notes, n.d., ASM(CIN), "History of U of D Heresy," 1967, D33, Day.

Darby's fourth point is the most troublesome. The commission report does not use the word "pastoral." The wording that is closest to the word "pastoral" is a reminder that the University of Dayton is an undergraduate institution. Darby's fourth point also eliminates the implication of wrongdoing on the part of those administering the university.

Previously, we saw that Darby's press release, after the archdiocese released the commission's report, caused a stir. Darby relayed to Humbertclaude that, in his press release, which he attached to the letter, he stressed the similarities between Roesch's letter following the university's investigation and the commission's report: (1) no finding of heresy, (2) corrective action needed although Father Roesch did not address it publicly, and (3) the ad hoc committee is a "sound, workable first step." Again, there is no indication that Darby included the commission's report in his letter to Humbertclaude.

Darby told Humbertclaude that, "as specifically recommended by the Archbishop's Commission.... [there will be] no dismissals." The archbishop's commission, however, used the following wording: "In view of certain presuppositions,... the commission has made no suggestions with respect to the dismissal of any professors involved in the investigation." The commission wanted it known that they did not call for the dismissal of any of the professors. Darby, however, turned their statement into a "recommendation" that no one be dismissed.

Darby indicated that "if [the commission] has a weakness," it is in drawing "too fine a distinction between the experts (theologians and philosophers) who may discuss and explore and what goes on perforce in these times in course-discussions on a largely undergraduate campus." He explains that American Catholic college students are exposed to a number of modern intellectuals by just reading the Catholic press.[71] It is "unrealistic to think that the subject matter in theology can somehow be simplified to exclude modern problems and modern writers. The University tries to guide the students through all this turmoil."

Darby recognizes that the controversy occurred because the two sides

71. Darby, notes, n.d. Darby lists Bishop Simonds, Charles Davis, Michael Novak, Karl Rahner, Cardinal Suenens, Father Nogar, Archbishop Roberts, Father Schillebeeckx, Father Häring, and Leslie Dewart.

could not come together. He tells Humbertclaude that the university is inviting "experts" and "scheduling closed seminar-type lecture discussions for faculty only on current theological matters embraced by the Magisterium and on philosophical matters that undergird the teaching of the Church." Darby hopes that these discussions will "serve as a bridge between the arch-conservatives and the progressives."[72] He continues, "Both groups, meanwhile, declare that they are 100% *in* the Church and they often meet in the same time for Holy Communion."

Darby concludes with comments on the press coverage—namely, "the coverage has been more provocative than informative." He relays that the archbishop was "deeply grieved over the manner in which the Dayton press covered this subject and a number of other subjects of special interest to the Church in recent years," the implication being that the press is responsible for Alter's "grief," rather than the actions or events being reported. Darby is confident that "sound steps are being taken to strengthen the two departments internally and to effect genuine and fructifying dialogue among the members of the two departments." These challenges are being faced on "every Catholic campus throughout the world."[73]

Father Humbertclaude responded to Darby on April 2, 1967. After thanking Darby for the report, Humbertclaude relayed that he helped Cardinal Marella make a report on it. With the continuing press coverage, however, Humbertclaude needed additional materials: (1) Darby's "press-conference on the decision of the archbishop's committee,"[74] (2) Father Roesch's talk to the faculty, and (3) Jesuit Neil McCluskey's speech sponsored by the ad hoc committee. Humbertclaude concludes with, "Let us pray and hope for a courageous and clean settlement of that [*sic*] question."[75]

---

72. There is no record that these discussions occurred. Bonnette, Chrisman, and Ulrich do not recall any such meetings. Perhaps the university administration did not see a need for the meetings once Bonnette left the faculty in summer 1967; Bonnette and Ulrich, emails to the author, September 7, 2003; Chrisman, email to the author, September 10, 2003.

73. Darby to Humbertclaude, February 1967.

74. Darby indicated that he attached his press release to the first letter to Humbertclaude, but since Humbertclaude asked for it in his second letter, it must not have been included in the first letter.

75. Pierre Humbertclaude to James M. Darby, April 2, 1967, ASM(CIN), "Statements," University of Dayton Theology [*sic*] Controversy, 1967.

Darby responded on April 17, 1967. He enclosed the three items requested, along with the *Ave Maria* article, Darby's "Letter to the Editor"
objecting to the *Ave Maria* article, and Darby's *America* article written at
the request of the editor (to be discussed in chapter 10). Regarding his
press release, Darby states that "the secular newspaper used a headline
that was a half-truth,[76] and a member of the archbishop's fact-finding
commission reacted to this headline by saying my position was an "unfortunate and wrong interpretation." Darby says the "commission member
should have called me" to see if the press coverage was accurate.[77] Darby
also pointed out that Father McCluskey does not represent the University
of Dayton position.

There is no record of further correspondence from Humbertclaude,
so, presumably, Humbertclaude passed the requested documents to Cardinal Marella, who passed them on to the CDF. There is also no evidence
that anything came of the report to the CDF: no response from the congregation to Darby, no correspondence to Bonnette that the CDF had
inquired into the case and considered it closed, no correspondence between the CDF and the archbishop, or any such action. The inquiry ended quietly, although it must have given Darby and Roesch some anxious
moments.

Several observations can be made about this exchange between the
Congregation for the Doctrine of the Faith and the Marianists. First, the
CDF's inquiry was discreet. A typed note on plain paper was given to a
cardinal to give to a Marianist to send to a Marianist provincial. Some
may consider this an indication of secrecy and "good-ole-boy" tactics operative in the church. On the other hand, the Congregation for the Doctrine of the Faith is the highest-ranking office in the church. A formal

---

76. The *Dayton Daily News* headline on the article on the release of the report is "Bishop's
Committee Clears UD Profs in Doctrine Dispute" (February 17, 1967). The next morning's
Dayton Journal Herald headlined their story: "Teaching Ruled Contrary: UD Pledges No Dismissal after Committee Report" (February 18, 1967). The *Dayton Daily News* article begins by
quoting Darby that the commission "clears the accused professors of any charge of heresy."
Although the article directly quotes the commission report that teachings contrary to the magisterium occurred, the headline writer apparently focused on Darby's quote in the opening
paragraph.

77. James M. Darby to Pierre Humbertclaude, April 2, 1967, ASM(CIN), "Statements,"
University of Dayton Theology [*sic*] Controversy, 1967.

inquiry into the controversy would have been out of proportion to the incident. An informal, confidential inquiry was adequate.

Second, the CDF's inquiry was separate from the archbishop's investigation, since it began prior to the completion of the archbishop's investigation. The congregation was aware of the basic facts of the situation prior to approaching the Marianists. We will never know how the CDF became involved, but perhaps Dennis Bonnette's letters to the pope and the Sacred Congregation of Seminaries and Universities were redirected to the CDF, since the issue was teaching contrary to the magisterium.

Third, how widespread was the knowledge that the Vatican was inquiring into the case? Marianist brother John Jansen was a member of the provincial council at the time. In an interview with the author, he indicated that the controversy "got to Rome." Once it got there, Darby wanted to "keep it from going too far"—that is, to keep from getting a "directive from Rome" on how to handle the situation.[78] It appears Darby was successful. The most likely person in the university to know about the Vatican inquiry was Father Roesch. Neither he nor Darby released the information that the Vatican was looking into the controversy, but, in a letter to the Marianist superior general nearly a year after the archbishop's fact-finding commission began its investigation, Roesch indicated that "the repercussions [of the controversy] reached even the Sacred Congregation," so he knew about the inquiries from Rome.

Finally, Darby's report minimizes Bonnette's and the fact-finding commission's emphasis on teachings "contrary to the teaching magisterium of the Church." Instead, Darby focuses on the lack of respect for the magisterium, which is a lesser offense. The statement attributed to Roesch calling for "stronger insistence" to "guarantee greater reverence for the Magisterium" fits in with Darby's focus on the magisterium.

SUPERIOR GENERAL OF THE MARIANISTS

Although Father Humbertclaude wrote directly to Father Darby, we can assume that Father Paul-Joseph Hoffer, the superior general of the

78. John Jansen, telephone interview with the author, March 10, 1999.

Marianists, knew of the communications. This is a reasonable assumption, given that both Humbertclaude and Hoffer were based in Rome. On March 31, 1967, nearly a month after Roesch's address to the faculty, Hoffer issued a circular to "all the religious of the Society." The occasions for the circular were the "150th anniversary of the founding of the Society of Mary and the nineteenth centenary of the martyrdoms of Saints Peter and Paul." Pope Paul VI "urged" the celebration of the latter and encouraged all to "offer the blessed Apostles a profession of faith both individual and collective, both free and conscious, both interior and exterior, both humble and outspoken."[79]

Father Hoffer wrote about the many speeches given by the pope "almost daily" on faith:

> Indeed, it is impossible to close one's eyes and ears to what is going on in the world. Many Christians experience a disquieting crisis of faith, occasioned at times by the imprudent language of certain Catholic intellectuals apparently indifferent to the reactions which their errors and their lack of discipline in the face of the directives of the Church's Magisterium arouse in the minds of the faithful, especially in the young.[80]

Hoffer continued with various quotes from Pope Paul VI, including a lengthy one from the pope's Apostolic Exhortation on the apostles Peter and Paul, issued on the feast day of their martyrdom, February 22, 1967:

> There can be seen here and there slipping into the field of Catholic doctrine new exegetical and theological opinions, often borrowed from outside philosophers, bold but blind. These opinions cast doubt upon or twist the objective meaning of truths which the Church teaches in virtue of her authority. Under the pretext of adapting religious thought to the modern mind, the directives of the ecclesiastical magisterium are lost from sight and theological speculation is stamped with a radically historical orientation. People go so far as to strip Holy Scripture's testimony of its historical and sacred character and endeavor to introduce a so-called post-conciliar spirit into the people of God. But this spirit fails to grasp the solid agreement between the broad and magnificent explanations made by the Council in

79. Paul VI, Apostolic Exhortation *Petrum et Paulum Apostolos*, February 22, 1967, quoted in Paul-Joseph Hoffer, "Circular," no. 36, March 31, 1967, 963.

80. Hoffer, "Circular," no. 36, 963–64.

doctrinal and legislative matters and the inheritance of the church's magisterium and discipline. It tends to make the traditional spirit of fidelity to the church disappear and to spread the misleading hope of giving to Christianity a new interpretation which could only be arbitrary and sterile. What would remain of the content of the faith if such attempts, slighting the authority of the Church's magisterium, were successful?[81]

Hoffer pointed out that, although the Holy Father was concerned about these "excesses," he did not intend to "dampen the enthusiasm for theological research." Hoffer hoped that in the future some of the Marianists might be able to "add their investigations to the reflections of theologians without fear of risking possible errors." He cautioned that theologians "should avoid broadcasting statements which are merely research hypotheses and raising questions with their pupils which they themselves cannot answer." Hoffer indicated that the Holy Father has the

duty of recalling to all who teach the faith that they must stop at certain impassable barriers. Be they theologians or mere preachers or even humble catechists, they must respect, not only the doctrines found in the Creed, but also the teaching of the Magisterium.[82]

Hoffer reflected on how Father William Joseph Chaminade, the founder of the Marianists, would look at the Holy Father's call for a year of faith and how the circumstances of the sixties were similar to those in Chaminade's lifetime. Chaminade gave the Marianists "valuable examples of respect for the guidance of the Magisterium and of fidelity to the content of the Creed." Hoffer quoted several writings by Chaminade and recommended what Chaminade recommended: reciting and meditating on the creed.[83] Hoffer included a quote by Paul VI on the creed, calling on Catholics to pray the creed, publicly and privately, during the year of faith.[84] Hoffer devoted the remainder of the circular to the upcoming general chapter of the Society of Mary.

At least one writer from the Cincinnati *Catholic Telegraph* interpreted

81. Hoffer, "Circular," no. 36, 964–65.
82. Hoffer, "Circular," no. 36, 965.
83. Hoffer, "Circular," no. 36, 966–67.
84. Hoffer, "Circular," no. 36, 968.

the circular as aimed at the University of Dayton. [85] This is a logical interpretation. It is also the correct interpretation. On December 4, 1967, Hoffer wrote Archbishop Paul-Pierre Philippe, second-in-command at the Congregation for the Doctrine of the Faith, and indicated that the circular was his response to the controversy at the University of Dayton.[86] He reiterated that the four accused were innocent of heresy but, as acknowledged by the archbishop's fact-finding commission, had taught opinions contrary to the magisterium. As for the university administrators, Hoffer thought they procrastinated too much and perhaps even supported the four accused.

As Dennis Bonnette's time at Dayton wound down, he wrote to Father Hoffer, sending him newspaper clippings about the controversy. Hoffer responded in mid-August with a letter that was forwarded to Bonnette in his new position at Niagara University. Hoffer stated that he had "followed very closely the happenings at the UD, but did not feel that [he] had to interfere in this matter." He hoped that "things will be settled during the coming school year according to the spirit of Vatican II and the welfare of the UD." He added that he was "sorry that [Bonnette] had to undergo such a trial and hope[s] that [he] did not suffer from any injustice."[87]

The escalation of the controversy became more complex as it moved from being a conflict among the faculty members to a conflict involving university administrators, the Marianist provincial, the university's board of trustees, local pastors, the archbishop, the apostolic delegate, the Marianist superior general, and the Vatican. The conflict involves two cultures: the academic and the ecclesiastical. The communications reviewed in this chapter show that Dennis Bonnette and his supporters—professors and local pastors—communicated with the church authorities on all levels. On behalf of the University of Dayton, Father James Darby was the liaison with the church.

85. George M. Barmann, "Marianist Superior Issues Guidelines on Magisterium," NC News Service story, May 30, 1967.

86. Paul-Joseph Hoffer to Paul-Pierre Philippe, December 4, 1967, AGMAR, Day 6, L58.

87. Paul-Joseph Hoffer, note to Dennis Bonnette, n.d., postmarked August 1967.

The restraint on the part of church authorities, both locally by the archbishop and more widely by the Vatican, is remarkable. The authorities could have recommended that some or all of the accused University of Dayton faculty be terminated from their positions. The Vatican, through the apostolic delegate, did just that when in 1943 it interfered in the case of lay philosophy professor Francis E. McMahon at the University of Notre Dame and successfully had McMahon terminated for calling Franco's government in Spain "Fascist."[88] Perhaps the church learned from public relations disasters like the McMahon situation that the strong-armed approach is not the way to go.

88. Philip Gleason, "A Question of Academic Freedom," *Notre Dame Magazine*, Spring 2013, accessed November 3, 2017, https://magazine.nd.edu/news/a-question-of-academic-freedom/.

CHAPTER 10

MEDIA COVERAGE

The more one probes the more [one] finds that ambiguity lies at the heart of any discussion—much less solution—of the problem of academic freedom at a Catholic university.

—John Reedy, CSC, and James F. Andrews, "The Troubled University of Dayton"

Throughout 1966 and 1967, newspapers, magazines, journals, radio, and television covered the controversy at the University of Dayton. While coverage was stronger in the local market, the story made national news in the *New York Times* and other national publications. As might be expected, there were more articles in Catholic sources than in non-Catholic publications. A review of the coverage is both interesting and important for understanding the conflict.

The majority of the articles focused on academic freedom in a Catholic university. The Dayton story was part of a continuum of stories about Catholic universities struggling to come of age in the American higher education arena of the sixties. The University of Dayton controversy followed the 1965 firing of thirty-one professors and subsequent strike by the faculty at St. John's University in New York City. The Dayton story preceded what would become a bigger story, the firing of Father Charles

Curran from the Catholic University of America. At the same time the University of Dayton story unfolded in the press, Webster College made the national news. Webster's president, Sister of Loretto Jacqueline Grennan, did not think it was possible for a Catholic college to have true academic freedom. Under Grennan's leadership, Webster renounced its Catholicity to become a secular college. Sister Jacqueline left the Sisters of Loretto and continued to lead the college. Would Dayton and other Catholic institutions follow suit? The reporters and authors covering the Dayton controversy recognized that the situation at Webster could have important ramifications for all institutions of Catholic higher education. The resolution mattered to the church and the University of Dayton.

Once the accusations were made to the archbishop, the media storm erupted quickly. Dennis Bonnette's letter to Archbishop Karl J. Alter, with a carbon copy to the apostolic delegate, was dated Saturday, October 15, 1966. The letter arrived in Cincinnati by Tuesday and in Washington, D.C., by Wednesday or Thursday of the same week. Father Roesch learned of the letter after the archbishop talked to the apostolic delegate by telephone on Thursday. Roesch then called a meeting of Bonnette, the accused, and their chairpersons on Monday, October 24, and issued the following statement on October 26:

> The attention of the University Administration has been drawn to an apparent difference of opinion on some basic Catholic principles between some members of the Departments of Philosophy and Theology. These differences have led to a direct charge by one of the members, Mr. Bonnette, that Mr. Chrisman, Dr. Baltazar, Mr. Ulrich and Mr. Lumpp are teaching and/or writing tenets that are contrary to the Church Magisterium.
>
> Father Roesch, the President of the University, has directed an investigation into the charges and the circumstances dependent thereon and is withholding any comment pending the outcome of the study.[1]

Father Roesch's statement did not say to whom the charge had been made. Roesch simply said the university was investigating the charge and

---

1. Aggie Taormina, "Fr. Roesch Investigates Bonnette's Charges," *Flyer News*, October 28, 1966, 1.

would not comment further until the study was completed. Roesch stuck by his statement. The university's next press release was issued nearly six weeks later, in early December.

The university's student newspaper, *Flyer News*, broke the story on Friday, October 28. Assistant editor Cay Wieland got wind of something going on, and feature editor Aggie Taormina covered the story, perhaps because she was in Lawrence Ulrich's class that semester.[2] *Flyer News* published the official statement and included comments from Chrisman, Baltazar, Ulrich, and Lumpp, who explained that the church was going through changes; that Bonnette should have brought his charges to them; that they had not been told any details about the charges; that the university has been fair in handling this issue; and that they have confidence in the University of Dayton. Bonnette declined to comment on the charges and the statement.

The local newspapers—the *Dayton Journal Herald* and the *Dayton Daily News*—and the local Catholic newspaper—the Cincinnati *Catholic Telegraph*—also ran stories on October 28. The source for most of their content was the *Flyer News* article. The major difference in the articles was that the *Telegraph*, which had inside information from the archbishop, indicated that there was "an inquiry about the charge from the office of the apostolic delegate in Washington, D.C., Archbishop Egidio Vagnozzi."[3] George M. Barmann, the author of the *Telegraph* article, also submitted his article—minus the paragraph about the apostolic delegate—to the National Catholic Welfare Conference (NCWC) press department in Washington, D.C.

CATHOLIC NEWSPAPER COVERAGE

In the sixties, the NCWC was a voluntary association of United States bishops that organized and coordinated the efforts of Catholics carrying out the social mission of the church in the United States.[4] The press department released stories to the Catholic media under the name "NCWC

2. Aggie Taormina, email message to the author, January 14, 1999, 2.
3. George M. Barmann, "UD Teachers Accused of Errors in Doctrine," *Catholic Telegraph*, October 21, 1966, A-10.
4. "National Catholic Welfare Council," in *1967 National Catholic Almanac*, ed. Felician A. Foy, OFM (Garden City, N.Y.: Doubleday, 1967), 591.

News Service," designated by the abbreviation "NC." Similar to the news services of the Associated Press (AP) and United Press International (UPI), in 1966 the NC news service reached 156 Catholic newspapers in North America with a total circulation of 6.25 million readers.[5] The majority of the papers were weekly diocesan papers. There were four national papers: *Our Sunday Visitor*, the *National Catholic Reporter*, *The Wanderer*, and the *Register*, which published thirty-four diocesan editions, including Cincinnati's *Catholic Telegraph*.

Dennis Bonnette recalls that a reporter from the *National Catholic Reporter* (*NCR*) contacted him within twenty-four hours of the Roesch meeting on Monday, October 24, during which the accused learned of the charges. Father Roesch's personal notes indicate that *NCR* contacted him and Baltazar in addition to Bonnette.[6] Someone had evidently leaked the story to *NCR*. When *NCR* ran their story nearly a week later, on November 2, 1966, they used the facts and quotes from *Flyer News*, but also indicated for the first time that Bonnette made the charges to the archbishop, who then referred the situation back to the university. Their source for this information was a "university spokesperson." Bonnette did not immediately comment on the dispute when contacted by *NCR*, but he did say that previously he had circulated a two-page document entitled, "Some principles relating to theology and philosophy at the University of Dayton."[7]

Dale Francis, director of the University of Notre Dame Press and director of the Bureau of Information for the NCWC, wrote about the accusations in the November 13, 1966, "Operation Understanding" edition of *Our Sunday Visitor*. He began his article by cleverly linking the University of Dayton controversy to Dayton, Tennessee, the site of the Scopes monkey trial over the teaching of evolution. He correctly predicted that academic freedom would be raised as a right of the faculty, but he took the "unpopular position" that the institution has a right to its identity:

5. "Circulation Goes Up: Catholic Press Registers Gains," *The Pilot* (Archdiocese of Boston), November 19, 1966, 11.

6. Raymond A. Roesch, "Chronology of the Bonnette Case," n.d., Roesch papers, series 91–35, box 5, AUD.

7. Dennis Bonnette, email message to the author, November 24, 2019.

A professor of philosophy at a Catholic institution should teach what reflects Catholic teaching, a professor of religion at a Baptist institution should teach what reflects Baptist teaching. Unless there is some precision in the boundaries drawn then the institution loses its meaning.

If each professor can determine his own philosophical beliefs, his own religious beliefs, then there might as well not be sectarian schools at all. As a matter of fact, the student is better off in a secular school for he'll not be led to believe he is getting a teaching in conformity with the religious beliefs of a sectarian institution.[8]

Only a few weekly Catholic papers picked up the initial story. The *Brooklyn (New York) Tablet* and two Ohio papers, Toledo's *Catholic Chronicle* and Youngstown's *Catholic Exponent*, ran modified versions of the NC press release. In early December, the press release on the clearing of the four faculty of the "heresy" charge was covered by six papers: *NCR* and diocesan papers in Ohio and nearby Detroit, Michigan. The press releases on the "Declaration of Conscience" and the censure led to the story being covered by Catholic papers in St. Louis, Boston, and Brooklyn. The San Francisco and Davenport, Iowa, papers—in addition to St. Louis, Boston, Brooklyn, and Ohio papers—reported on the appointment of the archbishop's fact-finding commission and the dissent of the University of Dayton's chapter of the AAUP.[9]

LOCAL NEWSPAPER COVERAGE

The *Dayton Daily News* and the *Dayton Journal Herald* followed the story very closely. In 1966, the University of Dayton was the only university in Dayton. It was very much a university of the community. What happened at the University of Dayton mattered to the community whether you were Catholic or not. The two local papers published sixty articles, six editorials, and seven letters to the editor over nearly a year of coverage of the conflict and its aftermath. The reporting was accurate and fair.

8. "Conflict in Dayton," Operation Understanding ed., *Our Sunday Visitor*, November 13, 1966, 5A.

9. The Archbishop of Cincinnati called the fact-finding group a "commission," while the University of Dayton called it a "committee." Throughout this chapter, both terms are used for the same group of people.

Both sides were given the opportunity to tell their stories. The editorials recognized the value of dissent and the university's handling of the controversy (December 6, 1966), supported the university in its commitment to academic freedom (December 8, 1966), took pride in the "lively controversy" that showed that people cared about what was involved (December 17, 1966), argued that the controversy was healthy and the university was improving as a result of it (January 10, 1967), complimented the university on sharing Vatican II's spirit of inquiry (March 12, 1967), and recognized that the university was redefining "its role as associated with but independent of the general functions of the church" (September 24, 1967).

NATIONAL NEWSPAPER AND PERIODICAL COVERAGE

The Dayton papers put the story on the news wires, and it was picked up by other papers, mostly in Ohio (at least fourteen newspapers) and a few other spots in the eastern states: Binghamton, New York; Camden, New Jersey; and Pittsburgh, Pennsylvania. Three articles were published in Sunday editions of the *New York Times*. The first stated that "the University of Dayton's academic tranquility, usually disrupted by no more than intense basketball fever, was caught in a liberal-conservative theological dispute." The article described the initial charges, the University of Dayton's response, and the declaration of a "whitewash" by Bonnette and his supporters. Bonnette was quoted as saying the controversy was "one of the negative results of the liberalizations which took place following the Vatican II Council."[10] A week later, a second article reported that Dennis Bonnette was informed his teaching contract may not be renewed for the following year.[11] The third article reported on Bonnette's resignation from UD, the fourth professor to do so as a result of the controversy. [The other resignations were Edward Harkenrider, Thomas Casaletto, and Hugo Barbic, all supporters of Bonnette.] After recounting the story of the conflict, the article ended by stating that the archbishop's fact-finding committee "opposed the university's position and upheld Professor Bonnette."[12] Since Dennis

10. "Religious Dispute Stirs U. of Dayton: Professor says 4 Colleagues Teach against Church," *New York Times*, December 11, 1966, 77.
11. "Dayton U. Teacher Faces Loss of Post," *New York Times*, December 18, 1966, 86.
12. "4th Teacher Quits in Dayton 'Heresy,'" *New York Times*, April 23, 1967, 42.

Bonnette's views figured prominently in the three articles, it appears he was the source for the article with no byline given. Bonnette recalls that he spoke to a local Dayton reporter who was a stringer for the *Times*.[13]

The Dayton controversy was mentioned in the *Wall Street Journal* (*WSJ*) in an article on changes in Catholic colleges. The author quoted Father W. J. Leonard, chairman of Theology at Boston College, saying that "too often theology was presented to students as a set of conclusions to be memorized and handed back.... Now, we try to treat students as adults who have legitimate questions; in fact, we encourage questioning." Dayton was used as an example that not all educators agree with the Boston College approach.[14]

In addition to newspaper stories, three secular magazines included the University of Dayton in articles on Catholic higher education. Similar to the *WSJ* article, Daniel Callahan wrote in April 1967 in the *New York Times Magazine* about the revamping of the theology and philosophy programs:

> Long a source of bitter student complaints—for their mediocrity, irrelevance and rigidity—these programs in particular are feeling the strong winds of the council. Less and less are Catholic students being taught a fixed set of Catholic "truths" in their theology classes and a packaged set of scholastic axioms in their philosophy courses. Scholasticism is giving way to existentialism, empiricism and phenomenology.

The University of Dayton was mentioned as an example of opposition to this trend. That Bonnette's charges were even investigated by the university was "a throwback to an earlier era," but the clearing of the accused and "the minority faction slapped down" was a sign of progress.[15]

The *U.S. News & World Report*'s article on May 8, 1967, was entitled, "Revolt in Some Catholic Colleges: What's Back of It All." The situation at Dayton was an example of a college in trouble. Self-described traditionalist Catholic Frederick D. Wilhelmsen wrote an opinion piece for the

---

13. Dennis Bonnette, email message to the author, February 23, 2017, and July 20, 2017.

14. Frederick C. Klein, "Catholic Colleges: Curricula, Campus Life Change as the Schools Alter Long-Held Views," *Wall Street Journal*, December 15, 1966, 16.

15. Daniel Callahan, "Sister Jacqueline Becomes Miss Grennan and Dramatizes a Crisis in Catholic Education," *New York Times Magazine*, April 23, 1967, 76.

"Speaking Out" feature in the July 15, 1967, issue of The *Saturday Evening Post*. In "Catholicism Is Right, So Why Change It?," Wilhelmsen laments academic freedom "taking precedence over the authority possessed by the Catholic Church." Dayton is used as the example: Father Roesch "publicly defied" the archbishop. "The heretics were vindicated, and the four professors making the charges have left the university."[16]

CATHOLIC PERIODICALS

Twelve national Catholic magazines featured full-length articles and editorials on the University of Dayton controversy. The first editorial was written by Jesuit Thurston N. Davis, editor-in-chief of *America* magazine, for the November 26, 1966, issue. After giving a short description of the controversy, Davis wrote:

> In an age like ours, when development and change are necessary and desirable, it is inevitable that doctrinal controversies—some of them violent—should break out on various campuses. UD gives us an early-warning flash that comes through loud and clear.[17]

Davis recommended that we "stock up on patience, understanding and charity" as they will be needed in the coming months. When "struggles" occur, he suggested that charges be talked out within the faculty before bringing in university administrators. He also recognized the "immense harm" that can be done when a professor takes his case to the bishop and predicted that going to church authorities will not put out these types of fires. Rather, such "handling of these disputes will bring discredit on our colleges and universities, as well as on Church officials and on the Church itself." He called on church authorities to have "an exquisite sense of restraint" and concluded by pointing out the "harm done by professors or students who make themselves responsible for what can degenerate into witch hunts on their campuses."[18]

---

16. Frederick D. Wilhelmsen, "Speaking Out: Catholicism Is Right, So Why Change It?," *Saturday Evening Post*, July 15, 1967, 10.

17. Thurston N. Davis, "Of Many Things," *America*, November 26, 1966, 672.

18. Davis, "Of Many Things."

A few weeks later, "Catholic Education and the New Enlightenment" was published in the December 8 issue of the *Wanderer*, an ultra-conservative national Catholic weekly out of St. Paul, Minnesota. The author was Paulist father Robert E. Burns, a weekly columnist for the magazine. This was early in the controversy, so Father Burns, without much actual information to report, described Bonnette's charges. He focused on situation ethics, since he suspected his readers did not know what it was. He quoted the *Theological Dictionary* definition of "situation ethics" and pointed out that it was condemned in the Holy See's recent letter to every bishop in the world.[19] For Burns, the problem was that in addition to situation ethics being applied to morals, existentialism was also being applied to interpretation of the Bible, particularly the gospels. He was concerned for "ill-equipped or immature students" and the "matter of parental rights in the education of their offspring."[20]

In its January 27, 1967, issue, *Commonweal* reported that the very fact that an investigation was undertaken implies that "the teaching of heresy is a punishable offense in a Catholic college," and, therefore, academic freedom is limited in a Catholic university.[21] The editors used Dayton's situation to support the secularization of Webster College.

TRIUMPH MAGAZINE

Triumph published "Storm over Dayton" in February 1967. *Triumph* was a conservative monthly magazine that the publishers described as having a traditionalist Catholic perspective. It was published from 1966 to 1975 by L. Brent Bozell Jr., brother-in-law of William F. Buckley, Jr. The article, written by assistant editor Gary K. Potter, looked at the controversy in more depth than the newspaper articles. Potter claimed the beginning of the controversy was Baltazar's lecture on Thomism in September 1963 and traced the events that escalated the controversy over the years. He detailed Baltazar's questionable teachings on Thomism, Teilhard de

19. He is referring to Ottaviani's letter discussed previously.
20. Fr. Robert E. Burns, CSP, "Catholic Education and the New Enlightenment," *Wanderer*, December 8, 1966, 5–7.
21. "Webster College," *Commonweal*, January 27, 1967, 442.

Chardin, contraception, and situation ethics, as well as Chrisman's on situation ethics and purgatory. The description of the most recent events indicates that Dennis Bonnette was his source. Potter knew that the letter to the archbishop was two pages long and described the contents in wording from the letter: "The situation ... now posed a threat to the faith and morals of the University community."[22] After describing the declaration of conscience, the censure by the faculty forum, and Harkenrider's resignation, the article ends with Chrisman telling Potter that there was no reason to call the witnesses against the accused because "we admitted all the charges." Chrisman concluded, "We all belong to the same Church, we're all Catholic. We must respect one another well enough to have dialogue.... It's been so long since we've had dissent that now when it comes, it comes with a roar."

After publication, Bozell sent a copy to auxiliary bishop Edward A. McCarthy in Cincinnati. The two had met previously in Rome.[23] McCarthy responded that he was "impressed by the thoroughness of Mr. Potter's examination of the situation and presentation of the facts up to date." McCarthy could not make additional comments because the fact-finding commission had yet to release its report. However, he ventured:

> It is of course distressing that some of the professors and students on the campus have so distorted a legitimate concern for academic freedom as to wish to usurp the Bishops (*sic*) chair as official representatives of the teaching of the church and to deprive the Bishop of his freedom to discharge his responsibility to the faithful of the Dayton community.[24]

McCarthy then wished *Triumph* "success as a constructive, balancing voice in some of the post-conciliar cacophony."[25]

Bozell continued the correspondence with a March 2, 1967, letter to Bishop McCarthy in which Bozell asked for a full copy of the findings. Bozell also asked for "your guidance in explaining how the archdiocese

22. Gary K. Potter, "Storm over Dayton," *Triumph*, February 1967, 12.

23. L. Brent Bozell to Edward A. McCarthy, January 25, 1967, "University of Dayton, general correspondence, 1966–1969," RG 1.6 ABP Alter, AAC.

24. Edward A. McCarthy to L. Brent Bozell, February 15, 1967, "University of Dayton, general correspondence, 1966–1969," RG 1.6 ABP Alter, AAC.

25. McCarthy to Bozell, February 15, 1967.

proposes to enforce orthodoxy at the university." He recognized that this was "an extremely delicate and difficult problem" and suggested that perhaps *Triumph* could say what the archdiocese could not. Bozell reassured the bishop that their "course will be determined by the single criterion of what seems to be in the best interests of the Church."[26]

Nearly a month later, since the material was given in confidence by those who appeared before the fact-finding commission, McCarthy responded to Bozell that he was unable to give him a copy of the report. McCarthy appreciated Bozell's offer of assistance, but said that it "would be most gratifying, of course, if the University could quietly solve its own problem, now that it has been exposed and the students and community are alerted to it."[27]

McCarthy indicated that "direct intervention by authority, if that must come, will, we know, be distorted in the news media as authoritarianism, become a rallying point for attacks on Catholic education, an occasion for still other intemperate statements, and an excuse for actions contrary to Faith and morals." He continued that there may be "wisdom in a cooling-off period, when, hopefully, saner minds will prevail, and those who are unorthodox will expose themselves more clearly by their own statements."[28]

Bozell hoped that a "cooling-off period" would work, but feared that the opposite may be true:

> that the failure of Authority to intervene may encourage a rash of rebelliousness through the Catholic academic community—to the extent, indeed, that the bishops will no longer be able to supervise the content of Catholic education. Certainly the events at The Catholic University...suggest this moment may be fast upon us.[29]

Triumph published a follow-up article, "Ohio Blows Up," in April 1967, written by the editors of the magazine. The happenings at Dayton since the original article have "driven the storm to hurricane strengths which

26. L. Brent Bozell to Edward A. McCarthy, March 2, 1967.
27. Edward A. McCarthy to L. Brent Bozell, March 28, 1967.
28. McCarthy to Bozell, March 28, 1967.
29. L. Brent Bozell to Edward A. McCarthy, May 15, 1967, "Controversy 'Academic Freedom, etc.,' 1966–67," Belmont Ave. general files, 1.6 Abp. Alter, AAC.

the University seems unwilling, and the Episcopal Authority unable, to control." The issues raised are what it means to be a Catholic university and "the necessary conditions for its continued existence."

> TRIUMPH believes that unless these issues are squarely faced, and unless they bring forth a vigorous reassertion of the Christian view of education and the search for truth, the chaos that today envelopes [*sic*] Dayton will in very short order swamp the entire Catholic educational establishment.[30]

The editors presented a bulleted chronology of events at Dayton beginning in late January 1967 and continuing through mid-March. The events listed for March stirred up their readers against the university. The editors quoted the *Dayton Journal Herald* announcing Father Roesch's "Declaration of Independence" for the faculty and described Father Neil McCluskey's lecture as "serv[ing] to drive home the University's defiance, and the Archbishop's humiliation." Again, they gave Eulalio Baltazar credit for starting the controversy in 1963 when he first lectured on Teilhard de Chardin. They were outraged that Baltazar, "the noisiest of Dayton's heterodox professors," was named the University of Dayton's professor of the year in 1967. The editors also mentioned the selection of the president of Chile, Eduardo Frei-Montalva, as the recipient of the 1967 Marianist Award as further evidence that the university had "surrendered to secularism." Previously, the award had been given to persons who made a contribution to Mariology. Beginning in 1967, the university planned to give the award to a person who "through his outstanding contributions to mankind, best exemplifies the goals and purposes of the University of Dayton."[31] Frei was given the award for his Christian social reform efforts in Chile.[32]

Following the chronology, the editors lamented the corruption of Catholic education. They blasted Kelly, Chrisman, Baltazar et al., saying:

> No one in their profession ever heard of these men before they decided to make the grade by advancing such bold doctrines for the twentieth century

---

30. The Editors, "Ohio Blows Up," *Triumph*, April 1967, 9.

31. "Ohio Blows Up," 11.

32. "Father Roesch Presents Marianist Award to President Frei-Montalva of Chile, 1967," Marian Library photograph collection, accessed September 15, 2017, http://ecommons.udayton .edu/imri_photos/20/.

as birth control, and by indulging such rash amusements as poking fun at Rome's authority. The daring boys! Like Siger de Brahant [*sic*], who taught heresy at the University of Paris in the thirteenth century, they pirouette before admiring adolescents (the phrase is St. Thomas's) as a substitute for serious scholarship.

[They] and their counterparts on Catholic campuses through the land... want to secularize their schools, the minds of their students, their religion—the better to accommodate "the modern consciousness"; and to this end they demand emancipation from ecclesiastical authority. Their position is enormously strong, moreover, because they wrapped themselves in the banner of Academic Freedom: they have prostrated themselves before the most powerful deity in contemporary American society; and that god faithfully, ferociously, protects its own.[33]

The article continues in this vein, calling the AAUP the inquisitors who

can be counted on to convoke an *auto-da-fé* at the first breath of heresy against academic freedom—as witness St. John's University. They can and do wither a university president with a disapproving glance—as witness the University of Dayton. They can and believably do tell a bishop of that other God to mind his place or prepare for ostracism by respectable society.[34]

Triumph does support, however, the academic freedom that is "a creation of Western Civilization, which is to say that it is a creation of the Catholic Church." Namely, scholars in Catholic institutions have the rights:

to explore their own disciplines in their own ways; to express their conclusions to their students without the petty recriminations that today so often follow in the wake of dissent from secularist prejudices; to be guaranteed, despite an unapologetic Christian commitment, both advancement and tenure; to speak in a language and in a style which are both personal and civilized, incarnating a commitment to the real that comes from the heart of men annealed in the wisdom of Christendom.[35]

In the minds of *Triumph*'s editors, the AAUP's version of academic freedom is a false god, since it "asserts the right to teach under Catho-

33. "Ohio Blows Up," 11.
34. "Ohio Blows Up."
35. "Ohio Blows Up," 11–12.

lic auspices doctrines that are contrary to both the structure of Being and the Lord of Being's representative on earth." They fear that secularists want "to uproot Catholic scholarship from the Magisterium and plant it in the soil of 'the modern consciousness.'" Since modern consciousness is hostile to the faith, it follows that "the Catholic university must accept the battle thus forced upon it, or agree that it has no further reason for existing."[36]

Ohio, continued the editorial, is the place for the battle to begin. The editors urged Archbishop Alter, "a descendant of the Apostles" and "custodian of God's truth," to defend orthodoxy at the University of Dayton. Matters have gone too far. The university has "scorned and repudiated" the archbishop's authority. Since there is "no place for the Archbishop on Fr. Roesch's 'organizational chart,'" there should be "no place in the Archdiocese of Cincinnati for Fr. Roesch's organization." If the Marianists want to keep their school, *Triumph* suggests that

> His Excellency can teach them how to do that. He can, and should, emulate Germanus, the Bishop of Auxerre in Belloc's drinking song, who "with his stout episcopal staff, so thoroughly thwacked and banged the heretics all, both short and tall, they rather had been hanged. Oh, he thwacked them hard and he banged them long, upon each and all occasions, till they in chorus bellowed loud and strong, their orthodox persuasions."[37]
>
> The editors hope that with the guidance above, "Catholic educators may learn to become a little less grim, a little less frightened of being 'left behind.'" They are on the right track if they remember that "Christ is *here*, in His Church.... There is no University worthy of the name that is not Catholic."[38]

According to Father John L. Cavanaugh, secretary to Archbishop Alter, the archbishop "found the article constructive and note-worthy—a real contribution to unraveling the confused situation at the University of Dayton." He requested a dozen reprints.[39]

The *Catholic Mind*, a monthly *Readers Digest*–type periodical pub-

36. "Ohio Blows Up," 13.
37. "Ohio Blows Up."
38. "Ohio Blows Up."
39. John L. Cavanaugh to L. Brent Bozell, April 5, 1967, "Controversy 'Academic Freedom, etc.,' 1966–67," Belmont Ave. general files, 1.6 Abp. Alter, AAC.

lished by the Jesuits through America Press, printed in full Father Roesch's December 3, 1966, letter to the University of Dayton faculty. By the time the letter was published, the controversy had escalated, and the archbishop had gotten involved. Still, publication of Roesch's letter to a wider audience was good public relations for the university.

OTHER CATHOLIC NEWSPAPERS AND PERIODICALS

In January 1967, the *Catholic Educator*, published by Joseph F. Wagner, founder of the *Homiletic & Pastoral Review*, included the University of Dayton controversy in their "Clips and Comments" section under the heading "Freedom in the Colleges." The editors pointed out that

> Within the space of two months, the Church has one university's accreditation placed on probation [St. John's University], another wracked by internal dissension [University of Dayton], and a third decided to abandon it all and turn into a secular college [Webster College in St. Louis], all revolving around the central issue of freedom—freedom to teach, freedom to conduct an institution in the manner which the administrators of the institution feel best.

The editors hoped that the "drive for freedom" will not "cause conflicts to the extent that colleges fold up.... If the Webster example is emulated, then it is said the Church will be throwing the investment of generations to the winds. We trust not."[40]

The *National Catholic Reporter* wrote news articles about every UD event as it unfolded in early 1967. It also included Dayton in a lengthy editorial, "Officially Catholic," on February 22, 1967. The editorial accompanied the *NCR* series "Issues that Divide the Church" and pointed out that three stories in the current issue—including Dayton and a similar situation at Rome's Lateran University—are "targets of official concern" and are "left of center in their views."[41] The question for *NCR* is "whether

---

40. "Freedom in the Colleges," Clips and Comments, *Catholic Educator*, January 1967, 4–5.

41. In the late 1950s and early 1960s, there was a controversy between the Pontifical Lateran University (a conservative institution) and the Jesuit-run Pontifical Biblical Institute (a liberal institution) over using modern critical methods for interpreting the Bible. Pope John XXIII addressed the biblical institute about the need for rigorous scholarship, along with submission

the modes by which authority in the Church has sought to keep inno-
vators in line will work any longer. Or, more profoundly, whether these
means were ever appropriate in the Church of Christ."[42]

NCR expressed support for the archbishop's fact-finding commission:
its "tone of reasonableness and restraint" and that "it contains no recommendations of punitive action." But it also expressed concerns: did the
fact-finding commission's qualifications match the qualifications of those
under investigation? and what is a teacher to do who "honestly cannot
accept some non-defined but standard element of the Catholic interpretation of reality"? The editorial concludes that

> Being a Catholic will always pose problems for anyone concerned to com-
> bine fidelity with personal integrity, teachableness with the spirit of inquiry,
> deference to authority with respect for freedom.... We don't much like the
> notion of outside investigating committees entering a university to check
> on the orthodoxy of teachers. And we hope that someday soon the Lateran
> university [*sic*] will be notified that the Inquisition is over.[43]

The *Catholic Educator* commented on the St. John's and Dayton situations again in April 1967. St. John's submitted the cases of its dismissed
faculty to the American Arbitration Association for final and binding decisions and remedies as recommended by the Middle States Association
accrediting agency. This action was viewed positively. The situation at the
University of Dayton, however, was one of "charges and counter-charges."
After detailing the happenings of January through early March, the editors were not sure "where and when this will end." The archbishop's
fact-finding commission found some instances of improper teaching:
"The university, however, is reluctant to acknowledge this and thus a
stalemate is forming from which each camp will hurl accusations and
denials from time to time." The last University of Dayton event reported
was Father Neil McCluskey's talk, which was "sure to raise the pitch of
the conflict."[44] The editors concluded,

---

to the deposit of the faith and the teachings of the magisterium; Joseph Pathrapankal, *Time and
History: Biblical and Theological Studies* (Eugene, Ore.: Wipf and Stock, 2005), 95.

42. "Officially Catholic," *National Catholic Reporter*, February 22, 1967, 3.

43. "Officially Catholic."

44. "Academic Freedom Con't," Clips and Comments, *Catholic Educator*, April 1967, 4.

It seems certain that Father McCluskey's talk will continue the controversy and may well lead to the full scale discussion of a subject much discussed these days, i.e., whether or not a Catholic college or university can in fact, grant academic freedom.[45]

AVE MARIA MAGAZINE

The most in-depth article was published in *Ave Maria*, a national Catholic weekly published by Ave Maria Press at the University of Notre Dame. The April 1, 1967, article was the cover story, "The Troubled University of Dayton," written by the editor, John Reedy, CSC, and managing editor, James F. Andrews, both of whom traveled to Dayton to interview the people involved in the conflict.

The left sidebar of the two-page magazine spread showed the chronology, starting with Bonnette's letter to the archbishop and ending with Roesch's address to the faculty. The authors begin by linking the Dayton "heresy trial" with the St. John's "faculty mess," quoting an unnamed Catholic university president who was concerned about the issues being raised, knowing his university also had to face them. No one wants his institution embarrassed like the University of Dayton was. The remainder of the article looked at the Dayton controversy as a case study of how to deal with "handling similar problems in other places and at other times."[46]

The core problem was described in multiple ways: What is the university's relationship to the hierarchy? What is theology's role in a Catholic university? What can academic freedom mean for a professor at a Catholic university? How can the authoritative teaching of the church ensure its adequate presence on the campus of the Catholic university? All are legitimate ways to look at the subject. Although recognizing the importance of the pastoral concerns, the authors chose to look at the subject from the perspective of academic freedom.[47]

The first view discussed was that of the archbishop, who has "a de-

45. "Academic Freedom Con't," 5.
46. John Reedy, CSC, and James F. Andrews, "The Troubled University of Dayton," *Ave Maria*, April 1, 1967, 9.
47. Reedy and Andrews, "Troubled University of Dayton."

fined, formal relationship [with a Catholic university] by tradition and law." The formal relationship was given to the archbishop by the university and "reinforced by canon law."

> The Archbishop maintains the traditional view of academic freedom in a Catholic university, a view founded on the expressed identity of the university as Catholic in its commitment, as well as on canon law and the provision of the American Association of University Professors for church-related universities.[48]

In other words, the archbishop believes that academic freedom is "limited by an institutional commitment to teach Catholic doctrine, a commitment clearly stated in its contracts with faculty." This means that "the administration has an obligation to investigate any deviations from this identity and correct the situation."[49]

The authors then quote the archbishop:

> Any aggrieved professors whose charges are not sustained by the administration have a right to appeal to higher authority. The first appeal, obviously, is to the administration itself. If satisfaction is not obtained, an appeal can be made to the Ordinary of the diocese in which the institution is established.[50]

Canon law paragraphs 1372, 1381, and 335–37 give the archbishop the right to investigate such appeals. "In [the archbishop's] view, this can best be carried out by a commission of inquiry which can proceed impersonally and with due safeguards to academic freedom." The authors indicate that the archbishop's actions in the Dayton case were consistent with his views on academic freedom. They wonder, however, what happens in the future if the university permits such teaching to continue.[51]

The university's view of academic freedom was presented by Father James Darby and Father Raymond Roesch. They agreed that the archbishop has a right to exercise pastoral concern on the campus. Then they made a distinction between the pastoral and academic dimensions. The

---

48. Reedy and Andrews, "Troubled University of Dayton."
49. Reedy and Andrews, "Troubled University of Dayton."
50. Reedy and Andrews, "Troubled University of Dayton."
51. Reedy and Andrews, "Troubled University of Dayton."

authors believe that Darby's and Roesch's statements "put them in agreement" with the view of Father Neil McCluskey, whom the authors properly identify as a visiting professor at Notre Dame. This put the University of Dayton at odds with the Archbishop of Cincinnati. The authors point out that while the distinction between the pastoral and the academic is "real and legitimate," it does not "answer the difficulties." Furthermore,

> The administration's dependence on this distinction has probably caused some of the confusion through the incident. For although it purported to seriously investigate Bonnette's accusation, its manner of handling the substance of his charges and the manner in which the accused professors were cleared on the basis of a technicality—that they were not guilty of heresy and therefore are cleared—shows that the administration was operating from Father McCluskey's view.[52]

Reedy and Andrews think that the University of Dayton had no other options, since the administration itself was under indictment as a result of Bonnette's appeal. They support this statement with a quote from Father Henry Kenney of Xavier University in Cincinnati, a member of the archbishop's fact-finding commission:

> The fact that the accused are not named in the Commission's statement indicated that the University is who was under study: The University administration allowed teaching contrary to the Magisterium. "The University manifested an inability to handle the situation. The *University* was clearly at fault when it approached their investigation the way it did."[53]

After seemingly taking the side of the archbishop, the authors ask, "Is either view adequate?" They then indicate that the archbishop did not take into account the "concrete sociology" of the circumstances. In other words, the archbishop did not take into account contemporary higher education and the implications of his actions. Higher education is "intolerant of interference," and "Catholic higher education is competing for stature, for professors, for students in that environment." The archbishop should keep that sociology in mind when he takes action.[54]

52. Reedy and Andrews, "Troubled University of Dayton," 20.
53. Reedy and Andrews, "Troubled University of Dayton."
54. Reedy and Andrews, "Troubled University of Dayton," 21.

They also wrote that the administration did not grasp the "sociology" of the situation. They do not explain how that is the case, moving on to say:

> The core of the matter was brought home to us when we tried to apply any of these positions to the concrete reality at the University. The facts do not admit of an ambiguous, doctrinaire solution. The more one probes the more he finds that ambiguity lies at the heart of any discussion—much less solution—of the problem of academic freedom at a Catholic university. Though one can disavow the reality at Dayton and wish that it offered a clear-cut issue, it simply doesn't. In a real sense, it may be fortunate that it doesn't, so that the complexity of the matter will come across to all concerned.[55]

The authors think that they have a "clue to the cause." The book *Academic Freedom and the Catholic University*, edited by Notre Dame professors A. Edward Manier and John W. Houck, had just been published by Fides in Notre Dame, Indiana.[56] Daniel S. Greenberg, then news editor of *Science*, the journal of the American Association for the Advancement of Science, contributed chapter 8, "The Drive for Academic Excellence: A Case Study." Greenburg analyzed the University of Pittsburgh's growth in academic excellence in the fifties under the leadership of chancellor Edward H. Litchfield. Pitt made great strides, but "in the process got a nervous breakdown and almost died from bankruptcy." The relevance for the University of Dayton is that "the strain on the University was too great, that growth must be organic if there is to be stability in the intellectual community." Book coeditor Houck, the president of the AAUP at Notre Dame, supported Greenburg's view: "Any discussion of academic freedom must be built on a presumption of competence, otherwise the whole thing crumbles. There has to be a tradition of academic dialogue before you can have academic freedom."[57]

Reedy and Andrews next tried to apply the question of "competence" or "tradition of academic dialogue" to the Dayton controversy. They answered by quoting Xavier's Father Kenney:

55. Reedy and Andrews, "Troubled University of Dayton."

56. University of Notre Dame press release, March 16, 1967, accessed September 20, 2017, http://archives.nd.edu/pr/pdf/PR_1967_03.pdf.

57. Reedy and Andrews, "Troubled University of Dayton," 21.

You've made the assumption that there's a university there—a genuine, viable dialogue of disciplines on a high level. We don't have it here (Xavier University) and they don't either (Dayton).[58]

Kenney thought this because of the lack of decorum on the part of the accused faculty, the lack of serious scholarship on the part of the accused and the accusers (Baltazar and Dieska being the exceptions), a legalistic approach to theology, the lack of sophistication on the part of the accusers, and the frustration on the part of the accusers to get a hearing for the authentic teaching of the church. To Reedy and Andrews, the conflict seems to be "an intradepartmental fight between philosophers of two differing commitments." The views of the accusers "toward philosophy and Thomism would not find sympathetic hearing even in many seminaries today."[59]

The problem at Dayton was bigger than the conflict in the Philosophy Department. The authors reviewed the recent happenings in the Theological Studies Department: William Doane Kelly's lecture, where he called on the pope and the archbishop to resign, Kelly's appointment to the ad hoc committee on academic freedom, and a lecture by an unnamed faculty member of the Theological Studies Department disparaging the magisterium, the pope, and church teachings on birth control. They also pointed out that of twenty-seven faculty in Theological Studies, eleven were thirty or younger.

Reedy and Andrews also blamed the administration for the way they handled the situation once the accusation was made. Dismissing the charges on a technicality was a mistake that led to Bonnette's appeal to the archbishop, putting the administration on the defensive.[60]

The conclusion of the article dealt with lessons for the future. First, "the church must develop (in chanceries and in educational institutions) a sophisticated, reasonable, forward-looking view of (1) academic competence, (2) the academic process, and (3) the value of open academic discussion." Second, both sides would do well to avoid "committed" posi-

58. Reedy and Andrews, "Troubled University of Dayton."
59. Reedy and Andrews, "Troubled University of Dayton," 24.
60. Reedy and Andrews, "Troubled University of Dayton," 25.

tions. Reedy and Andrews pointed out that once the archbishop launched an investigation, he was committed to seeing the situation through to a conclusion. And once it was determined that teachings contrary to the magisterium had taken place, presumably, the archbishop wanted the teachings to stop. Yet, in a recent lecture, a different University of Dayton faculty member used statements stronger than those of the accused. What happens if the teachings continue? What will the archbishop do? On the part of the university, by holding to its earlier investigation, it finds itself justifying some statements that the administrators "surely regard as objectively erroneous and irreverent."[61]

Third, *Ave Maria* does not think formal investigations and juridical rights will be "adequate to disputes in Church institutions of today." But they believe the archbishop "could probably insist that a group of University teachers be dismissed if he concluded that they consistently advocated positions which contradict the church's authoritative teaching." If Archbishop Alter did so, "it is hard to see how such a step could be taken without jeopardizing the whole academic life of the institution." The editors claim that "at least one of the accused indicates intent to appeal, claiming that he has been damaged in his professional reputation."[62]

Fourth, Reedy and Andrews believe that "viable solutions to such problems will have to rest as much on professional standards as on religious discipline." This implies that "truly professional scholars can achieve a working relationship with the Magisterium which will not do violence to their professional standards." The relationship has to work, or "the dream of a great Catholic university is impossible."[63]

Archbishop Alter wrote to Father Reedy shortly after the article's publication. He thought the "treatment of the University problem" was "fair and objective," but he did not find himself "completely in agreement with your observations":

> The issue of academic freedom does indeed affect all our Catholic universities, but I do not think that the solution to the problem will be found

61. Reedy and Andrews, "Troubled University of Dayton."
62. Reedy and Andrews, "Troubled University of Dayton." The author does not know who this person is.
63. Reedy and Andrews, "Troubled University of Dayton."

either in full secularization or in the removal of all restraints on the responsibility of a Catholic university to guarantee the integrity of Catholic doctrine to its student body and the public. There must be as large a measure of freedom as possible for professors in a graduate school to discuss questions of theology with their peers, but there must also be some authority in the event of doubt or disagreement to decide what is or is not Catholic doctrine according to the official pronouncements of the church's magisterium. If a Catholic university, by default, leaves the issue in doubt, then a formal appeal for an official decision is in order. Normally church authority need not take the initiative, but it cannot reject an appeal for a decision, when made from within the university or from the Catholic community.[64]

The May 13, 1967, issue of *Ave Maria* included seven letters to the editor. The authors point out the importance of civil dialogue; the dilemma for parents as to whether they should spend the money on a Catholic education for their children; and the need for new juridical structures regulating our Catholic institutions, the latter written by Holy Cross brother Raymond Fleck, then president of St. Edward's University in Austin, Texas. Several writers were from Dayton, Ohio. Ed Duffy pointed out that the "ringleader in the U. of Dayton rumble," namely, Dennis Bonnette, got his degrees from Notre Dame, but *Ave Maria* did not mention it. A Marianist, Father Edwin J. Weber, accused *Ave Maria* of "inconsistent procedure," since their March 11 editorial recommended that "everybody stop talking about [the controversy] for six months."[65] Less than a month later, Reedy and Andrews published their cover story. The cleverest letter—whose author's name was withheld—blames Notre Dame's article as payback over basketball players:

> Three years ago Don May [star player for Dayton] reduced his 70 offers of a basketball ride down to two schools (Dayton and ND in that order). Dayton won out, Johnny Dee [Notre Dame's basketball coach] tried suicide in the ND birdbath during the dry season and now in Dayton they consider your article as your means (as spokesman for ND) to get back for losing All-American May to Dayton. (Your article also came out one day after May's little brother with 125 different offers of basketball rides announced

64. Karl J. Alter to John L. Reedy, CSC, April 6, 1967, "Controversy 'Academic Freedom, etc.,' 1966–67," Belmont Ave. general files, 1.6 Abp. Alter, AAC.

65. "Letters," *Ave Maria*, May 13, 1967, 3.

he too was heading for Dayton.) Back to the gym to work on your timing which is way off.[66]

FATHER DARBY'S RESPONSE TO *AVE MARIA*

Marianist father James M. Darby, the University of Dayton's chairman of the board of trustees, responded to *Ave Maria* with a lengthy letter to the editor, published as an article, "Backtalk: The Troubled University of Dayton," in the May 20, 1967, issue. Darby assumed that "there is no intended relationship between the 'April 1' date, April Fool's Day, on the magazine and [the] cover title 'The Troubled University of Dayton.'" He considered "secretly regret[ting] the repeated inaccuracies in the reported word, suffering them in silence," but decided that would "not redress the wrong impressions they generate."

Darby felt the authors were trying to "draw a crowd" by "driving a wedge" between the Archbishop of Cincinnati and the University of Dayton administration, particularly by saying that Father Neil McCluskey's views were those of the administration. Darby said that McCluskey spoke "days after [Reedy and Andrews] left the campus," so how could McCluskey's views be those of the administration?[67]

Darby argued that the archbishop and the university authorities hold the same position:

> That the teaching of Catholic faith and morals must be within bounds clearly and practically set by the Magisterium and that the University is committed to accomplish this objective to the reasonable satisfaction of the Church authorities, as well as within the principles set forth by the AAUP.[68]

Darby took exception to the authors' view that because the University of Dayton supported academic freedom, the university was "likely to allow teaching contrary to the Magisterium to continue, or, for that matter, has allowed it in the past." He said "increased light and positive guidance" were needed from church authorities or other competent people with

66. "Letters," *Ave Maria*, May 13, 1967.
67. James M. Darby, "Backtalk: The Troubled University of Dayton," *Ave Maria*, May 20, 1967, 22.
68. Darby, "Backtalk."

knowledge of the magisterium. If there is a lack of "stable intellectuals" on the Universitiy of Dayton's or Xavier's campuses, what should the universities do? Close down? Not allow dialogue at all? Darby thought "an attractive possibility" would be "a workable built-in system of checks and balances, preferably operative within the confines of the University Community and according to the expressed purposes of the institution." Darby hoped the ad hoc committee would help on this front.[69]

Darby was also defensive about his statement to the press, which appeared to contradict the findings of the archbishop's commission. He said his statement "simply does not" represent a false position that the accused professors were innocent. If it did, he "would have had to refuse the Archbishop's report *in conscience* and appealed over his head for justice." As support for his position, Darby uses the quote from Father Kenney, who said the university was under investigation, not the accused, not the teachings, and not the pastoral effects themselves. Both the archbishop's commission and the university administration agree that the ad hoc committee is the way to begin resolving the issues.[70]

Finally, Darby expressed his opinion that "creative charity could have been in slightly greater evidence at spots" in the article. One spot is where the authors "stress that everything remains in turmoil and erroneous teachings continue." Darby felt that "If [the authors] try just a little harder to defend [their] thesis [they] will have pushed the whole business beyond the point of no return." Another spot is the "lack of any recounting" of what the administration has done and continues to do behind the scenes. A third spot is the reporting of a *Flyer News* article that was inaccurate and revised the next week by the professor in question.[71]

Darby concluded by recalling that he sent a telegram of appreciation to Reedy after his March editorial recommending everyone stop talking about the controversy for six months. Darby "had fully intended to take [the] advice seriously! Meanwhile, be assured, the University Community is following solid advice as she threads her way."[72]

69. Darby, "Backtalk," 22–23.
70. Darby, "Backtalk."
71. Darby, "Backtalk," 23.
72. Darby, "Backtalk."

On the same two-page spread, the editors replied to Darby's letter. They ignored the charge that they were trying to "draw a crowd" by driving a wedge between the archbishop and the university: "Civil discussion requires that charges of this kind be tested by the public facts and also by the consistent reputation of the *Ave Maria* and its editors."[73]

From there, the editors presented "factual difficulties" with Darby's response: (1) Father McCluskey's lecture was delivered while the editors were on campus. Furthermore, the editors did not say that McCluskey's views were those of the administration. They said, "We feel that [the administration's] actions and statements… put them in agreement" with McCluskey's view. The editors came to this conclusion after hearing Father Roesch's lecture to the faculty, where he made a distinction between pastoral and academic, by reading all the statements made by the administration, and by Darby's and Roesch's emphasis that the archbishop's report should have gone to Darby as provincial of the Marianists, not as chairman of the university's board of trustees. (2) Reedy and Andrews would have been happy to report on the "back-scenes work of the University administration, and did, in fact, report whatever [they] knew." They indicated that they interviewed as many involved parties as they could. "The only refusal came from the University president." (3) Last, Darby's calling them to task for reporting on Chrisman's lecture, which was reported inaccurately, was an error. Darby had overlooked that the faculty member in question was not part of the controversy. Rather, Reedy and Andrews reported on the lecture of William Doane Kelly, who "personally gave [them] the typescript of the speech in question." Kelly approved the published quote and mentioned to the authors that he had sent the lecture to "another national Catholic publication."[74]

Dennis Bonnette remembered that he and others were interviewed by Reedy and Andrews at a Dayton restaurant, where a large amount of alcohol was consumed. Presumably, the alcohol may have loosened the lips of Bonnnette and the other interviewees. Shortly after the article came out, Bonnette and Tom Casaletto stopped at the *Ave Maria* offices while

73. John L. Reedy, CSC, and James F. Andrews, "The Editors Reply," *Ave Maria*, May 20, 1967, 23.

74. Reedy and Andrews, "Editors Reply."

attending an American Catholic Philosophical Association conference at Notre Dame. Bonnette recalls that Father Reedy

> looked afraid for his life—thinking we had come there to attack him for publishing the article. We actually came to thank him for presenting a fairly balanced article, one revealing the shortcoming of UD's handling of the matter. He was relieved. We knew the article demeaned our competence to judge the issues involved, but really did not care what it said about us—just as long as the truth came out that teachings against the magisterium were, indeed, being offered at UD.[75]

AMERICA MAGAZINE

Father Darby also wrote an article, "Reflections on the Dayton Situation," that was published in *America* on April 29, 1967. He tried to counter the criticisms of the university. His stated purpose was to clarify "what are not among the true issues" at stake in the situation at the University of Dayton. First, there is no power struggle between the university and the archbishop. He went through the chronology event-by-event to show that throughout the controversy, the university and the archbishop agreed about what should be done. He concludes that the university was not "invaded" by the archbishop.[76]

Second, Darby stated that there "has not been a formal search to establish theological and philosophical deviations from the faith." Although the archbishop formed a fact-finding commission, Darby pointed out that the archbishop did not condemn any of the accused or recommend that anyone be dismissed. Darby claimed that his statement to the press that the accused were innocent did not contradict the statement by the archbishop's fact-finding commission that there were teachings contrary to the magisterium occurring on campus. In the end, he blamed the misunderstanding on the press reporting, which "oversimplified my position."[77]

Darby's third point was that the university has not been championing academic freedom. Considering that the university president Father

75. Dennis Bonnette, email message to the author, June 17, 1999.

76. James M. Darby, "Reflections on the Dayton Situation," *America*, April 29, 1967, 650–51.

77. Darby, "Reflections," 651.

Roesch proclaimed that the faculty have full academic freedom in his lecture to the faculty, this claim is the most bizarre. Darby recognizes that "everyone wants to be on the right side of the conversation" on this topic because "in its purest and simplest sense academic freedom means freedom of conscience." On a Catholic campus, the exercise of academic freedom is "in accord with the expressed purposes of the institution, with due respect, therefore, for the Church's teachings." Darby disagrees with members of the archbishop's fact-finding commission who, in Darby's opinion, said that "academic freedom connotes some sort of rarefied scholarly application to life on ultimate levels of university existence." Presumably, Darby is referring to the fact-finding commission's recommendation that the faculty limit what they say to undergraduates. Darby thinks theories are translated "rapidly and compulsively into understandable and negotiable language, to feed it into the blood stream of the common experience of all mankind." He downplays the topics raised in the Dayton controversy, saying they are "mostly from Teilhard de Chardin and Leslie Dewart," which are "headlined in the daily press since the close of the Council." He thinks it is up to a "professor with freedom of conscience" to "determine for himself where he goes from there." Someone "within earshot can take up the cause if it needs redressing, especially if there are some criteria to guide them fruitfully and forcefully."[78]

The fourth issue Darby clarified was that of competency. Darby took the position that "the Church as teacher feels the press of circumstances." He quotes Karl Rahner saying, "The road from universal principle to concrete prescription is longer than it ever was and … the Church by official teaching and guidance can accompany the individual to the end of this road much less often than formerly." Darby continues that "new and challenging dimensions of competence for all of us are stressed as the solution." The church will need to guide us as we move "forward, not back."[79]

Darby spent the majority of the article discussing the four issues he wanted to clarify. At the beginning of the article, however, he explained why the controversy happened. Darby said the

78. Darby, "Reflections," 652.
79. Darby, "Reflections."

plainest way of characterizing our difficulties would be to call them management problems and to add at once that they are being faced, we hope, with the sophistication and dignity befitting the institution. That is to say, the manner of the university's response to these internal pressures has become and continues to be a creative experience, an occasion for important growth within the broad and complex spectrum of true understanding and appreciation of human relations on a Catholic university campus.[80]

Presumably, admitting to a management problem is a lesser evil than allowing teachings contrary to the magisterium because the faculty have academic freedom.

The Claretian publication *U.S. Catholic* addressed academic freedom in a May 1967 article entitled, "The Bishops Have a Problem with Academic Freedom in the University." They alluded to John 11:48, where the chief priests and Pharisees said, "If we let him go on this way, everybody will believe in him and the Romans will come and destroy our place and our nation." The same has happened within Christianity: new ideas or developments destroy things. Witness Galileo and the discovery of cobalt-dating in the 1940s. What is a bishop to do when someone accuses a professor of teaching heresy? Archbishop Alter said he has the right and duty to investigate the charges. Jesuit Father Neil McCluskey said the archbishop should do nothing: "If the church is going to have a real regard for the truth, it can't go around muzzling professors who are attempting to reach it."[81]

The authors indicate that nonacademicians are "likely to be ill-equipped to gauge effective teaching methods." They gave as an example Jesuit Father William J. Wade from St. Louis University, who is regularly reported to university officials for teaching "heresy." Wade's goal is to teach the students to think. According to university president Jesuit father Paul C. Reinert, Wade was successful.[82]

In the past, if there were too many complaints against a professor, he would be reassigned as "a chaplain in a convent, or as assistant in a rural parish." This no longer works because

80. Darby, "Reflections," 650.

81. "The Bishops Have a Problem with Academic Freedom in the University," *U.S. Catholic*, May 1967, 56.

82. "Bishops Have a Problem."

many of the real "trouble-makers" are likely to be lay theologians like Stanford's Michael Novak; others are well-known priests (Brown University's monsignor John Tracy Ellis is an example) that can't very well be silenced without raising an international outcry.[83]

The authors also raised the recent situation of Father Peter O'Reilly, who failed to get the permission of his Chicago archbishop, John P. Cody, to teach at Illinois Teachers College in Chicago. O'Reilly was looking for a teaching position because he was one of the faculty dismissed from St. John's University after he organized a faculty strike.

U.S. Catholic quoted Father McCluskey extensively. They also quoted Eastern Rite archbishop Neophytos Edelby, an advisor to Melchite patriarch Maximos IV Saigh of Antioch, saying,

> In the Church there will always be people with a nose for heresy who find heresies everywhere. One should look ten times before declaring a doctrine heretical. The honor of condemnation should not be granted some thoughtless person simply because he has said something stupid.

Edelby deplores the abuses of freedom that occur, but he believes these are "mostly the result of doctrinal repression, long suffered in respectful silence but without conviction." The article included drawings of Galileo and the burning of heretics at the stake before the king of France in 1460.[84]

CHICAGO STUDIES JOURNAL

The academic journal *Chicago Studies* published "Academic Freedom and Apologetics" in its Summer 1967 issue. The author was Father George K. Malone, a professor of theology at St. Mary of the Lake Seminary. The article was the first in a series looking at the major problems being faced in the field of practical and scientific apologetics or fundamental theology. Malone looked at the definition of apologetics and the meaning of similar words such as polemics. The traditional approach to the field was becoming "impossible or at least undesirable" due to changes in biblical

83. "Bishops Have a Problem," 56–57.
84. "Bishops Have a Problem," 57.

studies and historical certitude.[85] He reviewed both and then discussed problem areas such as "proofs" of the preambles of faith, disillusionment with God, adaptation to ecumenism, and "the most pressing problem facing systematic Roman Catholic theology today," academic freedom.

Malone points out that the issue of academic freedom pertains primarily to the ordinary teaching authority of the church. Two incidents illustrate the question of academic freedom: Dayton and Little Rock, Arkansas. Malone gives no details on the controversy at Dayton. Rather, he begins with Father McCluskey's quote about there being no more academic justification for the archbishop to enter into theology than for the mayor to intrude into political science. Malone accepts this assertion from the point of view of a professional educator. But, "to the theologian this is a gross oversimplification," since, quoting Paul Tillich, "participation in a religious community is a presupposition of all theology."[86]

Malone sees two problems with McCluskey's remarks. The first is that within Roman Catholicism, a bishop has functions as taught by the Second Vatican Council.[87] Secondly, individual bishops "proclaim Christ's doctrine infallibly" when three conditions are met: "unity among themselves and with the pope; authentic teaching on a matter of faith or morals; and concurrence in a single viewpoint which must be held conclusively." If the three conditions are met "in a specific case of theological teaching, the local bishop not only can, but in fact must guarantee the teaching of this doctrine to his flock."[88] For Malone,

> McCluskey's remarks are nothing more than theological fantasy, for they ignore the structure of systematic Roman Catholic theology, in which the ordinary universal teaching of the episcopal college is one of the data with which this theology works.[89]

85. George K. Malone, "Academic Freedom and Apologetics," *Chicago Studies* 6, no. 2 (Summer 1967): 172.

86. Malone, "Academic Freedom and Apologetics," 183.

87. See Second Vatican Council, *Lumen Gentium* ¶25, and Pope Paul VI, *Pastorale Munus* ¶12; Malone, "Academic Freedom and Apologetics," 183.

88. Malone, "Academic Freedom and Apologetics," 183–84.

89. Malone, "Academic Freedom and Apologetics," 184.

In the Little Rock incident, the local bishop suspended a seminary professor, Father James F. Drane, from his priestly ministry because of articles on birth control that Drane wrote for the *Arkansas Gazette*, the daily Little Rock newspaper. The bishop wrote that since Drane taught and defended a doctrine forbidden by the Holy See, he was suspected of heresy. Since church teaching on birth control had not changed, Malone held that Drane should have upheld church teaching: "To go counter to this with the non-professional is not to be a heretic, but it is to leave the sphere of systematic Catholic teaching."[90]

Malone asked if the theologian had freedom or was "he bound merely to repeat and to parrot the teachings of his predecessors and contemporaries and simply to echo even the non-infallible pronouncements of the magistery?" He pointed out that in 1964 *Chicago Studies* established "theological norms according to which the professional theologian could dissent from authentic non-infallible teaching." Father Charles Curran applied those norms at the 1966 Catholic Theological Society of America convention when he presented an "exploratory discussion" on masturbation to his peers and was open to their criticism and questions.[91] In the Little Rock case, Drane disagreed with church teaching in a popular newspaper. Malone assessed that Drane's bishop was justified in removing him. Whether that was wise or desirable Malone left to others to determine.[92]

Malone concludes that both practical apologetics and academic freedom have a "common strain"; that is, "Roman Catholicism involves a creedal confession with certain intellectual and personal commitments.... To talk as if there were no reasoned explanation of our faith-preambles or as if the Catholic theologian enjoyed unlimited academic freedom is surely intellectually dishonest."[93]

At the close of the October 24, 1966, meeting in which the accused first heard they had been charged with teaching contrary to the magiste-

90. Malone, "Academic Freedom and Apologetics," 184–85.
91. Malone, "Academic Freedom and Apologetics," 185.
92. Malone, "Academic Freedom and Apologetics," 186.
93. Malone, "Academic Freedom and Apologetics."

rium, Father Roesch asked everyone to keep quiet about the accusations. All agreed. Within a day, the associate editor of *Flyer News* "heard" about the accusations and started pursuing the story with her feature editor. This forced Father Roesch to comment, and the coverage began.

Most of the reporting was accurate, perhaps because Dennis Bonnette spoke to the press as the controversy unfolded. One reason he spoke to the press was to clarify the charges as "teachings contrary to the Magisterium" rather than "heresy." Although Bonnette's accusation letter used language that indicated that John Chrisman's denial of purgatory could be heretical (Canon 1325), Bonnette claims he did not intend to call Chrisman a heretic. Rather, he was saying that denial of purgatory is a matter for heresy.[94] Once Canon 1325 was mentioned, however, Roesch needed to make sure the ecclesiastical charge was properly considered. He did so by consulting canon lawyer Father James O'Connor, who determined that there was no heresy involved. This consultation would later be used as a technical way out for the university. They could say that the faculty were innocent of the charge of heresy.

The university's initial statement on the controversy quoted Father Roesch saying that the charges were "teachings contrary to the Magisterium." The October news coverage in *Flyer News*, the Cincinnati *Catholic Telegraph*, *National Catholic Reporter*, and the Dayton newspapers also did not use the word "heresy."

In November 1966, Philosophy Department chair Dr. Richard Baker told *Flyer News*, "There is no such thing as a philosophical heresy but there are areas in philosophy that touch on theological doctrines." This statement was repeated in the *Catholic Telegraph*. Shortly after that, Dennis Bonnette issued a public statement that indicated that he was not talking about philosophical heresy but the theological implications of the teachings. He reiterated that his charges were "teachings contrary to the Magisterium."

Father Roesch's widely reported December letter to the faculty did not use the word "heresy," either, nor did the *New York Times*. So—when was the word "heresy" introduced into public discourse? It was used by

94. Dennis Bonnette, email message to the author, September 25, 2017.

the chairman of the board of trustees, Father James Darby, in his statement following the release of the archbishop's fact-finding commission's report in mid-February 1967. Darby said the commission supported the university's investigation in that the accused were cleared of heresy. In fact, they had never been charged with heresy, but the word stuck. When the March 1967 issue of the *UD Alumnus* arrived in the mailboxes of alumni, they opened the magazine to see an article entitled, "The 'Heresy' Affair."[95]

We have seen how Dennis Bonnette used the press to make sure the charges were presented accurately. Noticeable in the media coverage is the lack of comments by the accused. All four made comments in the original press report, but then said nothing throughout the remainder of the investigation.[96] They avoided appearing too radical, thus appearing to be more loyal to the university than the conservatives. It was important to faculty and administrators that the University of Dayton look good on a national level, and the publicity about the controversy did not make the university look good. The more Dennis Bonnette and his supporters went to the press, the worse the University of Dayton, and all American Catholic universities, looked.[97]

The publicity was not good for the church, either. Multiple articles in both the Catholic and secular press spoke of the Catholic universities as belonging to the church and that the church had a problem with its universities. Gary Potter, author of the *Triumph* article, pointed out that though Dayton was the first institution faced with such a crisis, the revolt against authority was building elsewhere. He saw Dayton's controversy as about upholding orthodoxy. No one had an appetite for it, either the bishops or the universities. The church wanted to avoid a scandal.[98]

Dennis Bonnette did not expect to go public with his charges, but

95. "The 'Heresy' Affair," *UD Alumnus*, March 1967, inside front cover.

96. One exception was a two-part story in the *Dayton Daily News* about Eulalio Baltazar and his research on Teilhard de Chardin.

97. Alfred Bannan, interview with the author, May 7, 1999. In 1966–67, Bannan was an assistant professor in the History Department at the University of Dayton and the first president of Dayton's AAUP chapter.

98. Gary K. Potter, interview with the author, February 8, 1999. Potter was the author of the February 1967 *Triumph* article "Storm over Dayton."

once the controversy was out in the open, he used the media to accomplish his goals. He made sure the charges were understood as multiple teachings contrary to the magisterium rather than only one charge of heresy. Bonnette and his supporters used the media to issue their "declaration of conscience," their appeal to the archbishop to reopen the investigation. Lastly, if Bonnette could not get the four accused to stop the teachings contrary to the magisterium, his use of the press informed parents of current and prospective students about what was happening at the University of Dayton. Then, as now, the media was used to pursue the agendas of all sides of the controversy.

CONCLUSION

Everything is the sum of the past and... nothing is comprehensible except through its history.
—Pierre Teilhard de Chardin, *The Future of Man*

The "Heresy" Affair is important for many reasons. For the University of Dayton and other Catholic institutions, the turbulent decade of the sixties changed Catholic higher education in the United States forever. In addition to helping Catholic institutions understand where they had come from, studying the Dayton controversy is useful for understanding why it happened and how to prevent future occurrences. It may also help institutions of Catholic higher education determine where to go in the future.

The "Heresy" Affair began in 1963 as a controversy among philosophers at the University of Dayton. Three years later, Dennis Bonnette wrote his letter to Archbishop Karl J. Alter. Once that happened, the controversy took on a life of its own. So, why did the controversy happen, and, specifically, why did it happen at the University of Dayton?

There are multiple contributing factors to the controversy. First, the cultural context of the Roman Catholic Church. As mentioned previous-

Pierre Teilhard de Chardin, *The Future of Man*, trans. Norman Denny (New York: Image/ Doubleday, 1964), 12, found in John Tracy Ellis, "American Catholic Clerical-Lay Relations," *Thought: A Review of Culture and Idea* (Autumn 1966): 329.

ly, new thoughts began bubbling up in the church in the forties and fifties. Pope John XXIII tapped into them when he called for "aggiornamento." The Second Vatican Council showed that the majority of the bishops were open to the church rethinking issues. Theologians who were silenced in the fifties—Henri de Lubac, Yves Congar, and American John Courtney Murray—gained prominence at the Council, and the role of the laity was recognized. The progressive faculty in the controversy (Eulalio Baltazar, John Chrisman, Lawrence Ulrich, and Randolph Lumpp) thought they were moving with the church. They wanted to update the church from within. In the language of the Vatican II documents, they thought they were helping to bring the church into the modern world. As laity and academics within the church, they felt responsible for bringing new approaches to the problems facing humanity. They thought new ways of thinking could contribute to the church by bringing it more in line with the current times. They believed they had the right and duty to question some church teachings. This is how Eulalio Baltazar, in particular, felt he contributed with his chapter in the book *Contraception and Holiness: The Catholic Predicament*, edited by Archbishop Thomas D. Roberts.

A minority of bishops at the Council, led by Alfredo Cardinal Ottaviani, tried to minimize the changes. After the Council, Ottaviani still led the Holy Office and continued to make statements that repeated some pre–Vatican II teachings. Dayton's traditionalists (Dennis Bonnette, Joseph Dieska, Father Richard Dombro, and their supporters), who were trying to make sense of the rapid change within the church, relied on Ottaviani. They believed that the church had already established the truth. As Catholics, they then were obligated to defend those truths and respect church leaders. Church teachings mattered because their own salvation and the salvation of those entrusted to them were at stake. More than anything, the traditionalists wanted official church teachings, especially on sexual morality, to be represented properly to impressionable students because the stakes were high.

While there is a long history of debates in the church, Vatican II marked a new era. Moreover, what changed in the sixties was the cultural context of secular society. In general, there developed a lack of respect for authority. As the decade wore on, citizens were aware that they were being lied to by government authority figures. Some lashed back in protest, but even those who did not protest lost faith in their leaders. They no longer believed everything they were told. This attitude carried over to all parts of their lives, including their spiritual lives.

At the same time, higher education in the United States experienced tremendous growth in the numbers of students and faculty. Institutions of Catholic higher education sought more respect from its secular counterparts. They needed funding to construct new buildings and develop new programs, and the federal government was a potential source of that funding. As a result, some leaders in Catholic higher education distanced their institutions from the church in order to qualify for the funding.

The increase in students required an increase in faculty. The religious orders that established and operated most of the Catholic colleges and universities not only had insufficient religious to staff the schools, but began losing membership. They began hiring many lay professors, some of them underprepared. While this was not a problem for most disciplines, philosophy and theology—the centerpieces of Catholic higher education—were different. The addition of laity to the faculty led to challenges that previously did not exist. If a religious got out of line, his religious superior had direct authority to correct the situation. That approach did not work with the laity. There was also little experience in place for how lay professors, especially in a troubled time of rapid change, should act within the Catholic academy. What was their role? What were their rights? These very issues were beginning to be intensely discussed at the University of Dayton as the controversy escalated.

One of the main issues for faculty was academic freedom. To gain academic credibility within American higher education, Catholic institutions needed to prove that their faculty had academic freedom. They also needed to increase academic quality, including in the areas of research and publication. These two factors led the university administration to support the progressives. Regardless of what the progressives said, the administration could not silence them without appearing to restrict their academic freedom. In terms of scholarship, Eulalio Baltazar was the most credible. His book on Teilhard de Chardin, along with the chapter in the

Contraception book and other articles, contributed to the national conversation in the church. This is what the administration encouraged the faculty to do, which became apparent when the president's three-man committee named Eulalio Baltazar "Professor of the Year" as the controversy ended in 1967.[1]

Turning from the cultural contexts of the church and American society, the various personalities of the participants contributed to the conflict. At the outset of the conflict, Joseph Dieska led the traditionalist cause. His Eastern European background fighting the Communists, at the risk of his own life, made him a formidable opponent. Once he knew that some professors were questioning church leaders, he was not willing to let it go. Dennis Bonnette and others such as Edward Harkenrider were committed individuals. They also were willing to challenge the progressives at great personal cost.

At least two of the progressives, John Chrisman and William Doane Kelly, loved to speak publicly, and they were often flippant toward church teachings and the hierarchy. Their attitude angered the traditionalists, who did not think church teachings were to be mocked.

In general, the students sided with the progressives who wanted the students to be "active learners." The traditionalists, on the other hand, tended to be authoritarian in the classroom. The way they taught Thomism was through rote memorization. When the students saw the traditionalists trying to silence the progressives, they too thought academic freedom was violated.[2]

As the controversy continued, communication between the two sides totally broke down. Traditionalist faculty member Hugo Barbic lamented, "We failed in that we weren't able to see both sides. We stopped talking, took sides. We could have handled the complexities better with-

---

1. The "Professor of the Year" title went to the Alumni Award winner chosen by a three-man committee appointed by the president. The 1967 committee was comprised of Dr. Rocco Donatelli, professor of history and chairman of the faculty forum; Dr. George Noland, chairman of the Biology Department; and Professor Erving Beauregard of the History Department and secretary of the faculty forum; University of Dayton press release, March 8, 1967, press releases, series 7J (A2), AUD.

2. Stephen Bickham, written comments to and interview with the author, September 25, 2015.

out alienation. There was no discussion in a rational way."[3] Recall that graduate assistant Robert Eramian described stereotyping by both sides, claiming the faculty called each other "the idiots" and "the heretics."[4]

Among the Marianists, brothers and priests sided with both factions in the conflict. The clearest examples are Fathers Dombro and Roesch. Roesch, as president, wanted to move the University of Dayton into a new era. He focused primarily on the academic issues. He expected there to be debate in an academic setting. Dombro, on the other hand, focused on the pastoral implications. He believed Roesch did not care about the pastoral implications. Dombro once told Roesch, "When I die, call a priest," which meant a priest other than Roesch. The traditionalists heard and repeated this story.

Another factor contributing to the controversy was the issues being discussed. The conflict began when Father Thomas Stanley, the dean and later provost of the University of Dayton, asked the progressives to lecture on the thought of Teilhard de Chardin and on existentialism. Both topics included philosophical issues that had been condemned at one time by the church hierarchy. At the Second Vatican Council, the church appeared to be more open to these teachings. To the dismay of the traditionalists and the local pastors, these lectures drew large crowds. The traditionalists tried to debate the progressives, but their arguments consisted mostly of citing condemnations, sometimes centuries-old church documents. In a discussion of controversial topics, the traditionalists were no match for the charismatic progressives.

As the controversy developed over time, the topics changed, and the progressives grew bolder in their challenges to church teachings. Baltazar, Chrisman, and their students wanted to move beyond Thomism. For the traditionalists, doing away with Thomism was incomprehensible. To them, Thomism provided fundamental support for church teachings. What would happen to the faith of the church and of the students? Teaching and studying Thomism was their life's work. How would they support their families if Thomism were to just disappear?

3. Hugo Barbic, interview with the author, April 28, 1999.
4. Robert Eramian, interviews with the author, January 22, 1999, and June 27, 1999.

By the end of the controversy, the topics had changed to moral and more contemporary issues: abortion, contraception, and situation ethics. These topics raised the stakes of the controversy because, presumably, wrong beliefs on these issues lead to wrong actions. The traditionalists believed that students were practicing contraception and that at least one student had an abortion because, as a result of hearing talks by the progressives, she believed it was not wrong. To the traditionalists, souls were in danger of being lost.

Throughout the controversy, the traditionalists tried to end teachings contrary to the magisterium. Early on, they took an academic approach, writing open letters to the progressives pointing out errors and quoting church documents. Initially, the traditionalists thought that if they educated the progressives, they would see the error in their thinking. The traditionalists also challenged the progressives in the question-and-answer periods following public lectures. When the progressives continued to spread their ideas, the traditionalists talked to several Marianist priests on campus. Father Richard Dombro went directly to Father Roesch in an effort to stop one particular lecture. There is no evidence that Father Roesch did anything in response to Dombro's request. A number of the traditionalists spoke to Father Charles Lees, the provost. Father Lees also attended and walked out of at least one lecture. Reportedly, Lees spoke to John Chrisman about Chrisman's behavior, but the teachings continued. Father Francis Langhirt wrote to the archbishop in spring 1966 after attending one lecture and was referred back to the university administration. Father John Elbert intended to bring the matter before the board of trustees in fall 1966 but died before he could do so.

The traditionalists also talked to their local pastors and, at the urging of Father Lees, wrote to a number of prominent theologians seeking their advice on how to handle the matter. Dennis Bonnette also wrote to the Vatican and to the apostolic delegate for advice. The traditionalists were running out of options for dealing with the situation. When Lawrence Ulrich and Randolph Lumpp gave their situation ethics lecture in October 1966, Dennis Bonnette decided to write to the archbishop. He knew Langhirt had done so in the spring and figured he would tell the archbishop that false teachings continued. For whatever reason, Bonnette sent a carbon copy to the apostolic delegate. Bonnette remembers that Joseph Dieska gasped when told about the carbon copy; he knew Bonnette's letter would not be ignored.

Where was the administration in the midst of the controversy? Father Thomas Stanley, the person who hired Chrisman and Baltazar, wanted to improve the intellectual climate on campus. Stanley encouraged the progressives to give lectures on the controversial topics and created the *University of Dayton Review* as a vehicle to publish their papers. The progressives were doing what he hoped they would do, and they were sure of Stanley's support. Stanley and Roesch also knew that Father John Nichols was nearing the end of his doctoral work in philosophy and would be coming to the university's Philosophy Department soon. They counted on Nichols, an impressive Marianist scholar, to broker the conflict within the department. Unfortunately, Nichols did not arrive in time to calm the conflict.

Provost Father Lees realized the teachings were contrary to the magisterium because he had consulted Father William Cole who told him that the existence of purgatory was part of the dogmatic teachings of the church.[5] Lees, however, was ineffectual in getting the progressives to cease. One wonders if Lees and Cole were keeping Father Roesch informed or whether Roesch was blindsided. Stanley recalled that Father Roesch was shocked upon hearing that some of the faculty went to the archbishop. Roesch wondered why the traditionalists did not come to him with their concerns. Given that Father Dombro had tried and failed and that Lees had been informed, it is not surprising that the lay faculty did not reach out to Roesch.

Upon receiving Bonnette's letter and talking to the apostolic delegate, the archbishop asked Father Roesch to investigate. Bonnette provided a list of witnesses to each of the lectures in question and expected them to be called to say what they heard at the lectures. Roesch, however, knew what had been happening. He wanted to deal quickly with the ecclesiastical issues and then handle the pedagogical concerns in an academic pro-

---

5. William J. Cole to Raymond A. Roesch, March 3, 1967, 1, Roesch papers, series 91–35, box 6, AUD.

cess. He recognized the archbishop's concerns, but also knew he needed to keep it from looking like the archbishop was interfering on campus. He knew that it would not look good if an authority external to the university limited the faculty's academic freedom. It was important to the academic legitimacy of the University of Dayton and all Catholic colleges and universities that Roesch handle this situation correctly.

Fortunately for Roesch, in his letter to the archbishop, Bonnette mentioned Canon 1325 §2, which defined a heretic. Roesch learned from the canonist that he could use this mention of the canon to avoid having formal ecclesiastical charges brought before the church. Unfortunately for Roesch, his declaration that the accused were innocent was so nuanced— he said the accused were innocent while simultaneously admitting that the accused did teach contrary to the church—that it enraged the accusers and local pastors and led to the involvement of the archbishop.

What did the rest of the University of Dayton faculty think of the controversy? At first, they dismissed it as philosophers arguing among themselves; after all, that is what philosophers do.[6] As the controversy escalated, however, the faculty were "embarrassed by the whole affair and felt [the] dean, provost and president should have stifled the accusers instead of letting the world know that the University was struggling with an affair that cheapened UD in the eyes of academics throughout the western world."[7] The faculty recognized that the progressives were more scholarly and that scholarship mattered a great deal to the reputation of the university.[8] The faculty forum censure happened because, on Phil Donahue's radio talk show, the traditionalists called the progressives incompetent. The censure was an act on the part of the faculty to defend themselves.[9] Within a month, the faculty formed a chapter of the AAUP, thus signaling a change in the way things would be done at the University of Dayton going forward.

The involvement of the local pastors occurred for several reasons. First, as mentioned, the traditionalists spoke to them and sought their ad-

6. Brother Joseph Stander, interview with the author, n.d.
7. Joseph Cooney, email message to the author, February 18, 2006.
8. Alfred Bannan, telephone interview with the author, May 7, 1999.
9. Bud Cochran, telephone interview with the author, May 7, 1999.

vice on how to handle the situation. The pastors also heard from parents of local University of Dayton students who were concerned about what their children were being taught at the university and at the local Marianist Retreat Center.[10] Father (later Monsignor) Lawrence K. Breslin, then a faculty member at Alter High School and an assistant pastor at St. Charles Borromeo parish in Kettering, a Dayton suburb, described the local pastors as "builders" of parishes. They were very pragmatic but not, in general, intellectual.[11] They did not trust the Marianists in part because the order was founded in France, which, in their minds, was liberal.[12]

To summarize, the controversy happened as a result of the changing cultural climate of the church and American higher education. The professors, mostly young and inexperienced, took opposing sides within those cultural beliefs. Most importantly, the issues involved were significant. When issues of importance are involved, people are more committed to their views and are willing to defend them vigorously.

It is appropriate to ask who the winners and losers were in this controversy. Dennis Bonnette and his supporters (faculty and local pastors) won, in that the archbishop's fact-finding commission upheld their accusations that teachings contrary to the magisterium were being presented at the University of Dayton and that the university administration allowed this to happen. Due to the subsequent publicity, parents of current and prospective students were alerted as to what was happening at the university.

Although the progressives lost when the archbishop's commission concluded that they were teaching contrary to the magisterium, they did not lose their positions, nor were they forced to change the way they were teaching. Eulalio Baltazar, the only true scholar in the group of professors accused, was recognized as the 1967 "Professor of the Year" at the Universi-

---

10. Lawrence K. Breslin, interview with the author, September 25, 2003. In 1967, a new retreat center building opened. The center was renamed the Bergamo John XXIII Center for Christian Renewal; "The History of the Bergamo Center for Lifelong Learning," accessed on November 10, 2017, http://www.bergamocenter.org/PDF/2017%20Bergamo%20History.pdf.

11. The one exception to this statement is Msgr. James E. Sherman, the pastor of Immaculate Conception parish in Dayton. See chapter 2.

12. Breslin, interview, September 25, 2003.

ty of Dayton. He was also given a visiting professorship by Bishop Fulton Sheen in the bishop's seminary in Rochester, New York, from January 1968 to June 1968.[13]

Bonnette and his supporters lost the controversy in that their idea of a Catholic university did not come to pass. The changes unleashed with Vatican II and the changes in American culture during the sixties led to changes in American Catholic higher education. The philosophy curriculum changed. As one undergraduate later commented, "Thomism could not defend its privileged position in the Catholic universities on its own merits when fairly brought into contact with contemporary Catholic and non-Catholic thought."[14] Losing their focus on Thomism was a real loss for the traditionalists.

The progressives' view of the church also did not come to pass. As time went on, the church reversed some of the hopes of Vatican II, particularly under Pope John Paul II. Their view of a Catholic university as evidenced in the ad hoc committee report also did not come to pass, since that report was rewritten by the administration. Indeed, the winner was Father Roesch and the University of Dayton. To the higher education community in general, the University of Dayton emerged from the controversy looking like a real university. Roesch affirmed that the faculty had academic freedom to pursue their research and teaching. However, Roesch still insisted on respect for the magisterium and the church's teachings as a part of the academic freedom as faculty pursued their work wherever it took them.

Faculty on both sides suffered personal losses as a result of the conflict. Edward Harkenrider gave up his faculty position, took an administrative position at Western Michigan University, and never taught philosophy again. Bonnette and Casaletto left the University of Dayton at the conclusion of the 1966–67 academic year, uprooted their families, and took new positions at Niagara University. Baltazar, after teaching at Bishop Sheen's seminary, returned to Dayton for a year and then accepted a position at Federated City College in Washington, D.C., now known as

---

13. Eulalio Baltazar, note to the author, n.d.
14. Bickham, written comments to the author.

the University of the District of Columbia. He never taught in a Catholic university again. Chrisman remained at the University of Dayton for a few more years but left when he was not granted tenure. He moved back to his native Northwest, was unable to find a teaching position in philosophy, and therefore changed careers.

We will never know the untold effects of the controversy on the lives of others. Surely, some parents refused to send their children to the University of Dayton. At least one religious community, the Missionary Servants of the Most Holy Trinity, intended to send their seminarians to the University of Dayton,[15] but, with the "Heresy" Affair underway in the spring of 1967, Archbishop Alter refused permission for the order to open a house there. Instead, the seminarians, including William L. Portier, went to Loyola University of Chicago.[16] Years later, Portier, after studying under Leslie Dewart in Toronto, would come to Dayton as a lay professor of religious studies and mentor this author. One cannot help but wonder if Portier's path would have been different if he had received his undergraduate degree from Dayton rather than Loyola.

Much has happened in Catholic higher education in the fifty years since the "Heresy" Affair. One of the most important events was the signing of the Land O'Lakes Statement in the summer of 1967. In the aftermath, most Catholic institutions began changing their articles of incorporation and constitutions to build lay boards of trustees and disconnect legally from their founding religious orders and the church.

The church, including Catholic higher education institutions, coexists within the secular culture. A question needs to be asked and considered: in the wake of the sixties, did Catholic colleges and universities give up too much in order to become academically legitimate, to be accepted by the secular academy? By the seventies, the founders of Christendom College in Front Royal, Virginia, thought they did. The founders, encouraged and supported by L. Brent Bozell of *Triumph* magazine, created Christendom College in 1977 "in response to the devastating blow inflicted on

---

15. The Missionary Servants of the Most Holy Trinity intended to purchase the residence of the Notre Dame nuns; minutes of the administrative council, series 87–83, box 3, AUD.

16. Portier, "Genealogy of Heresy," 1–2.

Catholic higher education by the cultural revolution which swept across America in the 1960s."[17] Then and now, Christendom's purpose is to "learn and live by the truth revealed by Our Lord and Savior Jesus Christ, 'the Way, the Truth and the Life,' as preserved in our deposit of faith and authentically interpreted in the magisterium of the head of the church Christ founded, our Holy Father, the Pope."[18]

Others such as Jesuit John T. Conley also answered yes to the question of whether Catholic institutions gave up too much to become academically legitimate. Conley pointed out that at the same time as Catholic colleges and universities were excluding Catholic bishops from having a say in their institutions, they were allowing in "the state, accrediting agencies, and professional organizations" such as the AAUP. Individuals, businesses, and corporations could also be added to the list. "The problem is not a lack of freedom. The problem is that we simply can't keep our eyes off Caesar and Mammon."[19]

EX CORDE ECCLESIAE

On August 15, 1990, Pope John Paul II called on Catholic higher education to renew itself by implementing *Ex corde Ecclesiae*, the Apostolic Constitution on Catholic universities. The two-part document dealt with (1) the identity and mission of the Catholic university and included (2) general norms based on the Code of Canon Law and other church legislation. The norms were to be applied by the bishops of each country with Catholic universities. Over a period of nine years, the United States Catholic bishops developed a process to implement the papal document. Ultimately, the National Conference of Catholic Bishops approved "The Application of *Ex corde Ecclesiae* for the United States" on November 17, 1999, with an "in force" date of May 3, 2001.

17. "Welcome to Christendom College," accessed on November 6, 2017, https://www.christendom.edu/about/.

18. "Christendom College: A Prospectus," 1976, 3. My thanks to Raymond P. O'Herron, one of the four founding faculty members of Christendom College, who provided the author with a copy of the prospectus.

19. John T. Conley, SJ, "Phony Academic Freedom," letter to the editor, *Commonweal*, December 17, 1993, 29.

One of the immediate concerns on the part of Catholic universities about the implementation of *Ex corde Ecclesiae* in the United States pertains to the topic of this book: respect by faculty for church teachings— specifically, the general norm expressed in Part II, Article 4, §3, which reads:

> In ways appropriate to the different academic disciplines, all Catholic teachers are to be faithful to, and all other teachers are to respect, Catholic doctrine and morals in their research and teaching. In particular, Catholic theologians, aware that they fulfil a mandate received from the Church, are to be faithful to the Magisterium of the Church as the authentic interpreter of Sacred Scripture and Sacred Tradition.[20]

In the application document, the bishops explained that the *mandatum* "recognizes the professor's commitment and responsibility to teach authentic Catholic doctrine and to refrain from putting forth as Catholic teaching anything contrary to the church's magisterium." The *mandatum* is issued privately to an individual in virtue of one's baptism; the bishop is not appointing, authorizing, delegating, or approbating the individual's teaching. Overall, the implementation has gone well for over twenty-five years.[21]

University of Dayton administrators and faculty were involved in discussions leading to the development of the Vatican document and its implementation. Then-Dayton president Marianist brother Raymond L. Fitz and provost/university chancellor Marianist father James L. Heft (at the time also a member and chair of the board of directors of the Association of Catholic Colleges and Universities) were both involved, along with other Catholic university presidents and administrators. In their dialogue with the bishops, they stressed a pastoral rather than juridical approach. Terrence L. Tilley, then chairperson of and professor in the University of Dayton's Religious Studies Department and president of the Catholic Theological Society of America, represented theologians in discussions

20. John Paul II, *Ex corde Ecclesiae*, August 15, 1990, http://w2.vatican.va/content/john-paul-ii/en/apost_constitutions/documents/hf_jp-ii_apc_15081990_ex-corde-ecclesiae.html.

21. "The Application for *Ex Corde Ecclesiae* for the United States," November 17, 1999, http://www.usccb.org/beliefs-and-teachings/how-we-teach/catholic-education/higher-education/-the-application-for-ex-corde-ecclesiae-for-the-united-states.cfm.

with the bishops.[22] Daniel E. Pilarczyk, Archbishop of Cincinnati and president of the U.S. Bishops' Conference (1989–92) participated as the chair of the bishops' Ad Hoc Committee on the Academic *Mandatum* (1999–2000). In this discussion, the involvement and contributions of the Archbishop of Cincinnati and the academic leaders of the University of Dayton helped formulate answers to the question raised in the University of Dayton philosophy controversy in the sixties: what is the relationship of the magisterium to individual theologians?

FIDES ET RATIO

As the bishops were working out the details related to the implementation of *Ex corde Ecclesiae*, in September 1998, Pope John Paul II issued his encyclical *Fides et Ratio*.[23] Addressed to the bishops of the Catholic Church, the encyclical explores the relationship between faith and human reason; that is, between theology and philosophy, throughout the history of Western thought. John Paul II emphasizes the traditional Catholic position—namely, that they are compatible and need to interact. The pope laments that their important symbiotic relationship is floundering. He calls on Catholic theologians and philosophers to "recover" their relationship if they are to find authentic wisdom and truth.[24]

Speaking to issues in the University of Dayton controversy, John Paul II recommends the philosophy of Thomas Aquinas, but insists that

> The Church has no philosophy of her own nor does she canonize any one particular philosophy in preference to others. The underlying reason for this reluctance is that, even when it engages theology, philosophy must remain faithful to its own principles and methods. Otherwise there would be no guarantee that it would remain oriented to truth and that it was moving towards truth by way of a process governed by reason.[25]

22. The other representatives on the Bishops' Ad Hoc Committee on the Academic *Mandatum* were Daniel K. Finn (St. John's University, Collegeville, Minnesota), James Conn, SJ (Pontifical Gregorian University), and Maureen A. Fay, OP (president, University of Detroit Mercy).

23. John Paul II, *Fides et Ratio*, September 14, 1998, http://www.vatican.va/content/john-paul-ii/en/encyclicals/documents/hf_jp-ii_enc_14091998_fides-et-ratio.html.

24. *Fides et Ratio*, ¶106.

25. *Fides et Ratio*, ¶49.

Father Roesch and the accused in the Dayton controversy would have supported this paragraph. On the other hand, Dennis Bonnette and his supporters saw it differently. They focused on wording from the same paragraph and drew a very different conclusion:

> It is the Magisterium's duty to respond clearly and strongly when controversial philosophical opinions threaten right understanding of what has been revealed, and when false and partial theories which sow the seed of serious error, confusing the pure and simple faith of the People of God, begin to spread more widely.[26]

Drawing upon the rich tradition of the interplay of theology and philosophy, the pope proceeds to review twentieth-century theological and philosophical teachings that contradict Christian doctrine, including fideism and some forms of existentialism, which were concerns of Dennis Bonnette and the Thomists in Dayton's Philosophy Department. John Paul II exhorted philosophers to examine critically such teachings and work with theologians so that together they could work for the "benefit and development of human thought."[27]

FIFTIETH ANNIVERSARY OF THE LAND O'LAKES DOCUMENT

More recently, on the fiftieth anniversary of the signing of Land O'Lakes, Villanova theologian Massimo Faggioli pointed out that the Land O'Lakes document "reflects ongoing intra-Catholic culture struggles," is "attacked as much as it is celebrated," and that it has aged and needs an update.[28] Faggioli claims that the statement is stuck in the Second Vatican Council theology of the sixties and the debate over the relationship of the universities and the church. We are in a different place now. Faggioli proposes that Catholic universities, including research universities and small liberal arts colleges such as Christendom, find com-

26. *Fides et Ratio.*
27. *Fides et Ratio,* ¶101.
28. Massimo Faggioli, "Showing Its Age? The Land O'Lakes Statement Could Use an Update," *Commonweal,* October 31, 2017, accessed November 16, 2017, https://www.common wealmagazine.org/showing-its-age.

mon ground in a more recent document, Pope Francis's *Laudato si*, an encyclical on the environment but also about political power and knowledge. Faggioli argues that Francis's ecclesiology is "an epochal shift in global Catholicism and therefore U.S. Catholicism." The encyclical, as did Vatican II, provides "a vision for the role of the Church in the world contending the emergencies of the time" and could be the basis of a new document on the future of Catholic higher education.[29] It remains to be seen whether a leader will answer Faggioli's call and step forward to lead Catholic higher education into the future, as Father Theodore Hesburgh did in 1967.

❦

In conclusion, the controversy known as the "Heresy" Affair is important for understanding the history of Catholic higher education in the United States, at least as it played out at the University of Dayton. The usual story in Catholic history is the clergy vs. the clergy or the clergy vs. the laity; the Dayton controversy was the laity vs. the laity. Therefore, the history of the controversy is the history of the laity. The traditionalists were trying to preserve and protect their understanding of Catholicism. They raised legitimate questions, although their methodology, including the use of the media to interpret and create the story, is questionable.[30] The progressives were trying to update the church and Catholic higher education; however, their pedagogical approach contributed to the escalation of the controversy.

Catholic higher education will continue to rely on the laity, even more so than in the sixties, as the number of religious declines. As church teachings continue to evolve, the debate about what it means to be Catholic will persist. In the early twenty-first century, Pope Francis has been attacked by both religious and laity, bishops, and even some cardinals. In such a volatile time, fueled by social media, authority figures should not be surprised that some people will take positions and register their disagreements in ways that seem unfathomable to others involved in the debate.

29. Faggioli, "Showing Its Age?"

30. My thanks to Debra Campbell and Father Joseph Chiminci, who commented on an earlier paper at the American Catholic Historical Association annual meeting in Washington, D.C., in January 2008.

STATEMENT RELATIVE TO THE CONTROVERSY TOUCHING ACADEMIC FREEDOM AND THE CHURCH'S MAGISTERIUM

This statement, prepared by the President of the University of Dayton, was drafted primarily for the use of the University Faculty. Portions of this statement were first presented in an address to the members of the University of Dayton faculty and staff at a Faculty Meeting on March 1, 1967.

PROLOGUE

Because it has become apparent that a number of professors on the staff of the University of Dayton and very many friends and alumni of the institution are unaware that there is a recognized question today both by ecclesiastical and academic authorities regarding the proper role of the Church's Magisterium on a university campus, I wish to present a position paper explaining some difficulties being encountered in this regard, and the diversity of opinion which exists. The traditional view seems well enough understood, but a newer viewpoint, primarily growing out of the spirit of Vatican Council II, seems little understood. In this statement I am presenting the arguments of reputable theologians and philosophers supporting this new position, but I am not necessarily implying the adoption of this position by all members of the faculty of the University. I seek only to show that this position is within the pale of Catholic theology and philosophy and actually advocated by leading authorities of Vatican Council II. If some of our faculty choose to defend this position, they are free to do so. If others choose to argue against it, such is the challenge of academic debate. My purpose is to clear the air and encourage true scholarship with all its interesting consequences.

I. CONSTITUTION ON THE CHURCH #25 RE THE MAGISTERIUM

Since the concept of the Magisterium was at the heart of the University of Dayton campus controversy, it is fitting to begin by quoting paragraph 25 of the *Constitution on the Church* which was referred to in the report made through Archbishop Karl J. Alter. "In matters of faith and morals, the bishops speak in the name of Christ and the faithful are to accept their teaching and adhere to it with a religious assent of soul. This religious submission of mind and will must be shown in a special way to the authentic teaching authority of the Roman Pontiff, even when he is not speaking ex cathedra; that is, submission must be shown in such a way that his supreme Magisterium is acknowledged with reverence, the judgments made by him are sincerely adhered to, according to his manifest mind and will. His mind and will in the matter may be known chiefly either from the character of the document, from his frequent repetition of the same doctrine, or from his manner of speaking."

Catholics accept that pronouncement of Vatican Council II. Its message is implicitly contained in the University of Dayton's statement in the Faculty Handbook that the faculty "may not advocate and disseminate doctrines that are subversive of the aims and purposes of this Catholic institution which is committed to the upholding of the deposit of faith and Christian morality."

The University recognizes that this abbreviated statement of its aims and purposes as here defined is not so exact and comprehensive as it should be. A faculty committee is currently at work on a reformulation of this statement whose wording seems to suggest a misleading emphasis on defense of doctrine and at the same time neglects to bring to the fore the dynamic aspect of developing academic efforts on the campus.

Even when such a direct statement is made and accepted, one is faced with the fact that one of the most vexing and highly debated questions in the academic world today is the exact and proper role of the ecclesiastical Magisterium. Some theologians, in making a distinction between the "infallible Magisterium" and the "authentic Magisterium," encounter difficulty in trying to identify the exact force of tenets which are positioned in the latter area. A representative treatment of the concept of the Magisterium today is Gregory Baum's Treatise in Volume XXI of the CONCILIUM. Two other conciliar *periti* (theological scholars), Bernard Haering of Rome and Eugene Maly of Cincinnati, concur that this exposition is widely accepted by scholars today. The opinion of these three recognized theologians, as well as other advisors on campus, have helped the administration present and clarify this position with confidence.

II. TASK OF THEOLOGIAN AND PHILOSOPHER

Despite concomitant difficulties, the Catholic theologian and philosopher today engages in theological inquiries, even if some of his conclusions challenge or reinterpret the apparent meaning of past conciliar statements or papal encyclicals. He has witnessed how Vatican II went beyond many doctrinal positions, some ancient and some more recent, proposed by the ecclesiastical Magisterium. At the same time the Catholic theologian wants to remain in union with the Catholic Church, and he has learned to express his positions in a tentative way—as questions, as contributions to dialogue—and he refuses to engage himself unreservedly in his own convictions, unless he knows himself to be accompanied by the Church. A scholar may respectfully, albeit forcefully, suggest a different formulation of doctrine or practice. This does not mean that he is trying to change a revealed truth, or that he seeks to defy authority. Pope Paul wrote in his *Mysterium Fidei*, #25, "They (doctrinal formulae) can, it is true, be made clearer and more obvious; and doing this is of great benefit. But it must always be done in such a way that they retain the meaning in which they have been used, so that with the advance of an understanding of the faith, the truth of faith will remain unchanged."

Father Bernard Haering, in an interview with the University's president on February 25, 1967, pointed out that doctrine must be constantly studied, otherwise the Church will be outmoded. However, he cautioned that only a person knowledgeable in the history of dogma should dare to challenge any of the past positions of the Magisterium. He explained how such a challenge was possible by emphasizing that these ecclesiastical pronouncements were directed toward certain problems at a specific time in history under known historical-social-cultural conditions. If any of the historical-social-cultural conditions change, there may rightly be question [sic] whether or not the pronouncement applies with equal force in the new situation. This, however, does not conflict with the accepted principle that solemnly defined Church doctrine can never change; otherwise infallibility has no meaning. This was declared explicitly in Vatican Council I's *Dogmatic Constitution on the Catholic Faith*, c. 4, "The meaning that Holy Mother Church has once declared, is to be retained forever, and no pretext of deeper understanding ever justifies any deviation from that meaning."

At the same time, the Church recognizes the possibility that in any historical situation, the repetition of an ancient credal formula may not in fact communicate the same truth. The tradition of faith is indefectible in the sense that it will never disappear from this earth. It is infallible in the sense that it communicates its unfailing message of salvation to the people who receive it. Father Haering stressed the idea that the teaching of the Gospel must apply to man's problems as he experiences them today. The truth of the message of Christ is universal. It applies to man's life in any age, but not necessarily in the same formulation. If the Magisterium is not responsive to human problems, it loses its role as a guide to daily living. It must seek to meet new problems with appropriate answers. It must be aware of the discovery of new knowledge and incorporate it into its teaching, once that new facet of learning has been proven to be true.

"Let them blend new sciences and theories and the understanding of the most recent discoveries with Christian morality and the teaching of

Christian doctrine, so that their religious culture and morality may keep pace with scientific knowledge and with the constantly progressing technology. Thus the knowledge of God is better manifested and the preaching of the Gospel becomes clearer to human intelligence and shows itself to be relevant to man's actual conditions of life." (Vatican Council II in *The Church and the Modern World*, #62) Thus it cannot be taken for granted that the continuity of the infallible and universal Magisterium necessarily implies the immutability of the wording of doctrinal formulae.

Father Haering called attention to paragraph 43 of the document *The Church and the Modern World*, "Often enough the Christian view of things (the Council speaking of the role of the layman) will itself suggest some specific solutions in certain circumstances. Yet it happens rather frequently, and legitimately so, that with equal sincerity some of the faithful will disagree with others on a given matter. Even against the intentions of their proponents, however, solutions proposed on one side or another may be easily confused by many people with the Gospel message. Hence, it is necessary for people to remember that no one is allowed in the aforementioned situations to appropriate the Church's authority for his opinion. They should always try to enlighten one another through honest discussion, preserving mutual charity and caring for the common good."

III. CERTITUDE AND THE MAGISTERIUM

Regarding certitude and the Magisterium, it is evident that a new attitude toward sacred truth has developed a quality of mind characterized by an awareness of a certain relativity of all human knowledge. A fact of our times, new in its emergence into our consciousness, is a new posture of realism about the limitations of human knowledge, whether this knowledge be of human or divine origin. This attitude is characterized by a positive openness to truth based upon the appreciation that no man and no institution has a monopoly on all truth.

Such an outlook reflects an epistemology representing a healthy development over the smugness of scientism and over the triumphalism of metaphysicism. It holds that truth is relative in several ways; that truth is relative by the quality of the possessor; that truth is relative in the limitations of the transmitter; that truth is relative in its applicability to the human situation.

Father Baum exposes this problem when he writes, "Doctrinal definitions must be related to the tradition of the Church. Such historical studies are only beginning. As yet, no hermeneutical principles for the interpretation of the ecclesiastical Magisterium have been identified. Since at this point of time no one knows what the application of form criticism will do to the doctrinal statements of the past, scholars are sometimes unable to answer in a definitive manner the question, 'What is the Church teaching on this or that subject?' even when such a subject has been treated in ecclesiastical documents."

He continues, "A deeper understanding of divine revelation at the Vatican Council has made the Catholic theologian more conscious of the transcendence of God's Word over any and every expression of it in the Church."

No one claims that this position is universally held. But it is a respected and acceptable position, one recognized as valid both theologically and philosophically. Should some of the faculty choose to defend it, they are at liberty to do so. The University as a moral body does not advocate any specific position, but considers it its duty to guarantee true freedom of position for any scholar on its campus.

IV. CRISIS IN THE ROLE OF AUTHORITY

The University of Dayton, as a Catholic university, does acknowledge an accountability to the local Ordinary in matters which pertain to the preservation and teaching of Catholic doctrine as such, which is recognized by some as distinct from the science of theology as an autonomous academic discipline. His Grace has publicly declared that he understands and respects the role of the scholar in theological research. As a member of the hierarchy he rightfully demonstrates a pastoral concern for the spiritual welfare of the members of his Archdiocese. "What is said on this topic by standard authors can be summed up in two points: (1) the authentic Magisterium of a bishop is limited to teaching and safeguarding Catholic doctrine, that is, truths concerning faith and morals that have already been defined or declared by the universal Magisterium; and (2) individual bishops have not the authority to settle theological controversies." So wrote Cardinal Lambertini, later Pope Benedict XIV, in *De synodo dioecesana*, Book 7, as reported in "Contemporary Moral Theology" by Ford and Kelly, v. I, pp. 35–36.

The president pointed out that the Archdiocesan ecclesiastical authorities did not actually interfere in the University's academic affairs, though such an impression might well be inferred from the news releases and articles which have appeared, and which were not refuted promptly by the University. Sole justification for this silence was that at that time the University authorities were respecting confidences which prevented them from publicly setting forth the full range of details, despite the ensuing embarrassment.

It is common knowledge that there is a crisis today in the role of authority. Scholars contend that legitimate authority does and must exist, but they do not believe that the role of authority is to silence those who are thinking, and reasoning, and studying. They agree with the pronouncement of the French hierarchy which pointed out that "condemnations will not make intellectual problems go away; that the job of teaching authority is not primarily to denounce errors, but to teach the truth; and that some traditional formulations of doctrine are insufficient, demand further research, and must be studied in relation to the true human problems of the time."

V. PASTORAL EFFECTS OF ACADEMIC FREEDOM

The University acknowledges that a detrimental spiritual or pastoral effect cannot be ignored on a Catholic campus. In regard to the pastoral role of a Catholic university, it is clear that Catholic institutions of higher learning have been less than successful in defining their pastoral influence without rendering suspicious their academic freedom. It remains to be shown that the Catholic university, which is distinct from all other institutions under Catholic auspicies [*sic*] by its academic nature, must not relate its academic role to its pastoral function, that is, must show to all that freedom in the academic realm is in the best service of the community of the faithful. It is imperative to relate and harmonize the academic freedom of our faculty and students with the spiritual well-being of the University community. The Catholic university is not the Catholic Church. Its *raison d'etre* is not identical or coterminous with that of the Church. One deals with the sanctification of man through faith in Christ, and the other deals with the civilization of intelligence through a humanistic and scientific process. These processes can be related, but they must never be confused. The guidelines which will be drawn up by the Ad Hoc Committee should clarify these roles.

Faculty members have asked whether or not the University was in accord with the contention that "since the University's orientation is primarily toward undergraduate education, complex issues which require a multinimity of responses, rather than a unanimity of responses, should be submitted to an inter-subjective dialogue only within the confines of graduate faculty gatherings." The University policy is that any scholar speaking on a topic in the field of his competence is free to voice his opinion provided he does so responsibly. In this case, this would certainly mean that he must judge the maturity and educational preparation of his audience and adjust his remarks accordingly.

It is expected that guidelines drawn up by the Ad Hoc Committee will make possible the full implementation of another recommendation of Vatican Council II's document, *The Church in the Modern World*, #62, viz., "In order that they may fulfill their function, let it be recognized that all the faithful, whether clerics or laity, possess a lawful freedom of inquiry, freedom of thought and of expressing their mind with humility and fortitude in those matters on which they enjoy competence."

In this regard, the University is convinced that the reaction of one's peers is a positive safeguard against any abuse of academic freedom. A man who is too proud to submit his reasoned conclusions to the scrutiny of his colleagues cannot be a true scholar.

VI. MISSION AND REPORT OF THE ARCHDIOCESAN FACT-FINDING COMMITTEE

The University of Dayton acknowledges the report of the fact-finding committee established by His Grace, Archbishop Alter. It is respected as the opinion of qualified theological and philosophical advisers whom the Archbishop selected to prepare a personal study for him. It is understood from his letter of December 15, 1966, that Archbishop Alter established his fact-finding committee at the request of several pastors of the Dayton area who "questioned the adequacy of the investigation of the University." Therefore, the purpose of the fact-finding committee was to serve as a personal reassurance to His Grace regarding the validity of the University of Dayton judgment.

The heart of the committee's conclusion was contained in this paragraph: "From the facts supported by testimony given to the commission, it is clear that there have been on some specified occasions teachings contrary to Catholic faith and morals, which teachings may not have been contrary to defined doctrines, but which were opposed to the teaching of the Magisterium. Moreover, in some public lectures a lack of respect for the Magisterium of the Church was manifested. (See paragraph 25 of the *Constitution on the Church*, Vatican II.) Among the disturbing aspects of the situation at Dayton is some evidence of a tendency to reduce the Magisterium of the teaching Church to a mere consensus of individuals, each teaching primarily in the light of his own insights. There is at the University more than a dispute between individual faculty members; the difficulty extends further into the University community."

VII. SCOPE OF THE UNIVERSITY'S STUDY, NOVEMBER, 1966

The Archbishop's fact-finding committee correctly emphasized that the academic problem, which the University originally identified as the pedagogical aspect of the controversy, was the more far-reaching one. At the Administrative Council meeting which followed immediately upon the telephone call received from His Grace, Archbishop Alter, on October 20, 1966, the U.D. administration decided that the charges presented both an ecclesiastical and academic aspect. Because the allegations against the four professors and the University were made, not to the University, but to the Archdiocesan authorities, it was decided to resolve the extra-mural phase first. Actually, it should be noted, the University provost had already acted upon earlier criticisms contained in a paper entitled "Some Principles Relating to Theology and Philosophy at the University of Dayton," sent by a member of the Philosophy Department to various members of the faculty and administration on September 26, 1966. The provost's investigation was being conducted quietly and confidentially, which probably explains why the accuser was of the opinion that his concerns were being ignored by the University authorities.

Since there was the possibility that the theological charges as made to the Archbishop could demand an ecclesiastical court disposition (the accuser had appealed twice in his letters of accusation to Canon 1325, which treats of heresy), the University of Dayton president, vice president and provost met personally with Archbishop Alter to determine the nature of the charges and how the Church wished to react. His Grace informed the three University authorities that his concern was only for that which attacked Catholic doctrine. He then identified two points in that category, namely, the statements pertaining to purgatory and abortion. The Archbishop then asked the University to ascertain the meaning intended by the authors of those two statements. If the professors were teaching contrary to the Church's doctrine, he directed that they should be admonished and corrected. Once that commission was carried out, the Archbishop declared that his involvement in the case was concluded. He acknowledged that the academic phase of the problem could well be handled on the campus scene.

In accord with the directive of the Archbishop, the University looked into the two charges touching faith and morals. This was done by trying to clarify the exact meaning of the statements challenged, by determining their full import in the context in which they were uttered. The juridical aspects of the case were put into the hands of Reverend James I. O'Connor, S.J., an expert in Canon Law attached to the Bellarmine School of Theology, North Aurora, Illinois. Father O'Connor is a consultant whose opinion is sought by the authorities of the Jesuit colleges and universities in the United States. His expertise in both canonical and academic affairs is widely recognized.

VIII. THE VALIDITY OF THE UNIVERSITY'S INVESTIGATION

It is apropos to explain why the University of Dayton contends that its investigation during the month of November was valid. It recognized immediately that it could not judge the dogmatic implications of statements taken out of context and interpreted by members of an audience. The four individuals accused were requested to submit copies of their prepared speeches, if they had them in written form, and to prepare a full explanation of their position in light of the charges made. Forty-five pages of documentation were received. Advisors, considered competent either theologically or philosophically, or both, who examined the 45 pages of evidence and testimony prepared by the accused professors, were of the opinion that there were no doctrines expressed contrary to the universal Magisterium.

The University also examined the credentials attesting the competence of these accused faculty members. It had ascertained their academic qualifications when it engaged their services in the first place, by receiving favorable recommendations from those who knew them. The institution continued to evaluate these men in the light of evidence reported by their colleagues, their chairmen, and their students each time it renewed their teaching contracts.

Canon 1325 regards not only the substance of statements advocated, but also the intention of the author. To this end the University inquiry touched the attitude of these men. As far as could be ascertained, evidence satisfactorily showed that they were active Catholics, who loved the Church, who wanted to advance the Gospel, and who sought the truth honestly, fearlessly, and openly. It was their intention to face the problems of the day. They proposed new solutions. They realized that many of their hypotheses could be questioned, but as scholars, they rightfully and openly expressed these hypotheses. They tried to support their hypotheses with solid reasons. They knew that truth might be found anywhere, even in areas previously considered "off-limits." They wanted to add their efforts to that of the Church learning of which they are a part. They were seeking that deeper and fuller meaning of the truth and revelation which demonstrates that the message of Christ is relevant to the lives of His followers in every age.

On the basis of the University's investigation the four professors were cleared of advocating doctrines contrary to faith and morals insofar as they had been accused in the original charges. With the Archbishop's acceptance of the decision on December 2, 1966, the University planned to plunge itself into the more far-reaching aspects of the pedagogical implications which were at the heart of the disturbance, by commissioning a committee to establish guidelines for scholarship on the University of Dayton campus.

The protest, however, of the eight dissenting professors and the six Dayton pastors to the University's settlement of the canonical charges, threw the entire affair back into the ecclesiastical realm. Then followed the inauguration of the Archbishop's fact-finding committee. While this work was being conducted, the University launched its Ad Hoc Committee on the academic phase of the problem.

The report of the fact-finding committee confirmed the University's decision that the mission of the Ad Hoc Committee was critical to the resolution of the controversy and that the charges against the individual professors were of secondary importance. It might be mentioned here that the divergence of the two judgments possibly stems from the fact that each was based on a different body of testimony.

IX. THE UNIVERSITY'S POSITION

On March 1, 1967, the President of the University of Dayton in a statement delivered to the entire faculty made clear the position that on the University of Dayton campus there must flourish genuine academic freedom. Professors need not confine themselves to a single viewpoint. He upheld as equally welcome the conservative and the liberal positions, as well as all those in between, but placed a strong emphasis on two points, namely, that those who speak should confine themselves to areas of their competence and that appropriate respect must be paid the proper role of the Church's Magisterium. Just how that respect is to be acknowledged is part of the task facing the Ad Hoc Committee.

The University accepts its responsibility to try to help solve the seeming conflict between academic freedom and the universal Magisterium of the Church. To this end, the University is planning a conference of academic and theological experts to discuss this problem in the Fall of 1967.[1]

University policy publicly supports the right, that the dissenting faculty members had, to voice their fears. It respects their conscientious disagreement with the conclusions reached by the administration. But, on the other hand, it objects strenuously to the procedures they employed in making their voices heard. Lodging accusations and criticisms through the public press seems entirely out of order for professional personnel.

X. ACADEMIC FREEDOM BRINGS RIGHTS AND RESPONSIBILITIES

The University administration was asked, "To what extent the four accused professors were going to have to alter their teachings?" In reply the administration contends that as long as professors confine their utterances to their area of competence, as long as they acknowledge, respect and pay due reverence to the Magisterium according to the guidelines which will be formulated by the Ad Hoc Committee, as long as their competence is continually attested to by their colleagues, chairmen, students and dean, they are free to teach as they see fit on the campus of the University of Dayton.

Correlative to the enjoyment of intellectual and academic freedom, the faculty has the obligation to distinguish between their personal convictions and generally accepted and proven conclusions. They have an obligation to present relevant data fairly to their students. This attitude will discourage sensationalism.

1. The proposed conference never happened.

273

Intellectual freedom does not rule out commitment, but rather makes it possible and personal. Freedom does not require neutrality, either on the part of the institution, or that of the individual. It does not even require neutrality toward the task of inquiry and learning, nor toward a value system.

The report of the Ad Hoc Committee will be submitted directly to the president, so that it may be published as an official, though at first tentative, document of the University. In general, its task is to demonstrate that paragraph 25 of the *Constitution on the Church*, as well as all the other recommendations of Vatican II, are fully applicable on a university campus. Once the Ad Hoc Committee has drawn up a satisfactory and logical explanation of the intent of the University contract pertaining to the preservation of the deposit of faith and Christian morality on campus, and once these guidelines are accepted formally by the entire faculty, they will be accorded the status of policy at the University of Dayton. Any action deliberately contrary to these guidelines will be considered a violation of one's contract. It is especially for this reason that it is considered most important that the faculty itself actively formulate these guidelines and that experts from outside our campus who are invited to testify, include some solidly Catholic authorities.

CONCLUSION

Regarding the future climate at the University of Dayton, The [*sic*] Very Reverend James M. Darby, S.M., chairman of the Board of Trustees, said in one of his interviews, that those who are not touch [*sic*] enough intellectually and spiritually to study under a true concept of academic freedom, be they faculty or students, may unfortunately be disturbed at the University of Dayton. Intense academic debate is not for the ill-informed or timorous. Until the time when all truth is discovered, the University fears the day when only one academic position is acknowledged by the faculty. Indoctrination would surely follow, and, without a challenge, scholars soon become demagogues. The conservative and traditionalist certainly has a podium on the University of Dayton campus.

He may teach his position with all the conviction he can muster. Many will welcome his position and find in it comfort and security. But he must also accept the challenge to engage in academic debate. He must both argue and listen. For the same reasons, the liberal is also welcome. He, too, must be ready to discuss, and prove, and revise, and meet every challenge hurled at him.

Despite the misunderstandings which appeared to dominate the scene, the University of Dayton community has learned much over those [sic] past few months. In his letter of December 3, 1966, the University president foretold that the result of this experience would have long-reaching effects on campus. It has. Rightfully a campus should be a lively place. To have a campus that cares about theology and philosophy is an honor and a distinction. May it ever be so.

The University is thankful to those of the faculty who do not profess the Catholic faith for their attitude during this controversy. It is apparent that they respected the sincerity that has been evidenced on both sides, and know that there will be no interference with their academic freedom.

In conclusion, as president, I reiterate the phraseology of Father Darby when he said, "The University of Dayton, while experiencing the tensions of the modern day, in no wise shrinks from her responsibility to her student body and the University community as a whole to reflect openly and objectively the living thought of our times. In such commitment, we accept unquestionably the risk demanded by a sincere pursuit of the truth."

Raymond A. Roesch, S. M.
President
April 10, 1967

BIBLIOGRAPHY

ARCHIVAL COLLECTIONS

American Catholic History Research Center and University Archives (ACUA). The
Catholic University of America, Washington, D.C.
Archives of the Chancery (AAC). Archdiocese of Cincinnati, Cincinnati, Ohio.
———. Series 1.6–10: Religious Communities. "Society of Mary, University of Dayton,
Unorthodox Teaching Investigation," 1967. RG 1.6, Abp Karl J. Alter.
———. Series 1.6–11: Belmont Ave. general files, "University of Dayton Controversy
'Academic Freedom, etc.'" RG 1.6, Abp Karl J. Alter.
———. Series 1.6–19: Scrapbooks, "University of Dayton Controversies," RG 1.6,
Abp Karl J. Alter.
Archivi Generali Marianisti (AGMAR). Rome, Italy.
National Archives of the Marianist Province of the United States. San Antonio, Texas.
Previously, Archives of the Society of Mary, Eastern Division [ASM(E)] and
Cincinnati Province [ASM(CIN)], Dayton, Ohio.
University Archives and Special Collections (AUD), University of Dayton, Dayton, Ohio.

OTHER SOURCES

Abbott, Walter M., SJ. *The Documents of Vatican II with Notes and Comments by Catholic,*
Protestant, and Orthodox Authorities. New York: Guild and America Press, 1966.
Baltazar, Eulalio R. "A Philosophy of Procession." In *New Theology* No. 2, edited by Martin
E. Marty and Dean G. Peerman, 134–49. New York: Macmillan, 1963.
———. "Contraception and the Philosophy of Process." In *Contraception and Holiness:*
The Catholic Predicament, introduced by Archbishop Thomas D. Roberts, 154–74.
New York: Herder and Herder, 1964.
———. "Teilhard de Chardin: A Philosophy of Procession." *Continuum* 2 (Spring 1964):
87–97.

———. "Re-examination of the Philosophy Curriculum in Catholic Higher Education." *University of Dayton Review* 1, no. 1 (Spring 1964): 27–40.

———. *Teilhard and the Supernatural*. Baltimore: Helicon, 1966.

Baum, Gregory. "The Magisterium in a Changing Church." In *Man as Man and Believer, Concilium: Theology in the Age of Renewal*, 21:67–83, edited by Edward Schillebeeckx, OP, and Boniface Willems, OP. New York: Paulist Press, 1967.

———. *The Oil Has Not Run Dry: The Story of My Theological Pathway*. Montreal: McGill-Queen's University Press, 2016.

Beauregard, Erving E. "An Archbishop, A University, and Academic Freedom." *Records of the American Catholic Historical Society of Philadelphia* (March–December 1982): 25–39.

———. *History of Academic Freedom in Ohio: Case Studies in Higher Education, 1808–1976*. American University Studies 14. New York: P. Lang, 1988.

Bonnette, Dennis. "The Doctrinal Crisis in Catholic Colleges and Universities and Its Effect Upon Education." *Social Justice Review* (November 1967): 220–36.

Bourke, Vernon J. *Ethics in Crisis*. Milwaukee: Bruce, 1966.

Bouscaren, T. Lincoln, SJ. *Ethics of Ectopic Operations*. Milwaukee: Bruce, 1944. Originally published in 1933.

Boyle, John. "The Ordinary Magisterium: Towards a History of the Concept." *Heythrop Journal* 20 (1979): 380–98, and 21 (1980): 91–102.

Brown, Mary Jude. "The 'Heresy Affair' at the University of Dayton, 1960–67: The Origins of the 'Affair' and Its Context." M.A. thesis, University of Dayton, 1999.

———. "An 'Inevitable' Campus Controversy: The 'Heresy Affair' at the University of Dayton, 1960–1967." *American Catholic Studies: Journal of the American Catholic Historical Society* (Spring–Summer 2002): 79–95.

———. "Souls in the Balance: The 'Heresy Affair' at the University of Dayton, 1960–1967." PhD diss., University of Dayton, 2003.

Buckley, G. A. "Heresy, Sin of." In *New Catholic Encyclopedia*, vol. 6. Palatine, Ill.: Jack Heraty and Associates, 1981.

Burtchaell, James Tunstead. *The Dying of the Light: The Disengagement of Colleges and Universities from Their Christian Churches*. Grand Rapids, Mich.: William B. Eerdmans, 1998.

Chrisman, John M. "A Study of Two Major Thomistic Attempts to Reconcile Stable Intelligibility with Evolutionary Change." Ph.D. diss, University of Toronto, St. Michael's College, 1971.

Conn, James Jerome, SJ. *Catholic Universities in the United States and Ecclesiastical Authority*. Rome: Editrice Pontificia Universita Gregoriana, 1991.

Connell, Francis J., CSsR. "Answers to Questions: Academic Freedom in a Catholic College." *American Ecclesiastical Review* (November 1966).

"The Council of Free Czechoslovakia." Wikipedia. Accessed June 10, 2016.

Danielou, Jean, SJ. "Pluralism within Christian Thought." *Theology Digest* (Winter 1962): 67–70.

Dewart, Leslie. "*Castii Connubii* and the Development of Dogma." In *Contraception and Holiness: The Catholic Predicament*, introduced by Archbishop Thomas D. Roberts, 202–310. New York: Herder and Herder, 1964.

———. *The Future of Belief: Theism in a World Come of Age*. New York: Herder and Herder, 1966.

Dieska, Joseph. "Teilhard de Chardin or Thomas Aquinas?" *Social Justice Review* (March 1967): 438–51.

———. "The Trojan Horse Within." *Social Justice Review* (November 1967): 238–39.

Dinoia, Joseph A. "Purgatory." In *The HarperCollins Encyclopedia of Catholicism*, edited by Richard P. McBrien. San Francisco: Harper San Francisco, 1995.

"L. Joseph Dieska." In *Gale Literary Databases, Contemporary Authors* [database-online]; accessed March 30, 1999, http://www.galenet.com.

Dolan, Jay P. *The American Catholic Experience: A History from Colonial Times to the Present*. Garden City, N.Y.: Doubleday, 1985.

Elbert, John A., SM. "Existentialism: Horizon or Dead End?" *University of Dayton Review* 1, no. 2 (Summer 1964): 11–18.

"Father Roesch Presents Marianist Award to President Frei-Montalva of Chile, 1967." Marian Library Photograph Collection. http://ecommons.udayton.edu/imri_photos/20/.

Fitzpatrick, Joseph P., SJ. *The Stranger Is Our Own: Reflections on the Journey of Puerto Rican Migrants*. Kansas City: Sheed and Ward, 1996.

Flannery, Austin, OP, ed. "Pastoral Constitution on the Church in the Modern World." In *Vatican Council II: The Conciliar and Post Conciliar Documents*, 903–1,014. Collegeville, Minn.: Liturgical Press, 1979.

Fletcher, Joseph. *Situation Ethics: The New Morality*. Edited by Robin W. Lovin, Douglas F. Ottati, and William Schweiker. Library of Theological Ethics. Louisville, Ky.: Westminster/John Knox Press, 1966.

———. "Situation Ethics Revisited." *Religious Humanism* (Winter 1982): 9–13.

———. "Memoir of an Ex-Radical." In *Joseph Fletcher: Memoir of an Ex-Radical: Reminiscence and Reappraisal*, edited by Kenneth Vaux, 55–92. Louisville, Ky.: Westminster/John Knox Press, 1993.

Ford, Charles E., and Edgar L. Roy Jr. *The Renewal of Catholic Higher Education*. Washington, D.C.: National Catholic Educational Association, 1968.

Fortin, Roger. *Faith and Action: A History of the Catholic Archdiocese of Cincinnati*. Columbus: Ohio State University Press, 2002.

Gaillardetz, Richard R. *Witnesses to the Faith: Community, Infallibility and the Ordinary Magisterium of Bishops*. New York: Paulist, 1992.

———, ed. *When the Magisterium Intervenes: The Magisterium and Theologians in Today's Church*. Collegeville, Minn.: Liturgical Press, 2012.

Gallagher, John A. *Time Past, Time Future: An Historical Study of Catholic Moral Theology*. Mahwah, N.J.: Paulist Press, 1990.

Gallin, Alice, OSU. *Independence and a New Partnership in Catholic Higher Education*. Notre Dame, Ind.: University of Notre Dame Press, 1996.

Gleason, Philip. "Academic Freedom and the Crisis in Catholic Universities." In *Academic Freedom and the Catholic University*, edited by Edward Manier and John Houck, 33–56. Notre Dame, Ind.: Fides, 1967.

———. "American Catholic Higher Education: A Historical Perspective." In *The Shape of*

Catholic Higher Education, edited by Robert Hassenger, 15–53. Chicago: University of Chicago Press, 1967.

———, ed. *Contemporary Catholicism in the United States*. Notre Dame, Ind.: University of Notre Dame Press, 1969.

———. *Keeping the Faith: American Catholicism Past and Present*. Notre Dame, Ind.: University of Notre Dame Press, 1987.

———. *Contending with Modernity: Catholic Higher Education in the Twentieth Century*. Baltimore: John Hopkins University Press, 1995.

Greiler, Alois, SM. "Marists at Vatican II." http://www.mariststudies.org/w/images/8/81/5 FN11Greiler.pdf.

Hardon, John A., SJ. "Nihil Obstat." In *Catholic Dictionary: An Abridged and Updated Edition of Modern Catholic Dictionary*. New York: Image Books, 2013.

Hassenger, Robert. "Conflict in the Catholic Colleges." *Annals of the American Academy of Political and Social Science* (March 1969): 95–108.

Hayes, Patrick J. Hayes. "Redemptorists and Vatican II: Two American Contributions." Le Concile Vatican II et le monde des religieux—Redemptorists and Vatican II: Two American Contributions. LARHRA, January 1, 1970.

Healy, Timothy S., SJ. "A Rationale for Catholic Higher Education." In *NCEA Bulletin* (August 1967): 63–67.

Hebblethwaite, Peter. *Paul VI: The First Modern Pope*. New York: Paulist Press, 1993.

Heft, James L., SM. "Academic Freedom and the Catholic University." *Current Issues in Catholic Higher Education* (Summer 1988): 26–38.

———. "The Response Catholics Owe to Noninfallible Teachings." In *Raising the Torch of Good News: Catholic Authority and Dialogue with the World*, Annual Publication of the College Theology Society, 32, edited by Bernard P. Prusak, 105–25. Lanham, Md.: University Press of America, 1988.

Hesburgh, Theodore M., CSC. "The Vision of a Great Catholic University in the World of Today." In *Thoughts IV: Five Addresses Delivered During 1967*. Notre Dame, Ind.: University of Notre Dame Press, 1968.

Houtin, Albert. *La question biblique chez les catholiques de France au XIXe siècle*, 129–34. Paris: 1902.

Hunt, John F., and Terrence R. Connelly. *The Responsibility of Dissent: The Church and Academic Freedom*. A Search Book. New York: Sheed and Ward, 1970.

Jencks, Christopher, and David Riesman. *The Academic Revolution*. Garden City, N.Y.: Doubleday, 1968.

John Paul II. *Ex corde Ecclesiae*, August 15, 1990. http://w2.vatican.va/content/john-paul-ii/en/apost_constitutions/documents/hf_jp-ii_apc_15081990_ex-corde-ecclesiae.html.

———. *Fides et Ratio*, September 14, 1998. http://www.vatican.va/content/john-paul-ii/en/encyclicals/documents/hf_jp-ii_enc_14091998_fides-et-ratio.html.

Kauffman, Christopher J. *Education and Transformation: Marianist Ministries in America Since 1849*. New York: Crossroad, 1999.

Kaufman, Abraham. "Teaching as an Intentional Serial Performance." *Studies in Philosophy and Education* 4, no. 4 (December 1966): 364.

Kisiel, Theodore J. "The Atheism of Heidegger, Sartre, and Thomas Aquinas." *University of Dayton Review* 1, no. 2 (Summer 1964): 19–31.

Knust, Edward H., SM. *Hallowed Memories: A Chronological Hisory of the University of Dayton.* Dayton, Ohio: University of Dayton, 1953.

Kohlbrenner, Bernard J., "The Catholic Heritage." In *Heritage of American Education*, ed. Richard E. Gross, 103–32. Boston: Allyn and Bacon, 1962.

Komonchak, Joseph A. "Ordinary Papal Magisterium and Religious Assent." In *Contraception: Authority and Dissent*, edited by Charles E. Curran. New York: Herder and Herder, 1969.

———. "The Struggle for the Council During the Preparation of Vatican II (1960–1962)." In *History of Vatican II*, vol. 1, *Announcing and Preparing Vatican Council II*, edited by Joseph A. Komonchak, 167–356. Maryknoll, New York: Orbis, 1995.

Kreyche, Gerald F. "The Philosophical Horizons Program at De Paul University." *New Scholasticism* (October 1965): 517–24.

Kroger, Daniel. "Scandal." In *The HarperCollins Encyclopedia of Catholicism*, edited by Richard P. McBrien. San Francisco: Harper San Francisco, 1995.

"The Land O'Lakes Statement." http://archives.nd.edu/episodes/visitors/lol/idea.htm.

Lewis, C. S. "Membership." In *The Weight of Glory and Other Addresses*. San Francisco: Harper San Francisco, 2001.

Malone, George K. "Academic Freedom and Apologetics." *Chicago Studies* 6, no. 2 (Summer 1967): 169–86.

Manier, Edward, and John W. Houck, eds. *Academic Freedom and the Catholic University*. Notre Dame, Ind.: Fides, 1967.

McBrien, Richard P. "Doctrine." In *The HarperCollins Encyclopedia of Catholicism*, edited by Richard P. McBrien. San Francisco: Harper San Francisco, 1995.

McCluskey, Neil G. *Catholic Education Faces Its Future*. Garden City, N.Y.: Doubleday, 1968.

———, ed. *The Catholic University: A Modem Appraisal*. Notre Dame, Ind.: University of Notre Dame Press, 1970.

———. "Preamble." *The Story of Notre Dame: The Idea of the Catholic University*. http://archivesl.archives.nd.edu/episodes/visitors/lol/idea.htm.

McCool, Gerald A., SJ. *From Unity to Pluralism: The Internal Evolution of Thomism*. New York: Fordham University Press, 1989.

McGannon, J. Barry, Bernard J. Cooke, and George P. Klubertanz, eds. *Christian Wisdom and Christian Formation: Theology, Philosophy, and the Catholic College Student*. New York: Sheed and Ward, 1964.

McGreevy, John T. "Productivity and Promise: American Catholic History Since 1993." *U.S. Catholic Historian* 21, no. 2 (Spring 2003): 121–26.

McInerny, Ralph, ed. "Introduction." In *New Themes in Christian Philosophy*, ix–xii. Notre Dame, Ind.: University of Notre Dame Press, 1968.

McLean, George F., OMI. *Teaching Thomism Today: The Proceedings of the Workshop on Teaching Thomism Today conducted at the Catholic University of America, June 15 to June 26, 1962*. Washington, D.C.: The Catholic University of America Press, 1963.

McMullin, Ernan. "Presidential Address: Who Are We?" In *Proceedings of the American*

Catholic Philosophical Association 41, ACPA, 1–16. Washington, D.C.: The Catholic University of America, 1967.

———. "Philosophy in the United States Catholic College." In *New Themes in Christian Philosophy*, edited by Ralph M. McInerny, 370–409. Notre Dame, Ind.: University of Notre Dame Press, 1968.

Murray, John Courtney, SJ. "Comments on the Declaration on Religious Freedom." In *The Documents of Vatican II with Notes and Comments by Catholic, Protestant, and Orthodox Authorities*, edited by Walter M. Abbott, SJ, 672–674. New York: Guild and America Press, 1966.

"Murray, John Courtney." In *Gale Literary Databases, Contemporary Authors* [database-on-line]; accessed May 28, 1999, http:// www. galenet. com.

"National Catholic Welfare Council." In *1967 National Catholic Almanac*, edited by Felician A. Foy, OFM. Garden City, N.Y.: Doubleday, 1967.

Nihil Obstat. In *Catholic Dictionary: An Abridged and Updated Edition of Modern Catholic Dictionary*, edited by John A. Hardon, SJ. New York: Image, 2013.

Noonan, John T., Jr. *Contraception: A History of Its Treatment by the Catholic Theologians and Canonists.* Cambridge, Mass.: Harvard University Press, 1966.

O'Brien, David J. *From the Heart of the American Church: Catholic Higher Education and American Culture.* Maryknoll, N.Y.: Orbis, 1994.

O'Connell, Marvin R. *Critics on Trial: An Introduction to the Catholic Modernist Crisis.* Washington, D.C.: The Catholic University of America Press, 1994.

O'Malley, John W., SJ. *What Happened at Vatican II?* Cambridge, Mass.: Belknap Press of Harvard University Press, 2010.

Orsy, Ladislas, SJ. "Magisterium: Assent and Dissent." *Theological Studies* 48 (1987): 473–97.

Pathrapankal, Joseph. *Time and History: Biblical and Theological Studies.* Eugene, Ore.: Wipf and Stock, 2005.

Pattillo, Manning M., Jr., and Donald M. Mackenzie. *Eight Hundred Colleges Face the Future: A Preliminary Report of the Danforth Commission on Church Colleges and Universities.* St. Louis: Danforth Foundation, 1965.

Paul VI. *Ecclesiam Suam.* August 6, 1964. http://www.vatican.va/holy_father/paul_vi/encyclicals/documents/hf_p-vi_enc_06081964_ecclesiam_en.html.

———. *Mysterium Fidei.* September 3, 1965. http://w2.vatican.va/content/paul-vi/en/encyclicals/documents/hf_p-vi_enc_03091965_mysterium.html.

———. *Apostolic Exhortation on the Nineteenth Centenary of the Martyrdom of SS. Peter and Paul: Petrum et Paulum Apostolos.* February 22, 1967. Washington, D.C.: United States Catholic Conference, 1967.

———. "The Christian's Response to Modern Philosophy." *Social Justice Review* (November 1967): 240–42.

Pauson, John J. "Duquesne: Beyond the Official Philosophies." *Continuum* 4 (Summer 1966): 252–57.

Pegis, Anton C. "'Who Reads Aquinas?'" *Thought: A Review of Culture and Idea* 42 (Winter 1967): 488–504.

Pius X. *Motu Proprio* "Sacrorum antistitum." September 1, 1910. Philadelphia: The Dolphin Press.

Pius XI. *Studiorum ducem.* June 29, 1923. https://www.papalencyclicals.net/piusi/p11studi.htm

Pius XII. *Humani generis.* August 12, 1950. http://www.vatican.va/holy_father/pius_xii/ encyclicals/documents/hf_p-xii_enc_12081950_humani-generis_en.html.

———. "Allocution to the Gregorian University," Discourse XV, 409–10. Also available at *Franciscan Studies* 14, no. 2 (1954): 204–9. http://www.jstor.org/stable/41974516.

Portier, William. "Reason's 'Rightful Autonomy' in *Fides et Ratio* and the Continuous Renewal of Catholic Higher Education in the United States." *Communio* 26 (Fall 1999): 541–56.

"The Genealogy of 'Heresy': Leslie Dewart as Icon of the Catholic 1960s." *American Catholic Studies* 113 (Spring–Summer 2002): 65–77.

Rahner, Karl. "On the Question of a Formal Existential Ethics." In *Theological Investigations*, vol. 2, *Man in the Church.* Translated by Karl-H. Kruger. Baltimore: Helicon Press, 1963.

Ratzinger, Joseph. "The Changeable and Unchangeable in Theology." *Theology Digest* (Winter 1962): 71–76.

Royce, James E., SJ. *Man and His Nature.* New York: McGraw Hill, 1961.

Ryan, Michael James. "Certitude." In *The Catholic Encyclopedia.* Vol. 3. New York: Robert Appleton, 1908.

"Statement on the Nature of the Contemporary Catholic University." *The Story of Notre Dame: The Idea of the Catholic University.* http://archives1.archives.nd.edu/ episodes/ visitors/lol/idea.htm.

Stritch, Alfred G., ed. *The Church of Cincinnati: 1821–1971.* Cincinnati: Catholic Telegraph, 1971.

Sullivan, Francis A. *Creative Fidelity: Weighing and Interpreting Documents of the Magisterium.* Mahwah, N.J.: Paulist Press, 1996.

Teilhard de Chardin, Pierre. *The Future of Man.* Translated by Norman Denny. New York: Image/Doubleday, 1964.

Thomas, Samuel J. "After Vatican Council II: The American Catholic Bishops and the 'Syllabus' from Rome, 1966–68." *Catholic Historical Review* (April 1967): 233–57.

"20th Century History." Slovakia.org: *Guide to the Slovak Republic.* Accessed November 11, 2019. http://www.slovakia.org/history6.htm.

University of Dayton Faculty Handbook. Dayton, Ohio: University of Dayton, 1966.

Vagnozzi, Egidio. "A Letter from Archbishop Vagnozzi." *American Ecclesiastical Review* (October 1961): 217–19.

Von Hildebrand, Dietrich, and Alice von Hildebrand. *Morality and Situation Ethics.* Chicago: Franciscan Herald Press, 1966.

Vorgrimler, Herbert, ed. *Commentary on the Documents of Vatican II.* Vols. 1 and 3. New York: Herder and Herder, 1967.

Young, Pamela C., CSJ. "Theological Education in American Catholic Higher Education, 1939–1973." Ph.D. diss., Marquette University, 1995.

INDEX

Heresy in the Heartland: The Controversy at the University of Dayton, 1960–1967 was designed in Sabon Next and Arvil display type and composed by Kachergis Book Design of Pittsboro, North Carolina. It was printed on 55-pound Natural Offset and bound by Maple Press of York, Pennsylvania.